IMAGES
of America

HAKONE ESTATE AND GARDENS

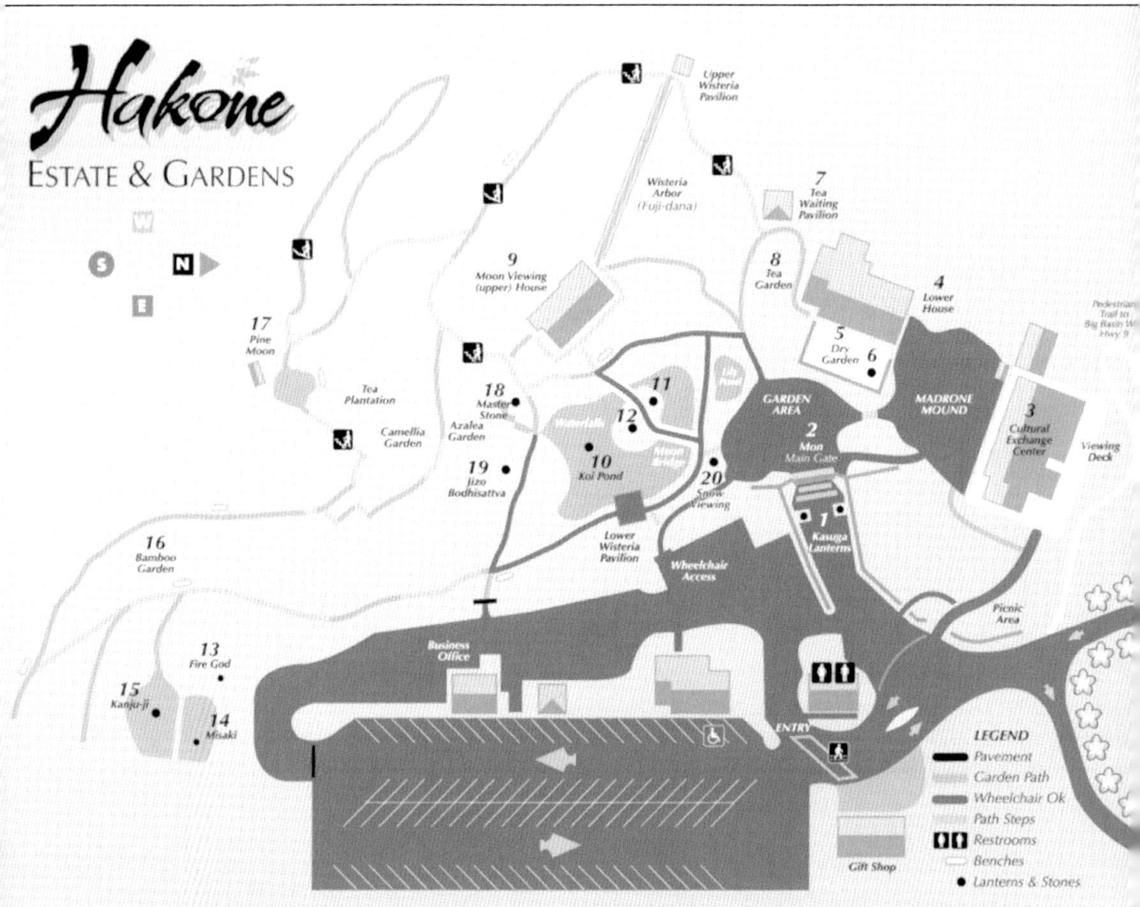

This map of Hakone Estate and Gardens shows the original buildings and pond of the Stine era: the Moon Viewing House (Upper House), Lower House, and koi pond. During the Tilden era, the Mon (main gate) was built. The Cultural Exchange Center (CEC), the Friendship Bamboo Garden (Kizuna-en), the walled Dry Garden (Karensansui) and the parking lot were built after the City of Saratoga bought the property. (Courtesy of Hakone Foundation.)

On the Cover: Hakone, in Saratoga, California, was the private estate of Isabel Stine, who was inspired by the 1915 Panama-Pacific International Exposition. After her trip to Japan to visit historic gardens and study Japanese theater, Stine oversaw the creation of her dream garden by master Japanese architects and artisans. This photograph shows the Moon Viewing House, designed by Shintani Tsunematsu, and the three Stine children posing on the hillside wearing Kabuki theater costumes purchased by their mother in Japan. (Courtesy of Peter Stine.)

IMAGES
of America

HAKONE ESTATE AND GARDENS

Ann Waltonsmith and Connie Young Yu

ARCADIA
PUBLISHING

ISBN 978-1-4671-0630-6

Published by Arcadia Publishing
Charleston, South Carolina

Printed in the United States of America

Library of Congress Control Number: 2020950109

For all general information, please contact Arcadia Publishing:
Telephone 843-853-2070
Fax 843-853-0044
E-mail sales@arcadiapublishing.com
For customer service and orders:
Toll-Free 1-888-313-2665

Visit us on the Internet at www.arcadiapublishing.com

This book is dedicated to Hakone's outstanding staff, volunteers, and foundation members, whose loving care has kept this garden flourishing and its mission vital.

Contents

Acknowledgments

This book was made possible by the many people who contributed their knowledge, expertise, and photographs in documenting Hakone's history. We gratefully acknowledge Peter Stine, Isabel and Oliver Stine's grandson, for his magnificent donation of the Stine family collection of photo albums and memorabilia to the Hakone Foundation. Our heartfelt thanks to Alexa Gregory for providing iconic photographs from the Tilden-Gregory Archives, along with historical background, and to Deon Gresham for sharing photographs and thoughtful recollections of Hakone in the last era of private ownership.

Thanks to these generous individuals who supported our photo documentation: Mike Story for personally taking so many wonderful photographs of Hakone and its events for the past 20 years; Peter Marra for saving all the old sister city pictures from many contributors; Brian Satoh, executive director of the Northern Culture Museum in Niigata, for sending historical photographs from Japan; and Ruthann Stolzman of Word Art for carefully scanning vintage photographs.

We are grateful to Shozo Kagoshima, executive director of the Hakone Foundation, for his contribution of photographs and technical support; to Jacob Kellner, Hakone's head gardener, for his counsel; and to Elaine Salter for her insights on Hakone's development and resource materials on the gardens. To the many community leaders and volunteers we interviewed on the history of Hakone and the city of Saratoga, we can only say we could not have done this book without you. Thank you, Karen O'Brien, for reading every chapter of the book in progress and editing. We are deeply grateful to Caroline Anderson, our steadfast editor at Arcadia Publishing, who guided us every step of the way.

Finally, we thank our respective husbands, Rick Waltonsmith and John Yu, for their unflagging support in our endeavors.

This book was inspired by the past owners' love of Hakone and the dedication of Hakone's staff, volunteers, donors, and foundation board members. We are proud to tell the dramatic story of how a Japanese garden in California was created, fought for, protected, and became a national treasure.

Introduction

Hakone, formally known as Hakone Estate and Gardens, is the jewel of Silicon Valley, California, an authentic Japanese garden set in the rugged foothills of the Santa Cruz mountain range. One of the oldest Japanese estate gardens in the Western Hemisphere, it is on the registry of the National Trust for Historic Preservation. Renowned for its beautiful, exquisite setting, Hakone is a public garden, a tourist attraction, and a popular site for weddings, special celebrations, and corporate retreats.

Hakone also has a little-known, marvelous history. It is an enchanted garden, a secret garden, a garden of indomitable strength and endurance. Throughout a century, the garden survived a national depression, racist policies, and threats of land redevelopment. A traditional Japanese garden estate, Hakone was saved for posterity by three separate non-Japanese ownerships over its first 50 years. These were extraordinary individuals who pushed back against the prejudice, xenophobia, and nativism of their respective times. They possessed a moral compass and gave Hakone its soul.

Not until Hakone's centennial celebration (2015–2017) did the garden's history of challenges, struggles, and triumphs come to light. Through oral history interviews, photographic collections, and archival research, the hidden history of Hakone has now been documented, serving to enhance and deepen the visitor's experience. There is an intrinsic essence in this century-old garden that is the soul of Hakone.

Isabel Stine's inspiration for Hakone is legend—how the Japan Pavilion of the 1915 Panama-Pacific International Exhibition in San Francisco gave her the idea to have her own splendid Japanese garden estate. But not revealed is how she defied the anti-Asian sentiment of her times by hosting Japanese cultural events at Hakone and in San Francisco in opposition to her neighbor, US senator James Phelan, whose legacy was anti-Asian legislation. Stine had many Japanese friends and employed Japanese landscape architects and artisans at Hakone, while Phelan, who built his European-inspired estate, Montalvo, just down the road, ran his campaign for reelection with the slogan "Keep California White."

In 1932, the new owner of Hakone was the prominent Maj. Charles Lee Tilden, founder of the East Bay Regional Parks District, saving thousands of acres of land for the public to use, a legacy benefiting the Bay Area to this day. Major Tilden purchased Hakone from Isabel Stine Leis during the Great Depression and enhanced the garden by building the Mon, the majestic main gate. He protected Hakone during World War II, when Japanese gardens across the United States were being destroyed. He kept in touch with his Japanese gardener, James Sasaki, and his family when they were sent to relocation camp, and after the war, he brought the Sasakis back to Hakone.

Japan's attack on Pearl Harbor launched the United States into World War II. There were fears of a Japanese invasion on the West Coast and the potential threat of Japanese Americans being used as spies and aiding the enemy. Executive Order 9066, signed by Pres. Franklin Roosevelt on

February 19, 1942, forcibly evacuated 120,000 people of Japanese heritage to relocation camps in desolate areas of the United States. The Sasakis, living in Santa Clara County, were assigned to the camp at Heart Mountain, Wyoming. James, born in Japan, knew he had to go, but he did not expect that his American-born wife, Shizue, and their four young children would also be incarcerated as potential enemies. The executive order was for "all persons of Japanese ancestry." The Nishiura brothers, Shinzaburo and Gentaro, devout Buddhists who built Hakone's entrance corridor and Mon, lived in San Jose and thus were sent to Heart Mountain as well. They could only take what they could carry and had to sell or give away the priceless tools of their trade. The Sasakis applied to be evacuated with relatives in the East Bay, so their designated camp was Topaz, Utah.

Hakone was a scene of heartbreak in March 1942, as the Sasakis were given 48 hours to report to their area's assembly center for transportation to camp. Digging a pit in the orchard, now Hakone's parking lot, James Sasaki built a fire and burned everything Japanese his family owned: beloved heirlooms, his wife's and daughters' kimonos, his son's practice bamboo kendo swords, books, and pictures. His seven-year-old daughter, Betty, begged him not to throw her Japanese children's books in the fire, but he said to her, "I have no choice." Ordered to report to an assembly center in the East Bay, the family of six piled into a Ford Model A, each with a suitcase. The mother said each child could take one toy, and the father told the children they were not to cry.

In September 1945, the Sasakis, along with hundreds of other Japanese Americans, were released from Topaz and put on a train to Oakland. The windows were covered so they could not see out and no one could see them. They had no idea what would happen to them after three and a half years of incarceration. Most were without any resources and faced hostility and anger from white Americans who lost loved ones in the war. But when the Sasakis stepped off the train, they were met by Marion Mitchell, Major Tilden's stepdaughter, who drove the family of six back to their home in Hakone. James Sasaki resumed his career of cultivating a traditional Japanese garden, bringing Hakone to its height of perfection in the 1950s.

The last private owners of Hakone (1961–1966), the least understood and most misrepresented owners, were a partnership of two white couples—Joseph and Clara Gresham and their son Eldon Gresham and daughter-in-law Deon—and four Chinese American couples—George and Marie Hall, Johnny and Helen Kan, Dan and June Lee, and John and Mary Young. They employed Charlie Ray, who was African American, as Hakone's live-in gardener. This diverse group of individuals raised fears among the community that they were going to raze the gardens and build a Chinese restaurant at Hakone.

They purchased Hakone at a critical moment, when Saratoga was becoming a residential area and parcels of land were being subdivided. The partners used Hakone as their private retreat, meticulously maintaining the gardens and buildings. This book reveals, through photographs, how dedicated they were to keeping Hakone authentic, and it also tells about their careers and contributions to society. The partners saved Hakone from being subdivided by offering it for sale solely to the City of Saratoga.

Through the leadership and foresight of Mayor Bill Glennon, the city purchased Hakone in 1966 to be used as a public park. The challenge facing Saratoga, incorporated merely 10 years earlier, of managing Hakone without a parks and recreation department was formidable. The city government turned to volunteers for help, and concerned citizens stepped up. The Hakone Gardens Japanese Cultural Society was formed, and then Hakone's first foundation began taking steps toward supporting and managing the gardens. There was a cultural shift in American society, with the civil rights movement, ethnic studies, and increased immigration from Asia, and Hakone began to become an important cultural center. In 1983, Saratoga established a sister city relationship with Muko, Japan. In 2000, the city council established a second nonprofit foundation to take on the responsibility of fundraising, managing the garden, and showcasing Hakone to the wider San Francisco Bay Area. This book illuminates the stages of Hakone's development as a public park and how the foundation and the City of Saratoga established Hakone as a renowned Japanese garden and cultural center open to all.

Originally 15 acres of natural California oak and redwood forest, the land had been completely logged when the Stines bought the property in 1915. Isabel Stine began to establish the Japanese landscaped garden at the center of the acreage, leaving a circle of natural woodlands to regrow around the new garden and buildings. It remains that way today, a Japanese garden surrounded by a forest of big oak trees and redwoods. Hakone is now 17 acres of beauty, receiving a land parcel donation for a new section of bamboo garden and additional parking spaces to accommodate daily visitors and events.

One

Hakone's Beginnings

Isabel Stine Builds a Japanese Garden in California

Isabel Longdon Stine achieved something never done before by creating an authentic Japanese garden estate on a rugged California hillside. She named it Hakone, after Fuji-Hakone National Park in Japan. Independent and audacious in an era when American women did not have the right to vote, Stine defied society's conventions. According to legend, she was inspired by the Japan Pavilion at the 1915 Panama-Pacific International Exposition, but in truth, her interest in Japanese culture developed earlier, when she was a young music student in San Jose, enthralled with the sounds of bells and chants from a Buddhist temple in Japantown. Her husband, Oliver Stine, a San Francisco real estate developer, supported her pursuits.

In 1915, the Stines purchased 15 acres in Saratoga to build a country estate. Isabel traveled to Japan with her young son John MacLeod in 1917 to visit historic Japanese gardens and to study Kabuki theater in Tokyo. Tragically, the following year, her husband suddenly died. With three young children and Oliver's finances to manage, Isabel continued her pursuit of building an extraordinary garden, hiring the finest Japanese landscape architect and artisans.

Just over the hill from Hakone, Sen. James Phelan was building Montalvo, his European-style country estate. Phelan, three-time mayor of San Francisco and US senator, advocated for immigration bans on Asians and the passage of California's Alien Land Law. In his unsuccessful run for reelection to the Senate, he promoted such racist slogans as "Keep California White" and "Save Our State from Oriental Aggression." Meanwhile, Isabel Stine was promoting Japanese culture and garden design at Hakone as well as understanding and acceptance. She married Francis Leis at Hakone in 1925. A patron of the arts in San Francisco, Isabel was largely responsible for establishing a permanent opera in the city and the 1925 West Coast premiere of Puccini's opera *Madama Butterfly*.

During the Great Depression, Stine could no longer afford to keep her beloved Hakone. She sold her dream garden to Maj. Charles Tilden, a friend who would love and care for Hakone, ensuring that her legacy would endure.

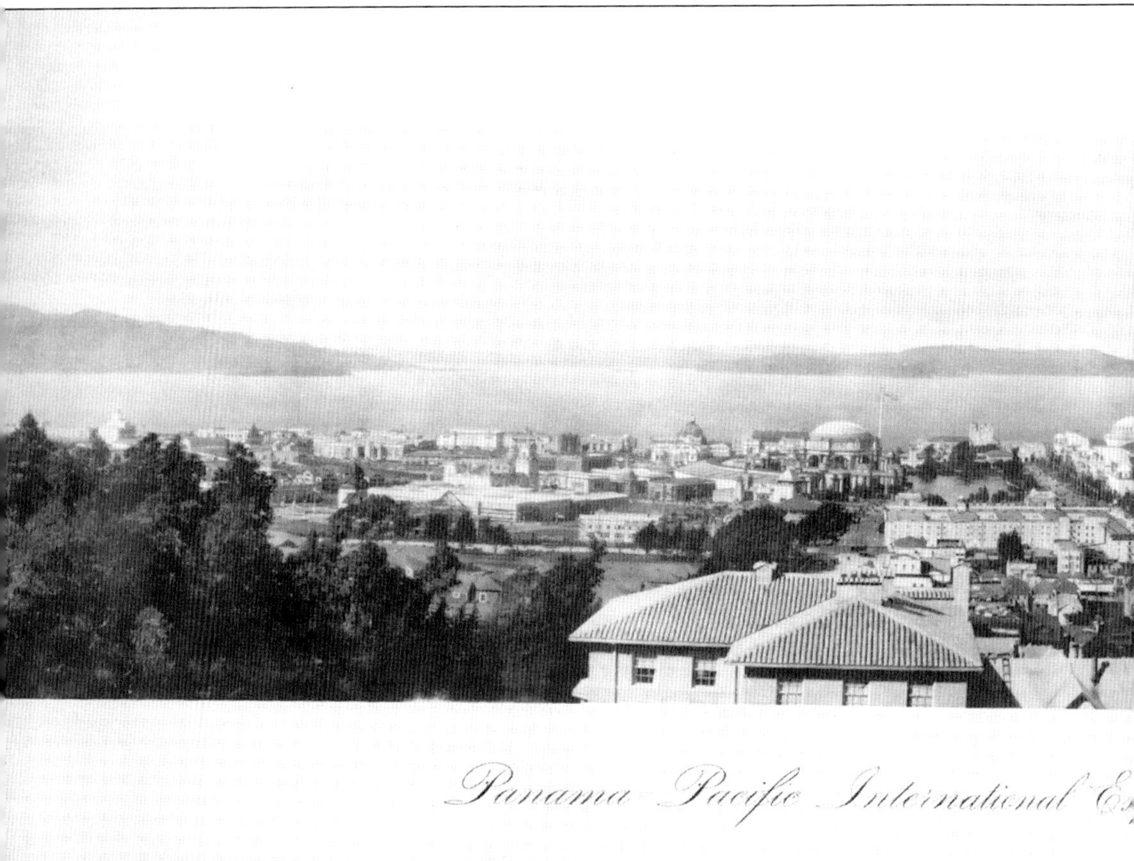

The Panama-Pacific International Exposition, the 1915 world's fair celebrating the completion of the Panama Canal, was San Francisco's grand opportunity to showcase the city's economic recovery from the 1906 earthquake and to promote new commerce and international trade. It was a spectacular success. The fair was constructed on a 636-acre site along the northern shore of San Francisco, between the Presidio and Fort Mason, now known as the Marina District.

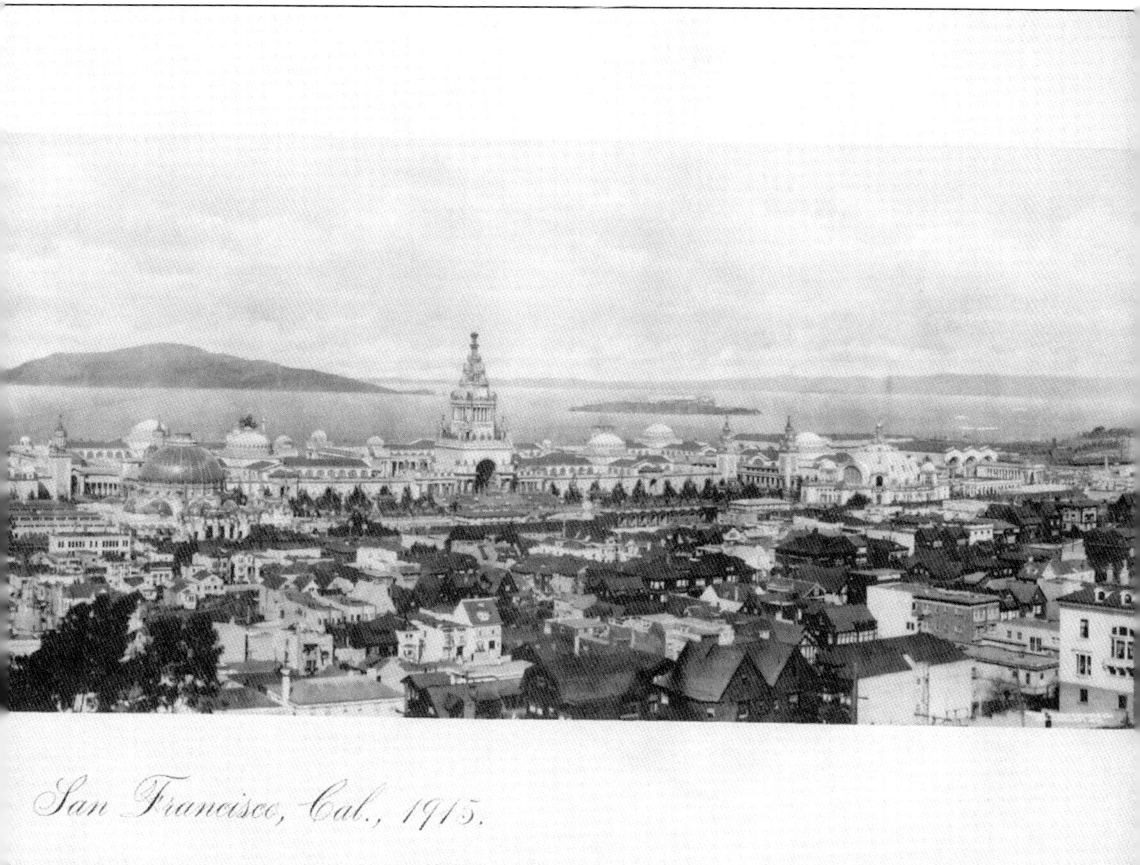

Oliver C. and Isabel Longdon Stine, a wealthy San Francisco couple and future owners of Hakone Garden in Saratoga, were enthusiastic supporters of the exposition. It was a city within a city with spectacular foreign pavilions. One of the most visited sites was the Japan Pavilion, particularly admired by the Stines. (Courtesy of Peter Stine.)

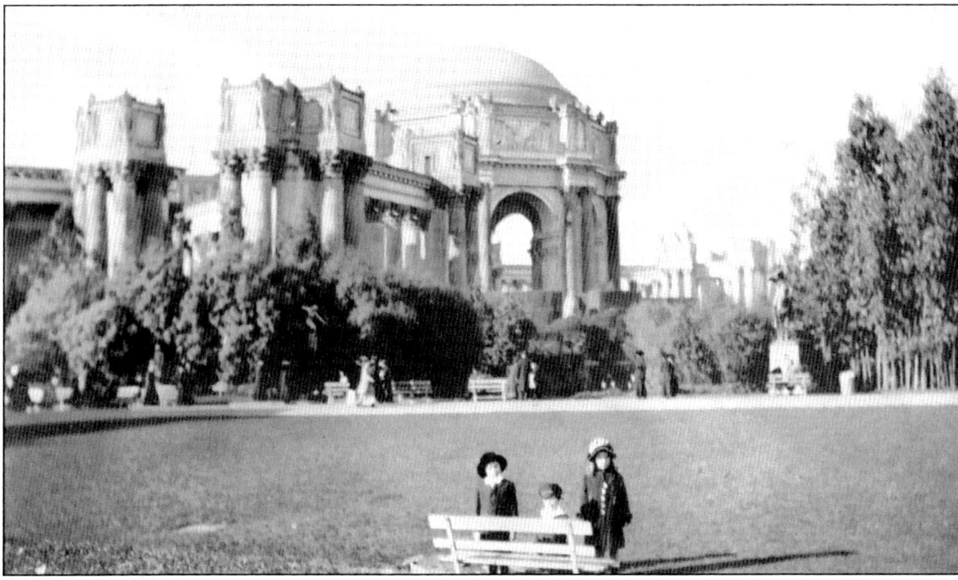

The Stine family, residing in a mansion on nearby Russian Hill, visited the Panama-Pacific International Exposition frequently. The three Stine children (from left to right), John, Oliver, and Helen, are pictured in front of the iconic Palace of Fine Arts. There were monumental buildings and pavilions representing 48 states and 21 countries. The Palace of Fine Arts is the only building from the exposition still standing. (Courtesy of Peter Stine.)

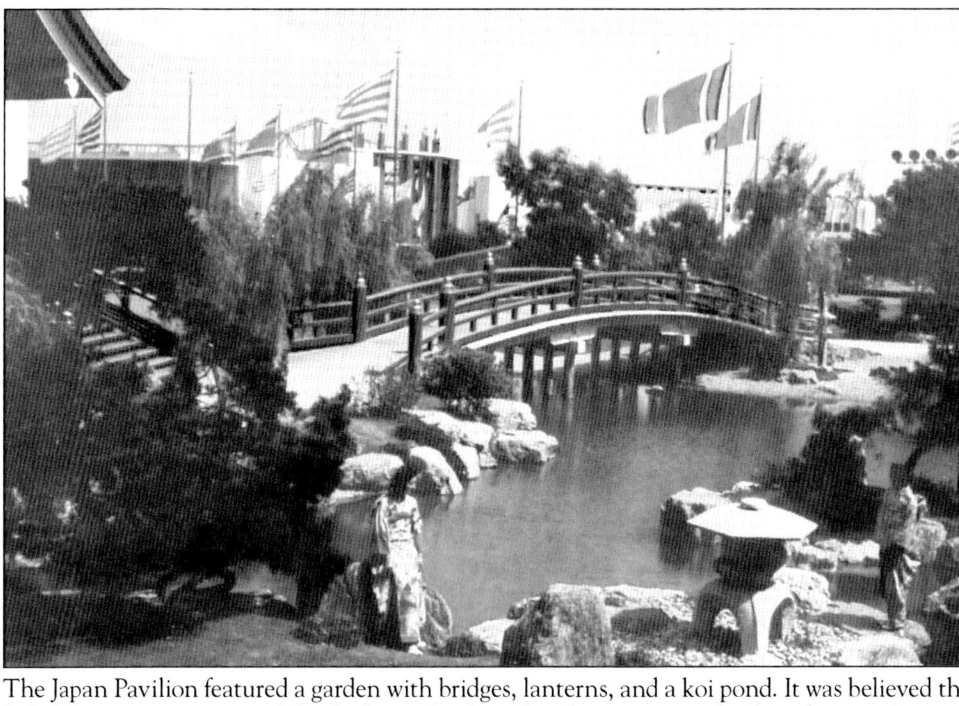

The Japan Pavilion featured a garden with bridges, lanterns, and a koi pond. It was believed that Isabel Stine was so awestruck by the Japan Pavilion that she was inspired to have her own Japanese garden estate. In actuality, she was enchanted by Japanese culture before the fair and shared her interest with her husband. The Stines proceeded in 1915 to purchase 15 acres in Saratoga for a Japanese-style summer home. (Courtesy of Peter Stine.)

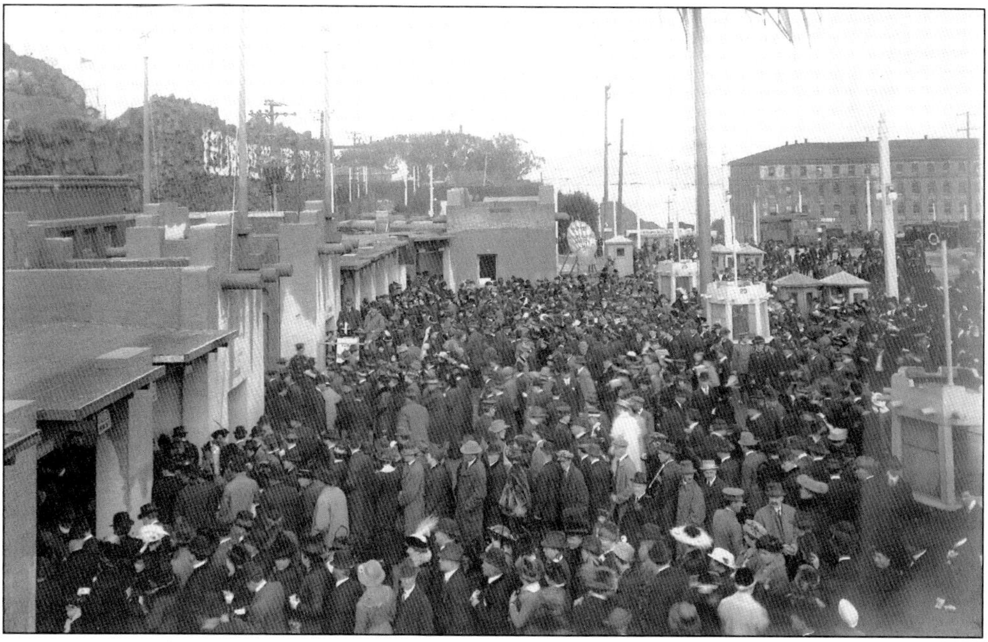

Enormous crowds from near and far gather at the entrance of the Panama-Pacific International Exposition. In the background is San Francisco Bay. Statistics indicate that 19 million visitors from all around the world attended the fair, which lasted from February 20 to December 4, 1915. (Courtesy of Peter Stine.)

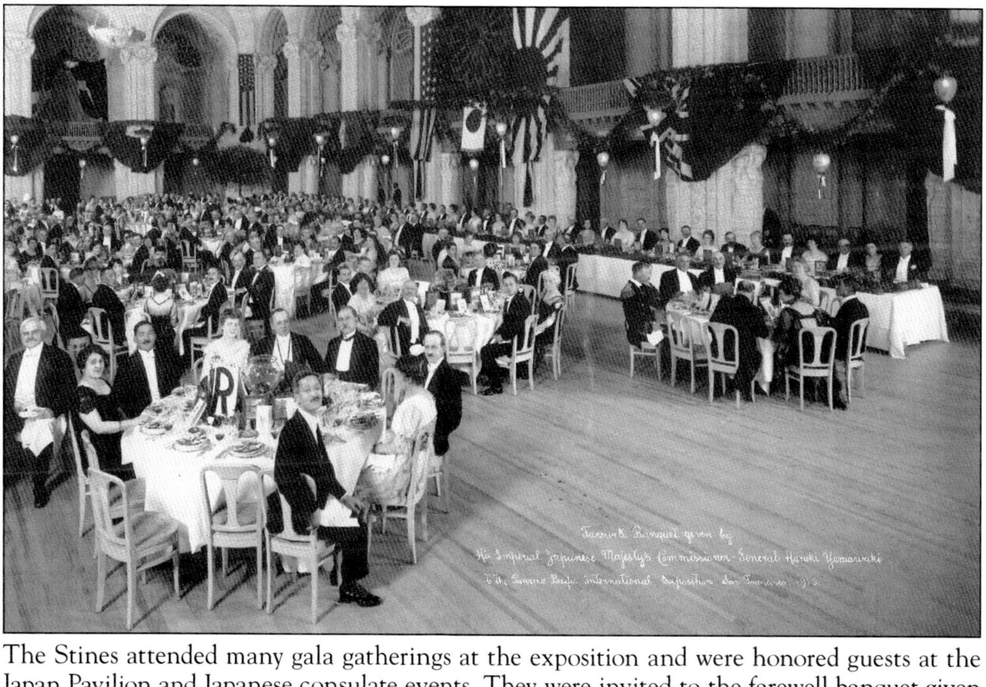

The Stines attended many gala gatherings at the exposition and were honored guests at the Japan Pavilion and Japanese consulate events. They were invited to the farewell banquet given by the Japanese emperor's commissioner, Haruki Yamawaki. Isabel Stine became friends with the Japanese cultural emissaries and maintained a correspondence and connection with them over many years. (Courtesy of Peter Stine.)

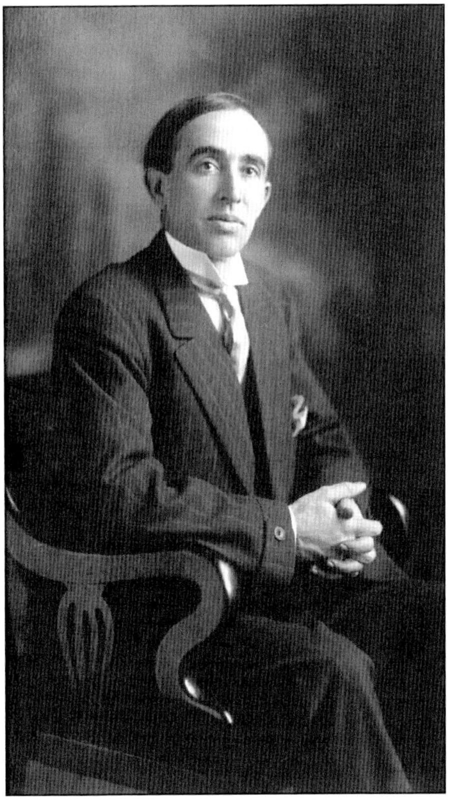

Oliver Charles Stine, born in Pennsylvania in 1877, received a law degree from George Washington University in Washington, DC. Coming to San Francisco, he turned to real estate, establishing O.C. Stine Real Estate Company. He was committed to residential planning. A millionaire, he was well connected in San Francisco political circles, with membership in the exclusive Bohemian Club. (Courtesy of Peter Stine.)

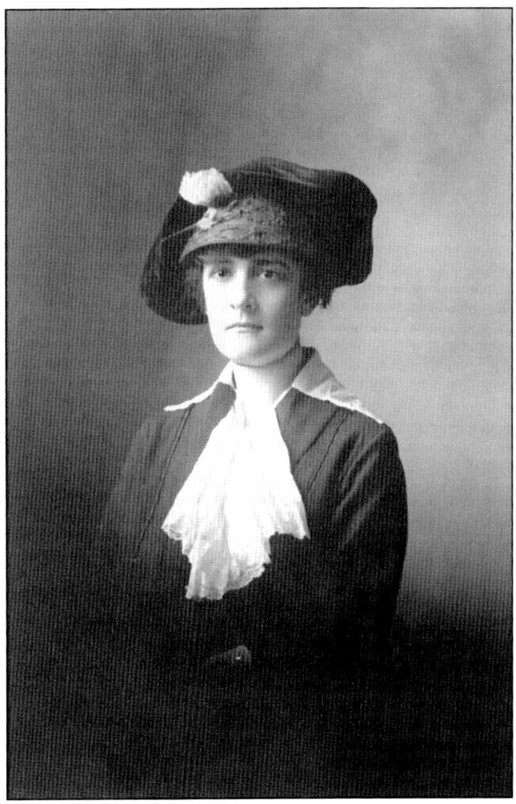

Through her marriage in 1905 to Oliver Stine, Isabel moved in exclusive San Francisco social circles, but she remained independent and individualistic, attending the Japanese community's Kabuki plays in the city. Her husband encouraged her interest in Japanese culture, which reached a high point while attending the Panama-Pacific International Exposition. Their marriage was a true partnership; Hakone was the dream project for both of them. (Courtesy of Peter Stine.)

Isabel Longdon, born in San Francisco in 1880, was raised in San Jose. She had one sibling, younger brother John Longdon. A gifted pianist and composer, she attended King Conservatory of Music in San Jose. She was intrigued by the Japanese music and rituals she observed in San Jose's Japantown. According to family lore, young Isabel listened to the sounds as she stood outside the Buddhist temple. (Courtesy of Peter Stine.)

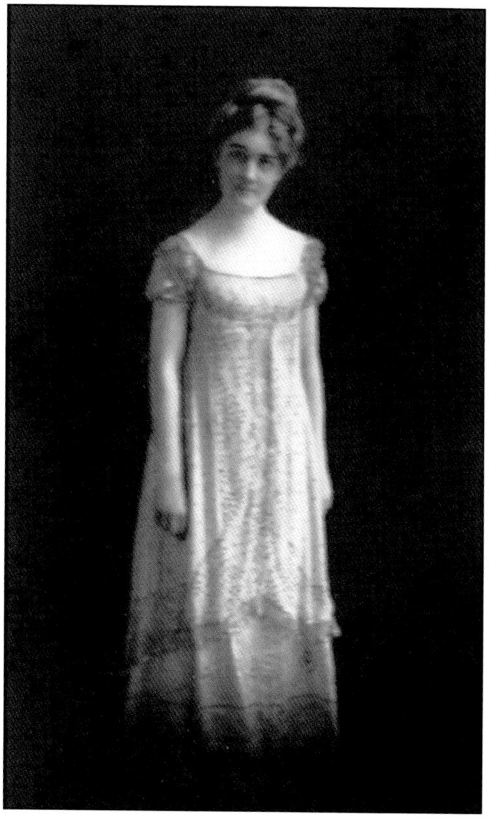

This charming piece of memorabilia, a "cutting portrait" of the Stine family in silhouette, was made at the 1915 exposition. The Stines and their children, John, Helen, and Oliver, are shown in profile, with elegant, fashionable attire. Silhouette cutouts were a popular novelty in the 19th and early 20th centuries, until the camera became more accessible and affordable. (Courtesy of Peter Stine.)

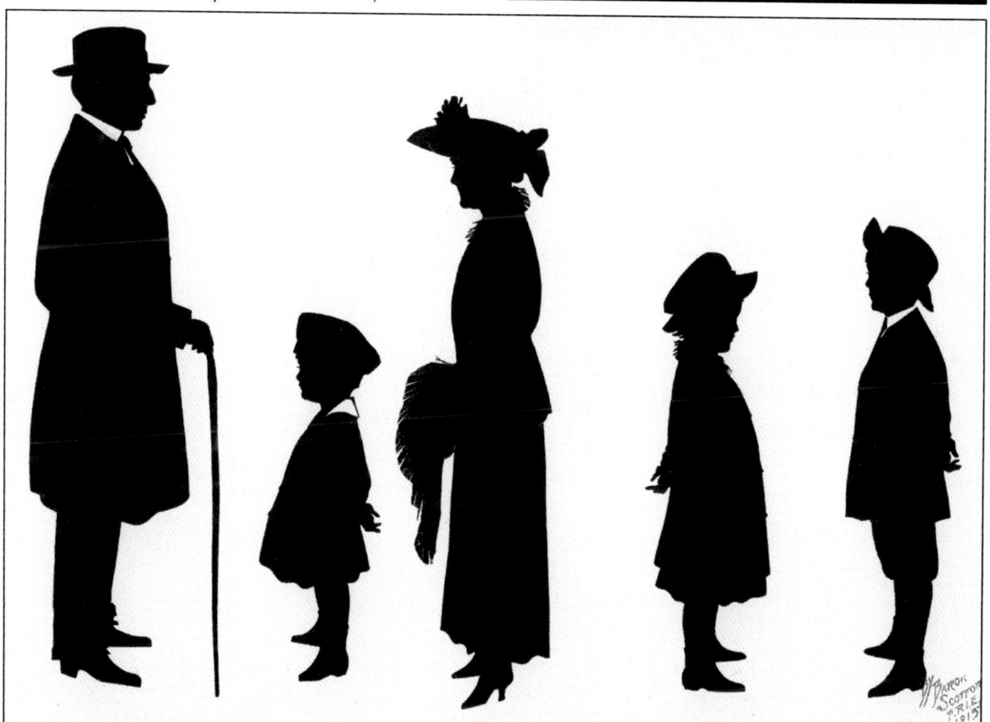

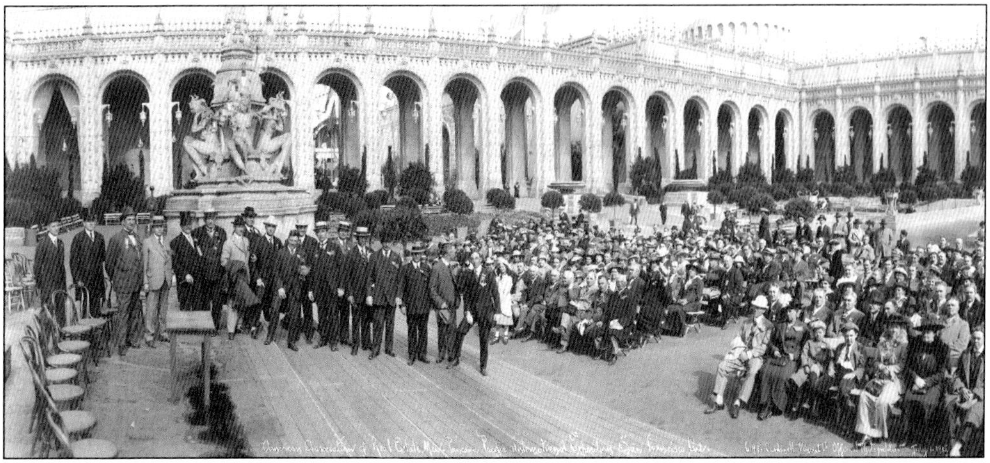

Members of the American Association of Real Estate gathered at the Court of Abundance at the Panama-Pacific International Exposition with Oliver Stine (standing, far right) as their president. The exposition was a momentous event for the real estate community, showcasing a variety of architectural styles and drawing affluent tourists and visitors from all over the United States and the world. (Courtesy of Peter Stine.)

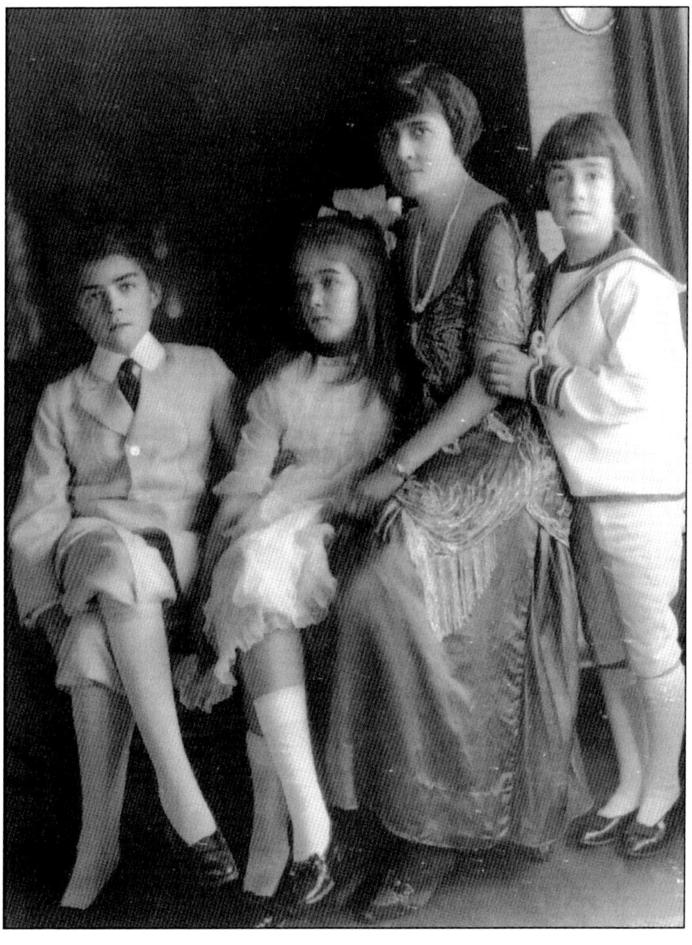

Isabel Longdon Stine was a devoted, loving mother widowed at the age of 37, with three children to raise alone after her husband's premature death in 1918 at the age of 40. Pictured from left to right are John, Helen, Isabel, and Oliver, nicknamed "Tommy." The children attended private school in San Francisco, and the family spent the summers at Hakone, their new Japanese garden estate. (Courtesy of Peter Stine.)

Isabel Stine and son John toured historic sites in Japan. Pictured at a shrine, from left to right, are John, Lilian de Havilland, and Isabel Stine. Isabel studied Kabuki theater in Tokyo and became friends with de Havilland, an actress and English citizen who was married to an attorney working in Japan. They renewed their friendship when de Havilland and her two daughters moved to Saratoga. (Courtesy of Peter Stine.)

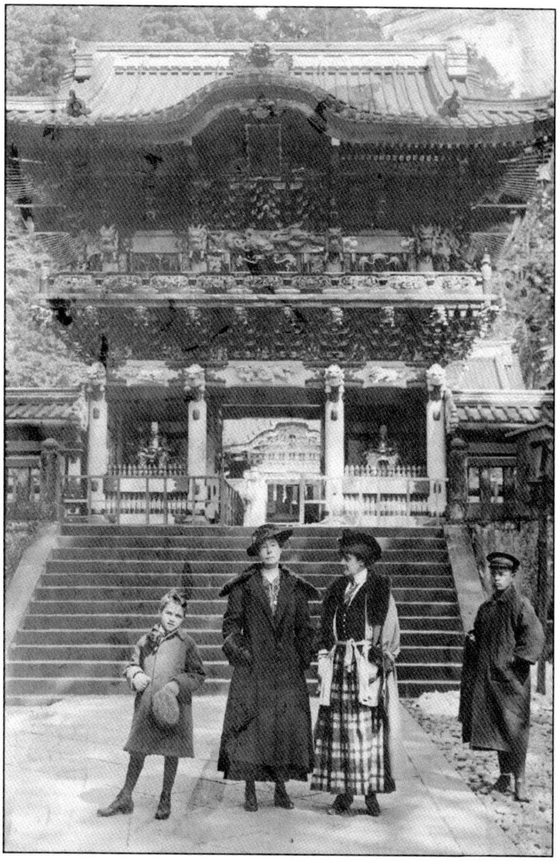

For young John Stine, the Japan trip was a grand adventure. He wrote in his diary on February 6, 1917, "In the morning I was the first one to see the Mount Fuji. It was awfully pretty the snow mountain rising above everything. I saw hundreds of Japanese boats all around and saw a fort and lots of other things. When we were docked, we got off in a rickshaw and beat it to the hotel." (Courtesy of Peter Stine.)

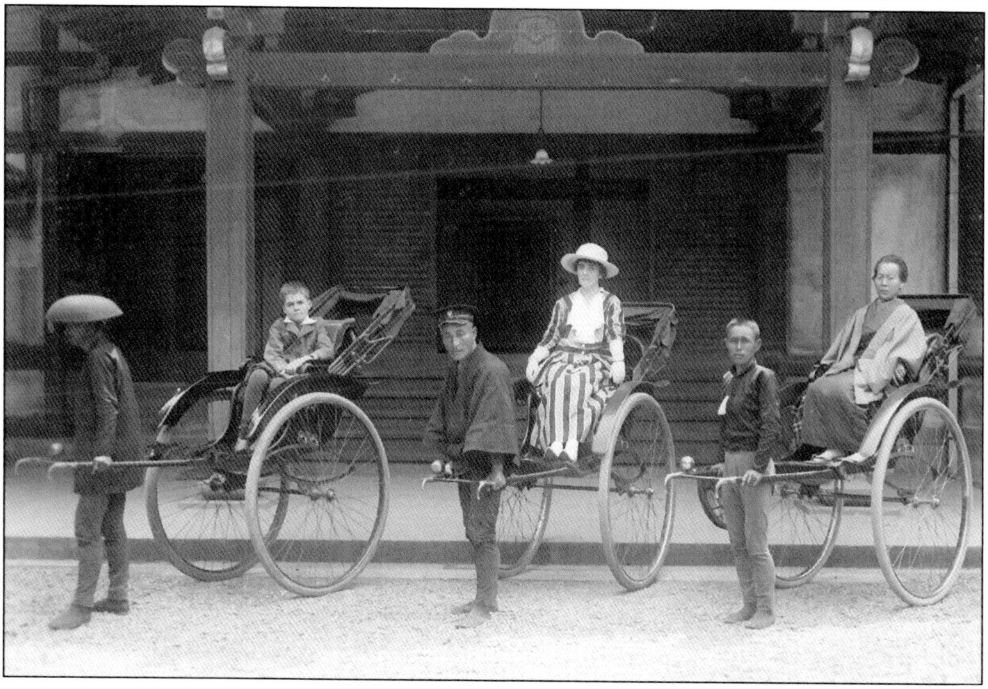

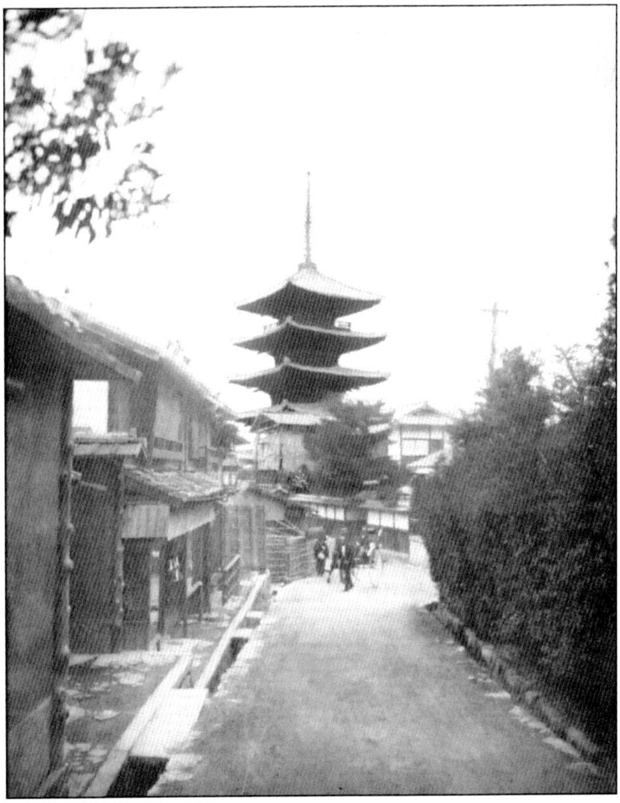

Isabel and John rode in a rickshaw past traditional houses, shops, and a Shinto shrine tower. Isabel purchased many Japanese artifacts, decor, and exquisite fabric and clothing to bring home. John wrote of one shopping trip in his diary on February 20, 1917: "Bought some kimonos. 2 for me and a lot for mother and 4 for sister and two for Tommy." (Courtesy of Peter Stine.)

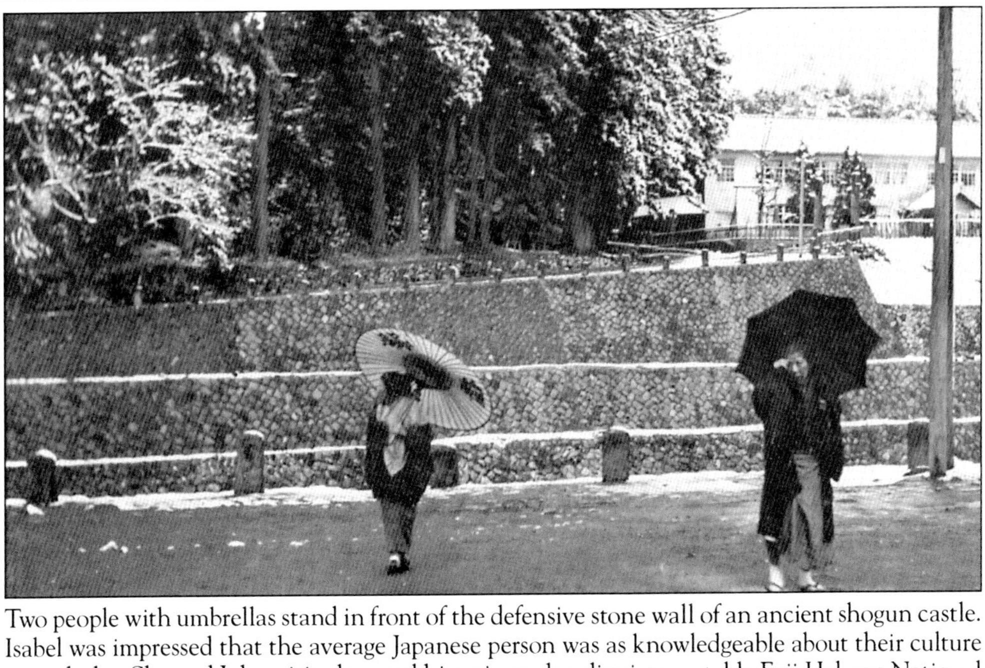

Two people with umbrellas stand in front of the defensive stone wall of an ancient shogun castle. Isabel was impressed that the average Japanese person was as knowledgeable about their culture as a scholar. She and John visited several historic garden districts, notably Fuji-Hakone National Park. Seeing this enchanting region, she must have been inspired to name her own Japanese estate after it. (Courtesy of Peter Stine.)

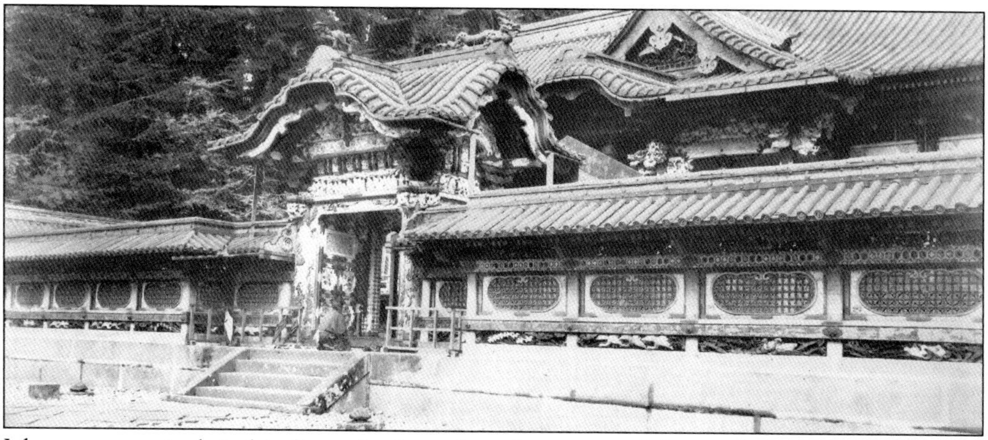

John wrote sparingly in his diary after busy days of touring with his mother to ancient Buddhist and Shinto temples. His entry for Saturday, March 9, 1917, is brief: "Went to a temple. Hundreds of shops in front and inside the gates." He also wrote of attending performances in Tokyo, including a Noh play, jotting down, "I liked it a lot." (Courtesy of Peter Stine.)

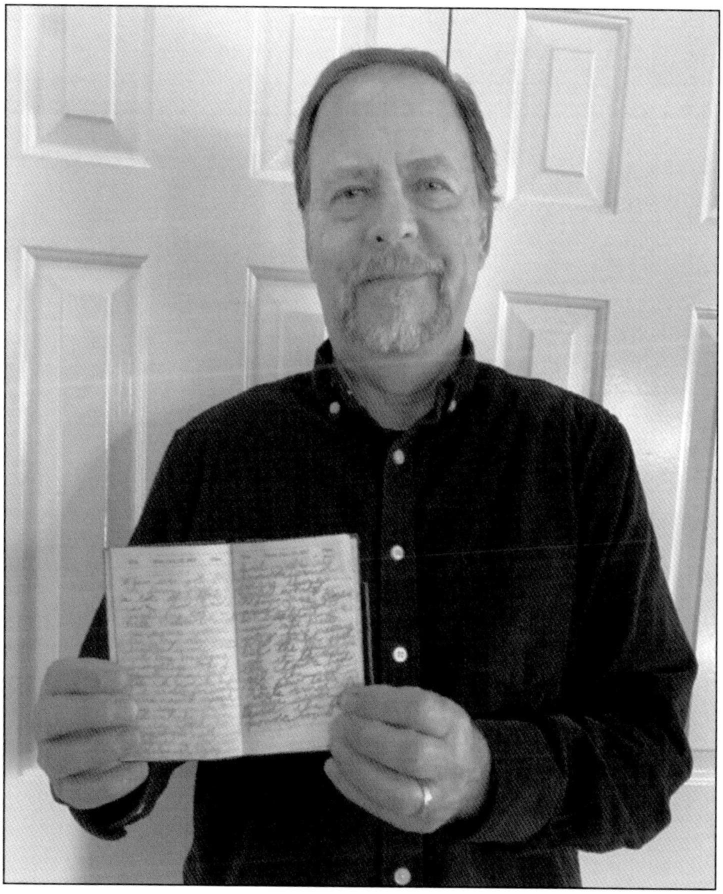

Peter Stine holds the 1917 diary his father, John MacLeod Stine, kept during the Japan trip with his mother, Isabel. John, age 10, wrote sporadic but vivid entries, giving glimpses of their six months' stay in Japan. Dr. Stine is a retired research ecologist with the USDA Forest Service, Pacific Southwest Station. He generously donated Isabel Stine's albums of photographs and memorabilia to the Hakone Foundation. (Courtesy of Peter Stine.)

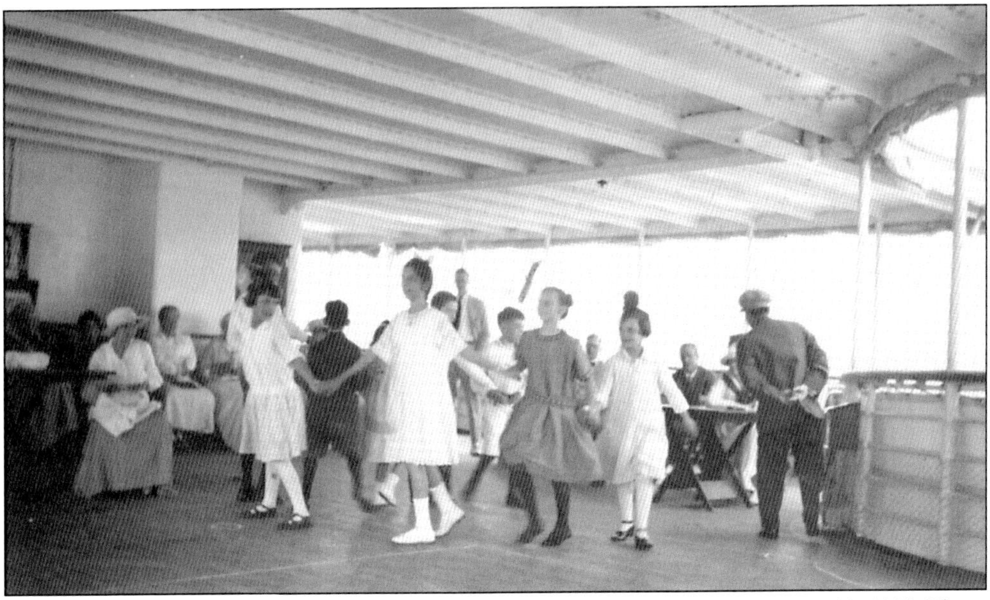

Isabel and John traveled by ship to and from Japan, starting their trip on January 22, 1917. There were other wealthy American families on board. John (center in white outfit) is pictured here. The passengers entertained themselves on the weeklong trip across the ocean. In his February 5 diary entry, John wrote, "Mother played the piano a lot and a lot of people sang." (Courtesy of Peter Stine.)

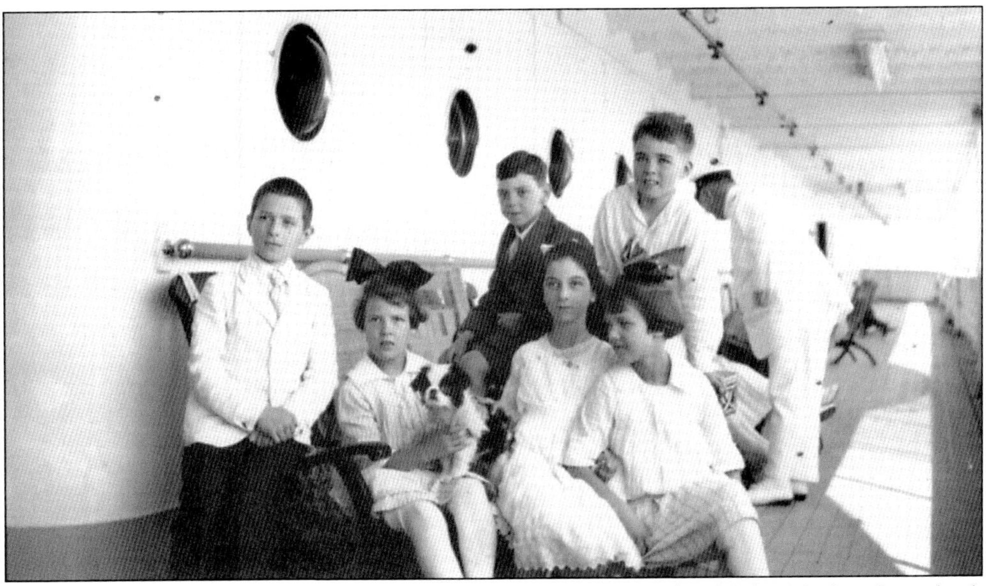

The children on board the steamship played deck games and socialized. John MacLeod is in back on the right. He and his mother traveled first to Vancouver, Canada, by train, and then boarded the ship to Japan. They would reverse the long trip on the way home six months later, with unusual memories, artifacts, and a deeper understanding of Japanese culture. (Courtesy of Peter Stine.)

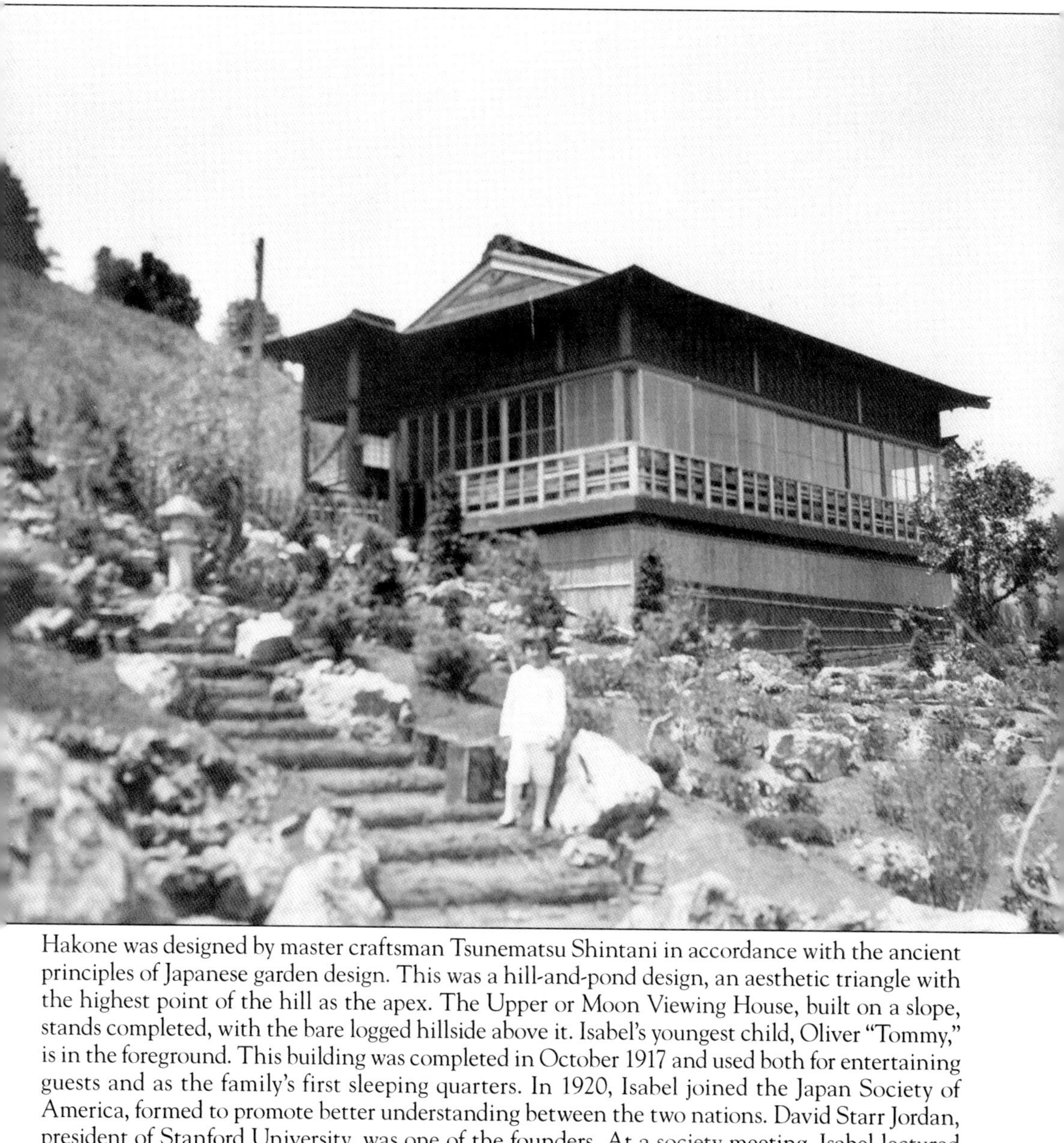

Hakone was designed by master craftsman Tsunematsu Shintani in accordance with the ancient principles of Japanese garden design. This was a hill-and-pond design, an aesthetic triangle with the highest point of the hill as the apex. The Upper or Moon Viewing House, built on a slope, stands completed, with the bare logged hillside above it. Isabel's youngest child, Oliver "Tommy," is in the foreground. This building was completed in October 1917 and used both for entertaining guests and as the family's first sleeping quarters. In 1920, Isabel joined the Japan Society of America, formed to promote better understanding between the two nations. David Starr Jordan, president of Stanford University, was one of the founders. At a society meeting, Isabel lectured on Kabuki theater, showing slides from her 1917 stay in Tokyo studying Japanese performing arts. (Courtesy of Peter Stine.)

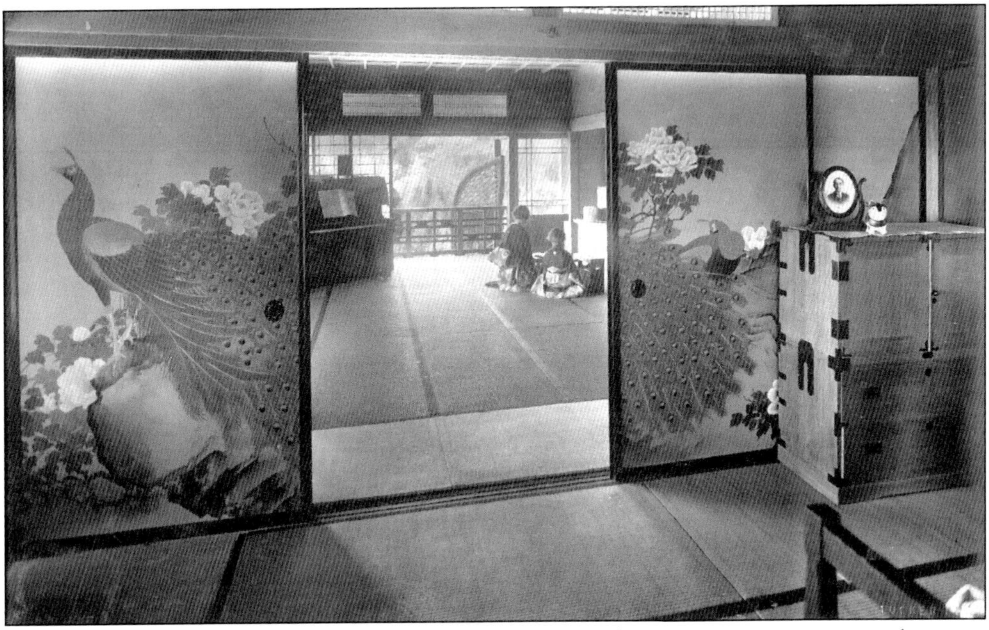

In the interior of the Upper or Moon Viewing House, with one room opening into the next, the Stine children can be seen. A photograph of their late father, Oliver Stine, is on top of the Japanese chest of drawers at right. The peacock-design screens on the sliding door are identical to the those inside the Japan Pavilion of the Panama-Pacific International Exposition of 1915. (Courtesy of Peter Stine.)

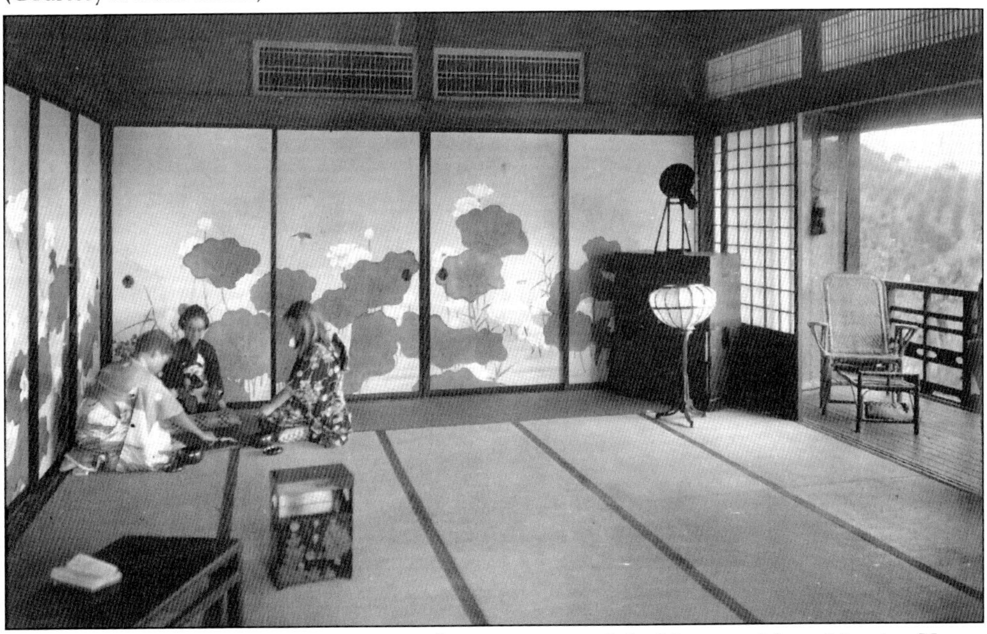

The Stine children sit on tatami mats in the main room of the Upper or Moon Viewing House playing a game of Go (Japanese chess). They wear the kimonos their mother purchased for them on her trip to Japan in 1917. The surrounding panels are painted with elegant floating lotus pads. With traditional Japanese flooring, everyone removes their shoes before entering the room. (Courtesy of Peter Stine.)

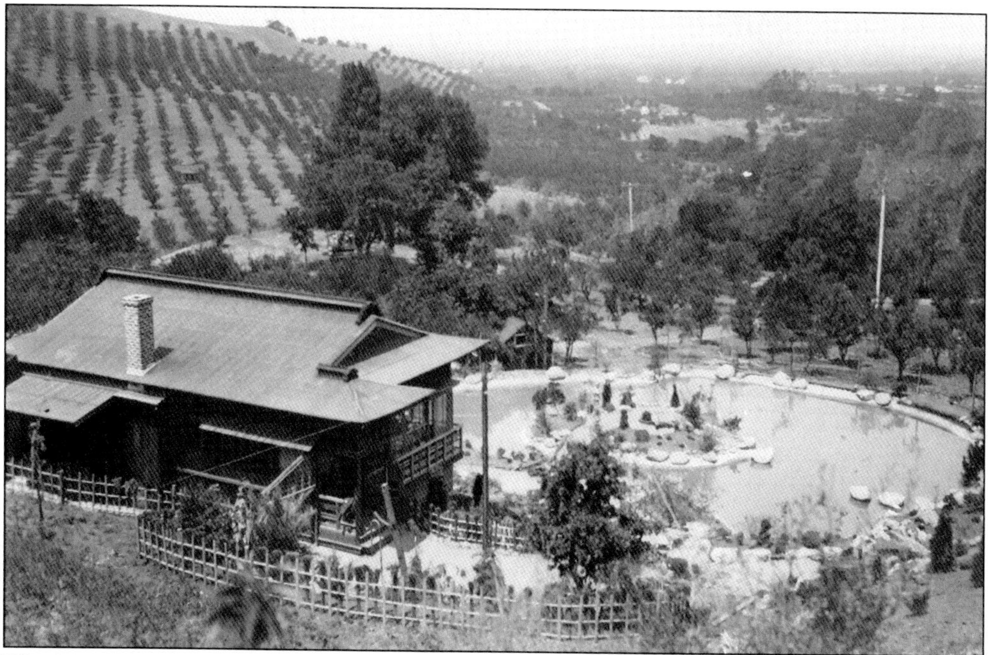

The Moon Viewing House looks east and down on the newly constructed pond. Beyond is Saratoga and the valley. The cookhouse for meals is partially hidden down the hill. The iconic arch bridge has yet to be built. Note the hillside with rows of fruit trees. Agriculture was the business of fertile Santa Clara County, which was known as the "The Valley of Heart's Delight." (Courtesy of Peter Stine.)

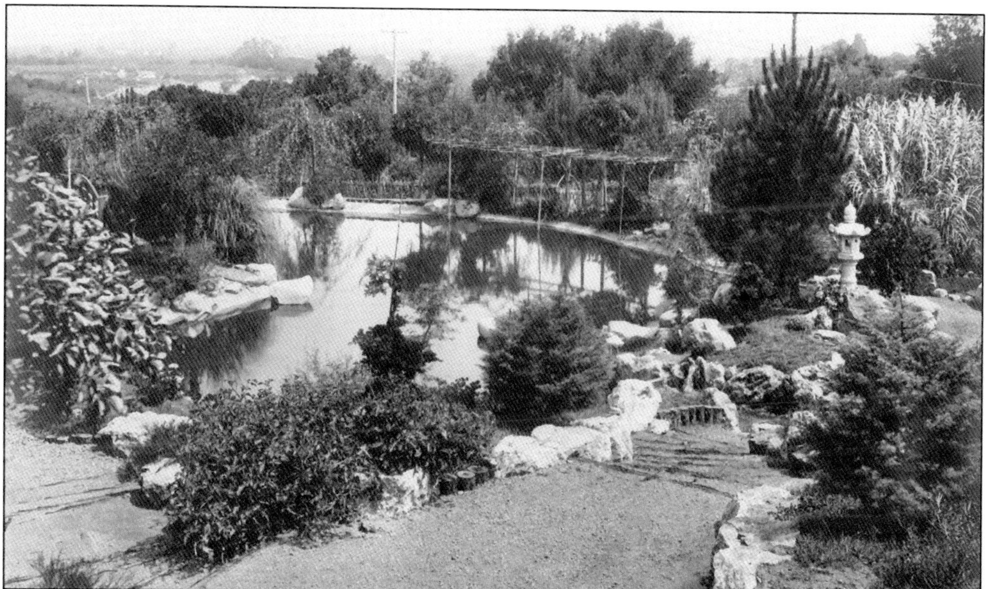

The pond and wisteria platform are visible from the Upper House. The strolling garden faces east, so a rising moon can be seen. The arch bridge is in the background. Naoharu Aihara set the gardens on 15 acres of bare logged hillside. Aihara, from a family of imperial gardeners, designed Hakone in the style of the late Endo period, 17th-century Japan, and it was completed in 1919. (Courtesy of Peter Stine.)

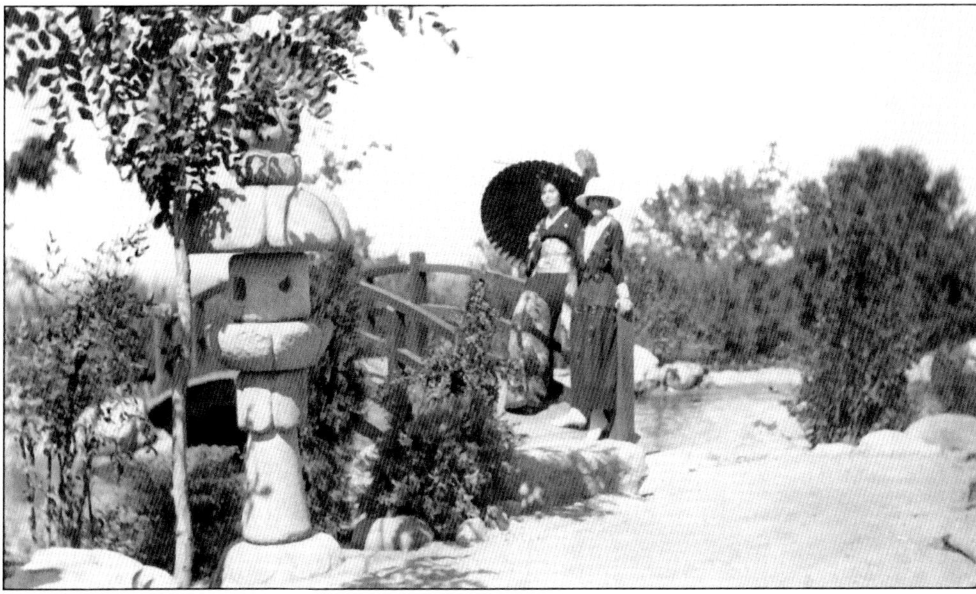

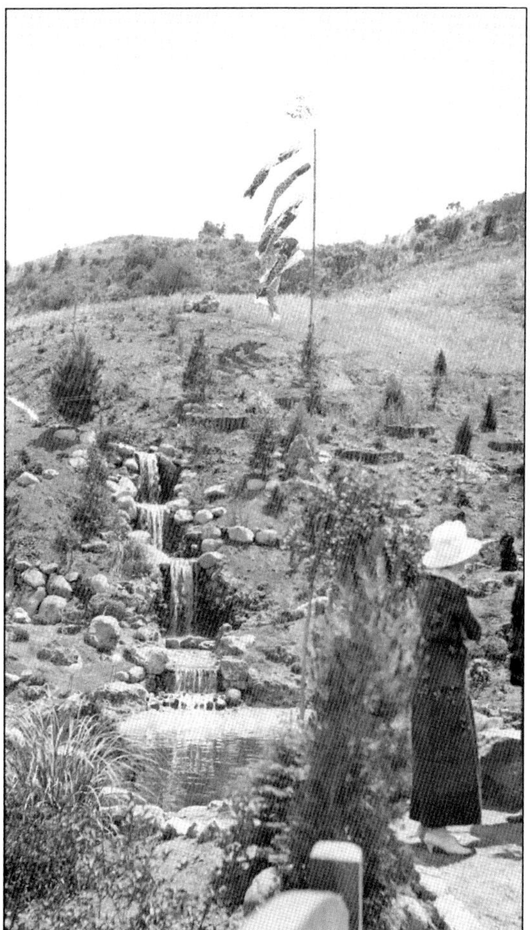

Isabel Stine, in western dress, stands with a friend in Japanese costume on the new arched Moon Bridge over the pond. The pedestal lotus lantern in the foreground represents the sacred water flower, a Buddhist symbol. The lantern, significantly placed on the island, is part of a triad of lanterns around the pond. The Japanese vegetation for shade has yet to mature. (Courtesy of Peter Stine.)

Isabel Stine celebrates Boys' Day, May 5, by flying a carp flag above the waterfall in honor of her two sons, John and Oliver. In Japanese culture, the carp is a male symbol of strength and fortitude. Stumps of redwood trees are still visible on the hillside. The land was logged before the Stines bought the property. (Courtesy of Peter Stine.)

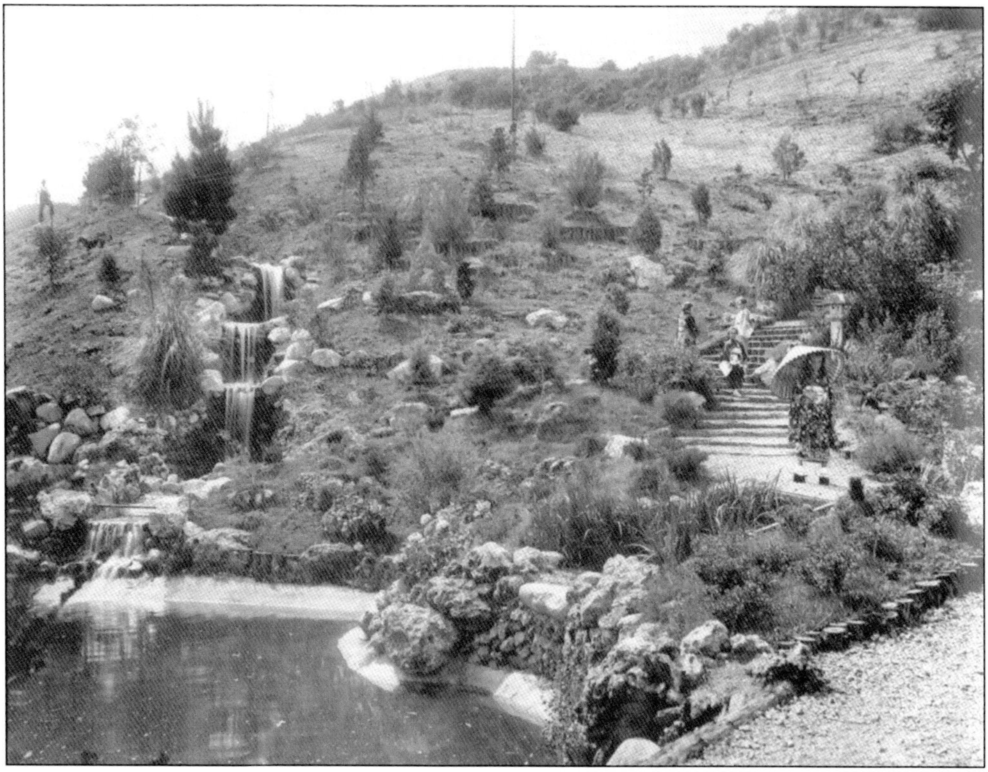

The exquisite Japanese garden is nearing completion, with the waterfall, or *konogari*, flowing into the pond. This was a momentous moment, and Isabel Stine staged a dramatic scene to be captured for posterity. The Stine children (from front to back), Helen (with umbrella), John, and Oliver, are descending the newly constructed steps wearing the Japanese costumes their mother purchased for them in Japan. (Courtesy of Peter Stine.)

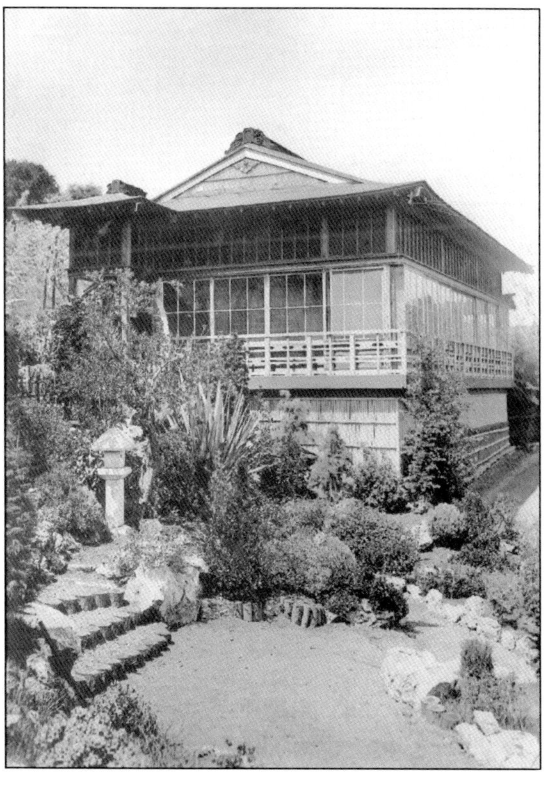

This is the southern side of the Upper House, also known as the Moon Viewing House. Note the newly planted vegetation and steps made of redwood log sections. Designed in classic Japanese garden style with Buddhist principles and Taoist cosmology, there is an aesthetic triangle with the moon hill at its apex. Landscape artist Aihara imported lanterns, trees, plants, and fencing materials from Japan. (Courtesy of Peter Stine.)

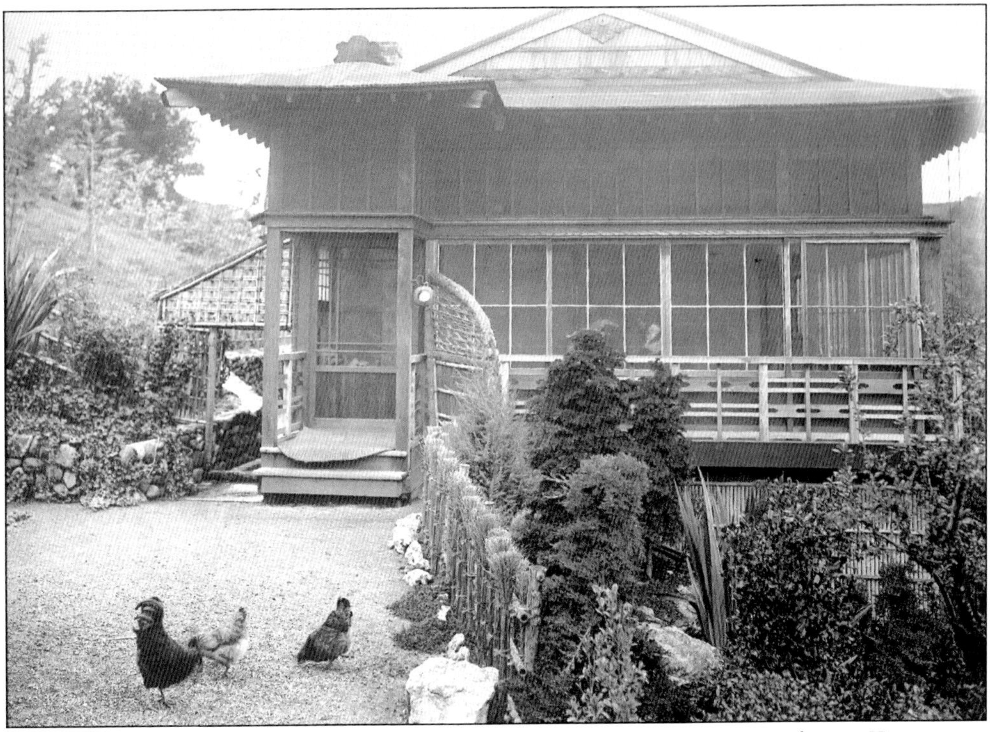

A southern view of the newly built Moon Viewing House, designed by master craftsman Tsunematsu Shintani, shows a country atmosphere, with chickens wandering about pecking at the earth. It was the Stines' residence for summers and on weekends. In the formal garden, there was a harmonious placement of plants, stones, and water, with a California influence. (Courtesy of Peter Stine.)

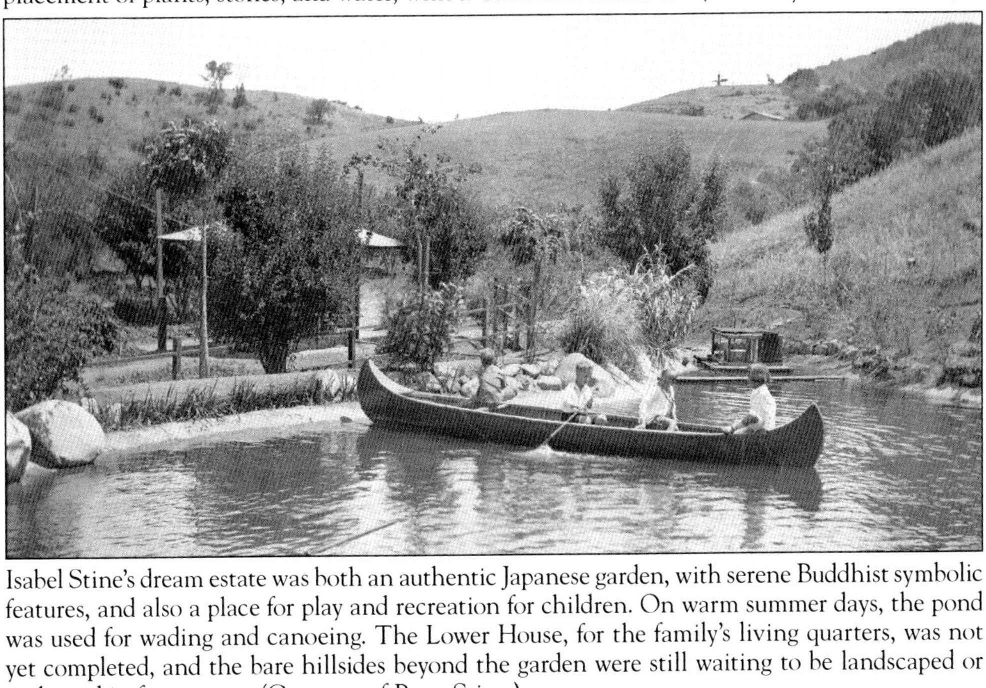

Isabel Stine's dream estate was both an authentic Japanese garden, with serene Buddhist symbolic features, and also a place for play and recreation for children. On warm summer days, the pond was used for wading and canoeing. The Lower House, for the family's living quarters, was not yet completed, and the bare hillsides beyond the garden were still waiting to be landscaped or replanted in forest trees. (Courtesy of Peter Stine.)

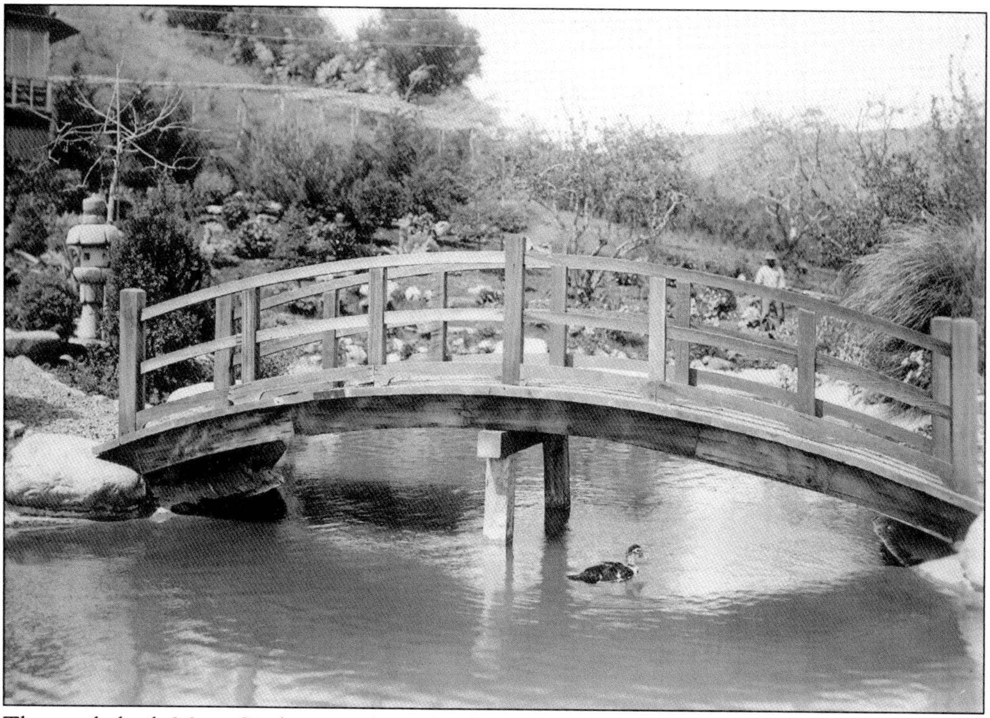

The newly built Moon Bridge completes the design of Hakone. The Japanese garden originated with the introduction of Buddhism to Japan from China in the fifth century AD. The Moon Bridge is a variation of the Chinese arched bridge. The lotus lantern on the left is part of a triad of lanterns around the pond in the sacred triangle motif. (Courtesy of Peter Stine.)

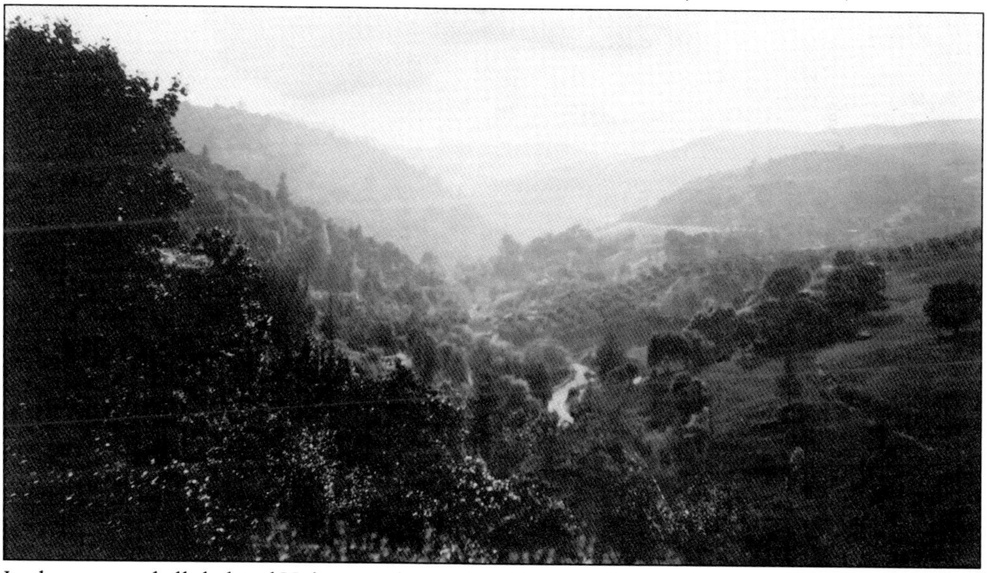

In the western hills behind Hakone is the road to Congress Springs Inn, one of the famous public vacation spots in the area, and on to Santa Cruz. While Hakone is designed in the hill-and-pond style of mid-17th-century Japan, with two authentically constructed Japanese houses, there is no denying it is in California, surrounded by redwoods and oak forests. (Courtesy of Saratoga History Museum.)

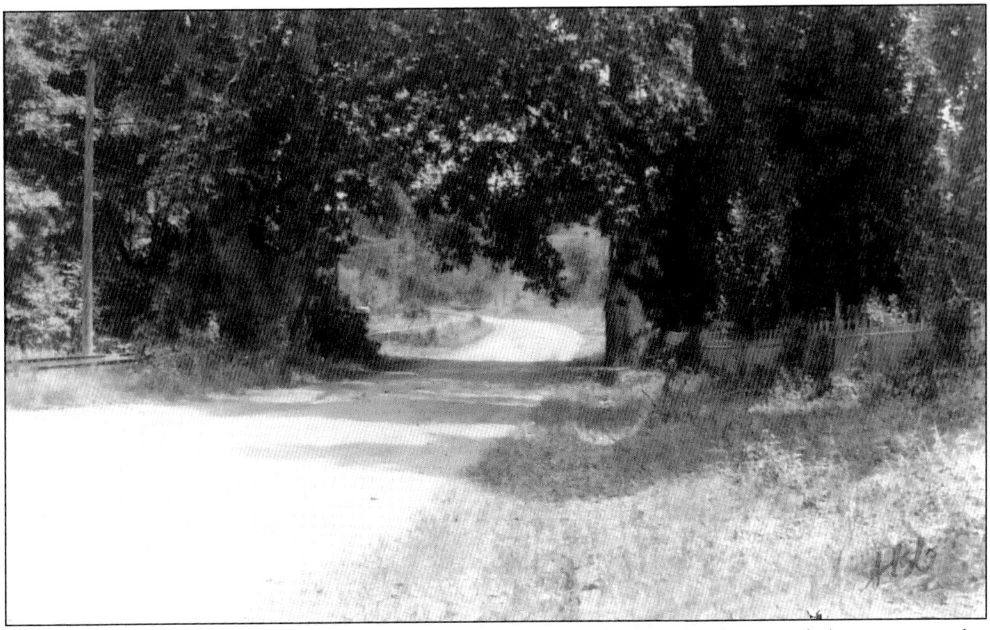

This is a view of the road in front of Hakone's entrance, looking back toward the curve in the road to the village of Saratoga. Note the electric Interurban Peninsular Railroad rails for the line that serviced Hakone and the community. The railway was built as a complex system connecting to the steam locomotive line going up to San Francisco, over to San Jose, and beyond. (Courtesy of Peter Stine.)

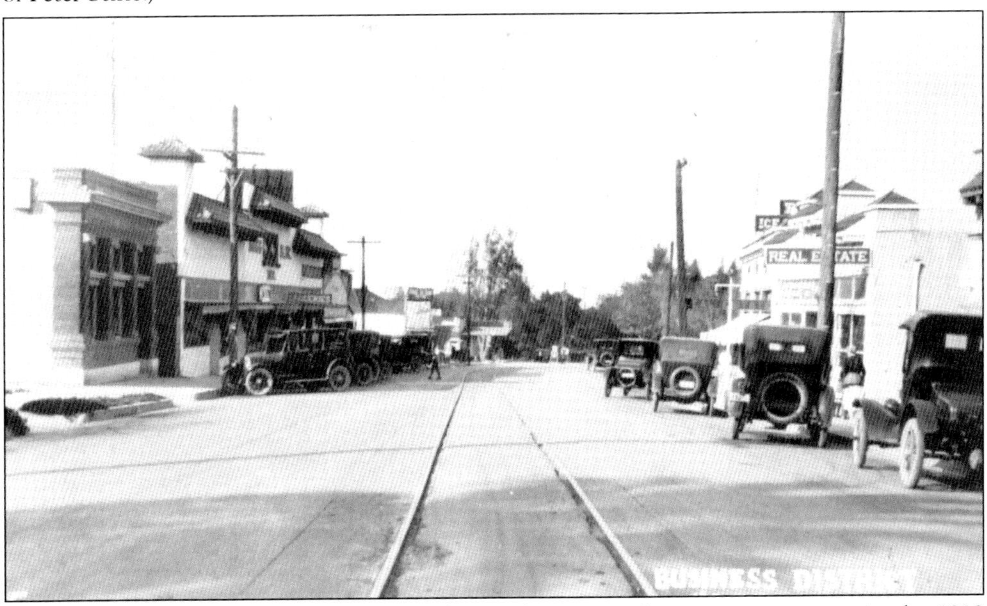

The poles and rails of the electric interurban railway are a dominating presence in the 1918 business district of Saratoga. With two rail systems, Southern Pacific and Peninsular Railroad, coordinating their services hauling freight and passengers, people began living along the rail lines. A growing wealthy class in San Francisco sought warmer vacation land on the peninsula, finding the climate and scenery of Saratoga and Los Gatos very desirable. (Courtesy of Saratoga History Museum.)

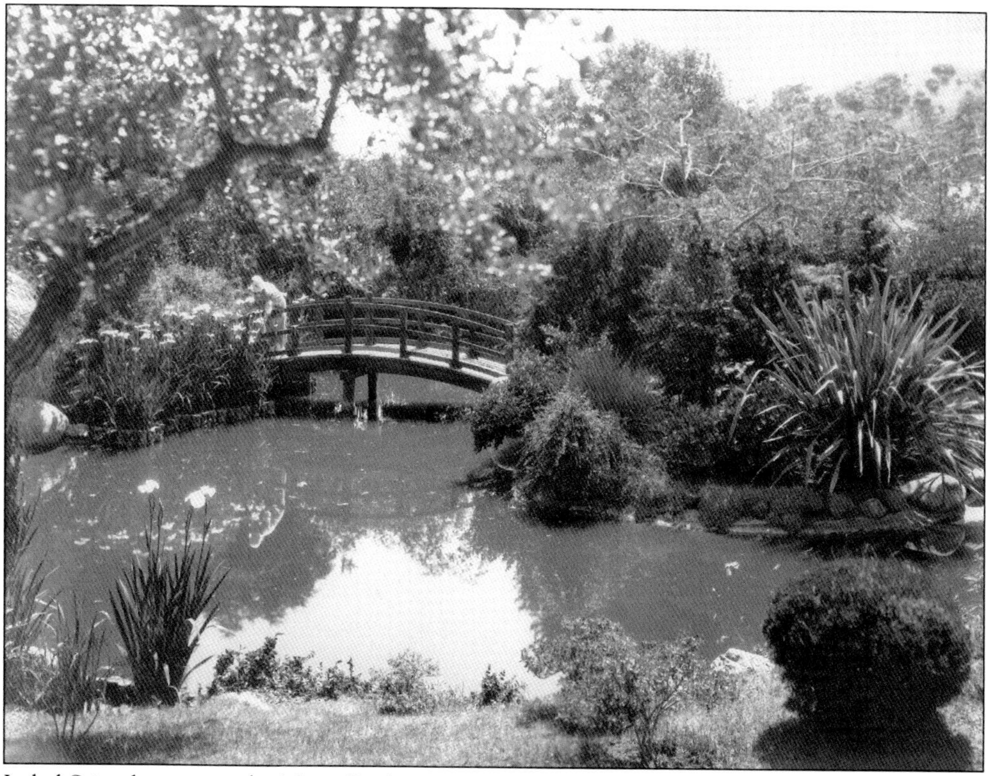

Isabel Stine leans over the Moon Bridge, picking Japanese iris that grow prolifically around the pond. She could now enjoy the completion of her Japanese estate, as the landscaping finally matured and covered the original logged area. Note the serene pond reflecting the image of the bridge, which was intentional in the Japanese design. (Courtesy of Peter Stine.)

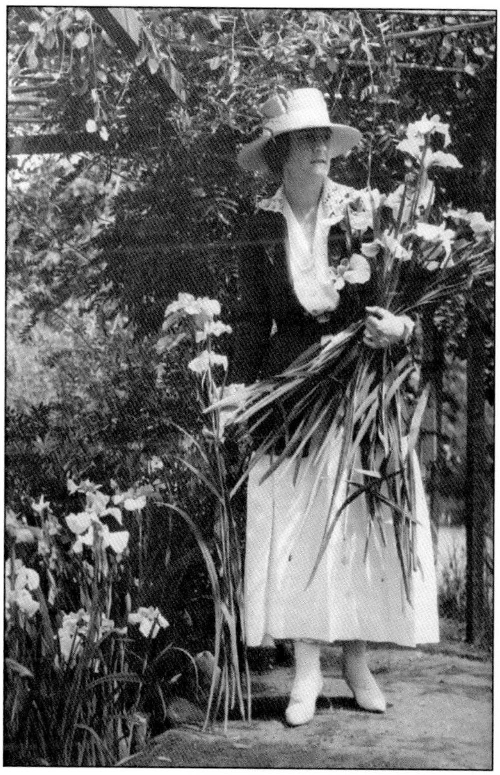

Isabel Stine poses in her dream garden with a bouquet of Japanese iris she has gathered. Hakone's garden designer, Naoharu Aihara, planted them around the pond and returned on occasion to give advice on the garden. The year-round temperate climate of California promoted the lush landscape, which was Stine's heart's desire. (Courtesy of Peter Stine.)

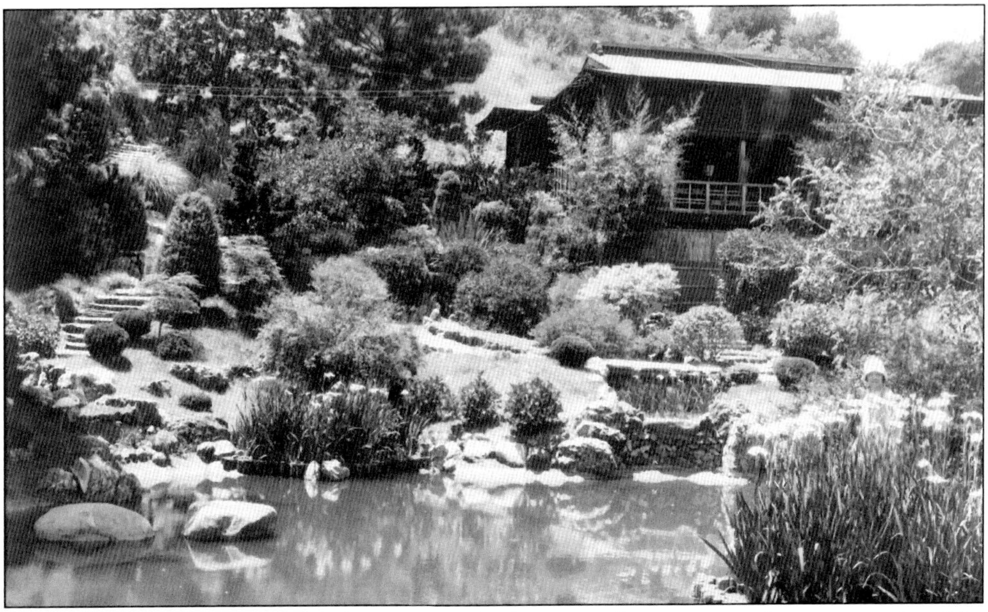

Isabel Stine is peeking over her Japanese iris bed enjoying her maturing Japanese garden. She wanted Hakone to exemplify the beauty and value of Japanese culture and aesthetics. The ideals she promoted were in direct opposition to those of politicians and their supporters advocating for ending Japanese immigration with the Exclusion Law of 1924. Stine was an active member of the Japan Society of America. (Courtesy of Peter Stine.)

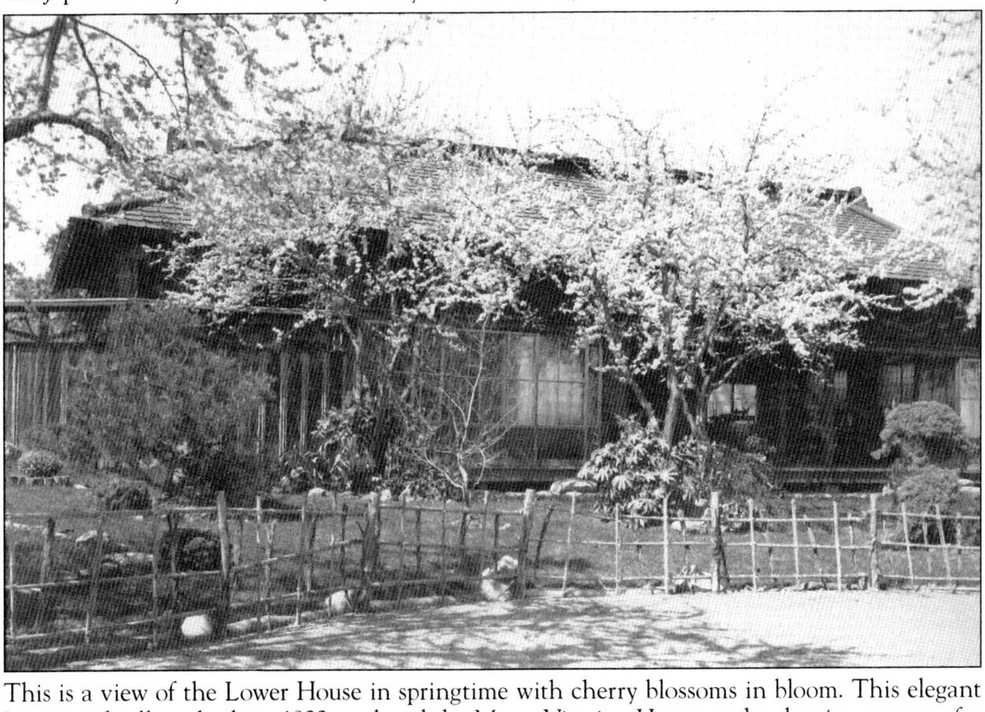

This is a view of the Lower House in springtime with cherry blossoms in bloom. This elegant Japanese dwelling, built in 1922, replaced the Moon Viewing House as the sleeping quarters for the family. Hakone was now a complete country estate for Isabel to enjoy with her children and share with her large circle of friends. (Courtesy of Peter Stine.)

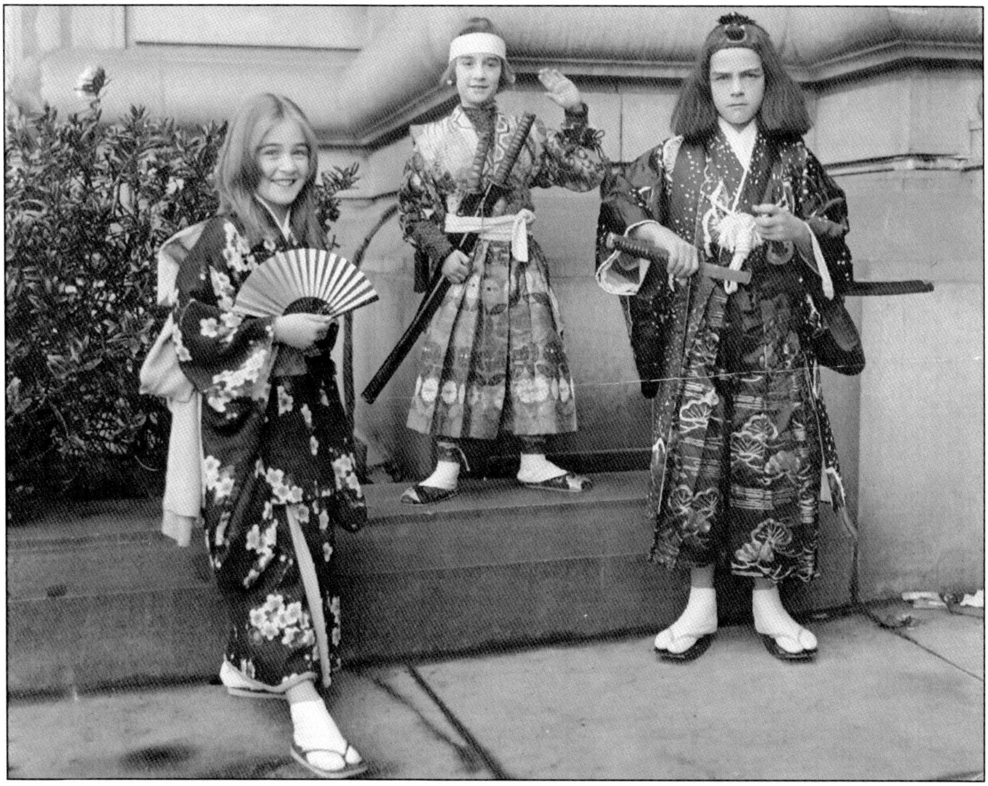

The Stine children (from left to right), Helen, Oliver, and John, who attended private school in San Francisco, are wearing the ornate theatrical costumes their mother brought back from Japan. As reported in the *San Francisco Examiner* on December 28, 1919, they attended a "Fancy Dress Costume Holiday Party at the Fairmont Hotel along with other children who will be the future Belles and Beaux of Society." (Courtesy of Peter Stine.)

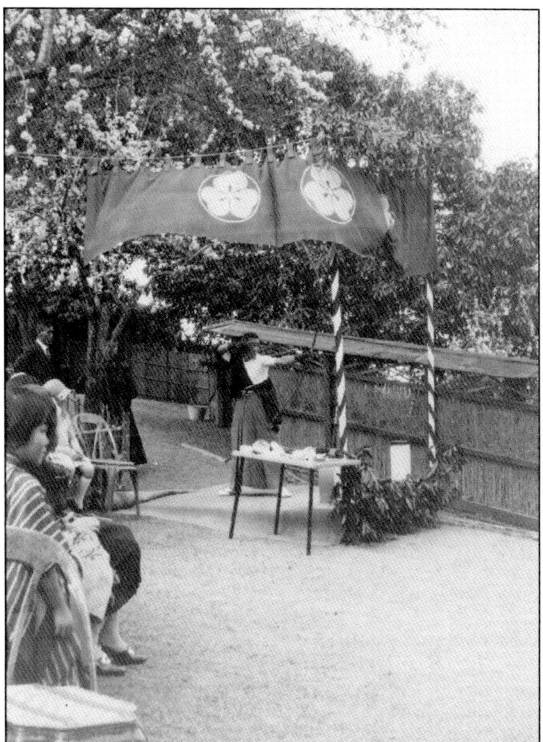

Isabel Stine, by hosting Japanese cultural events at her splendid Hakone, promoted intercultural understanding in California at a time of anti-Asian sentiment and immigration exclusion. Here in the garden is master archer Imazumi, dressed in ceremonial *haori* and *hakama* costume exhibiting a traditional art. He and other Japanese Kyudo Club members held exhibition tournaments at Hakone, demonstrating their archery skills and mental discipline. (Courtesy of Peter Stine.)

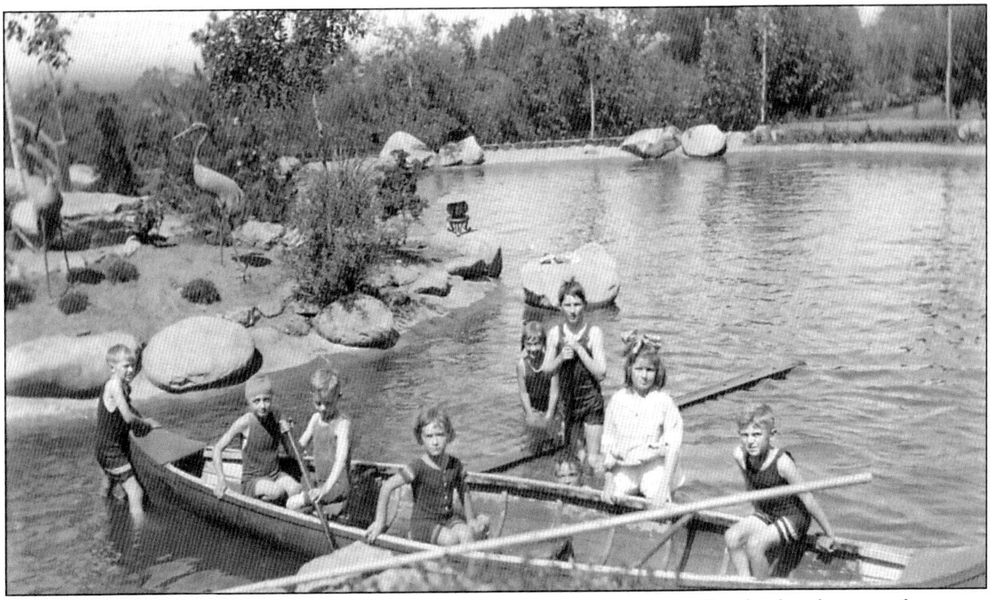

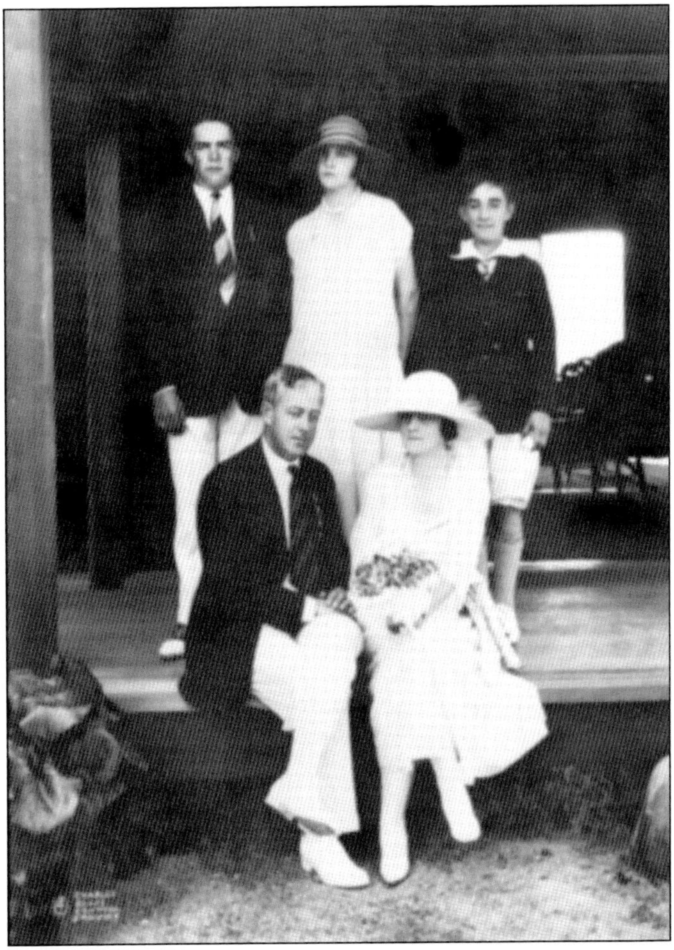

As the landscape of Hakone was developing in traditional Japanese style, the Stine children and their friends continued to use the pond for canoeing, wading, and swimming on hot summer days. In the background on the island is the bronze crane and other garden ornamentation imported from Japan. The crane is still standing regally in the pond today. (Courtesy of Peter Stine.)

Isabel Stine married Francis Leis at Hakone in 1923. This formal portrait of the newly wedded couple with Isabel's children (from left to right), John, Helen and Oliver, was taken in front of the Lower House. Isabel gave a copy of this wedding photograph to her friend, Maj. Charles Lee Tilden, who would purchase Hakone from her nine years later. (Courtesy of Peter Stine.)

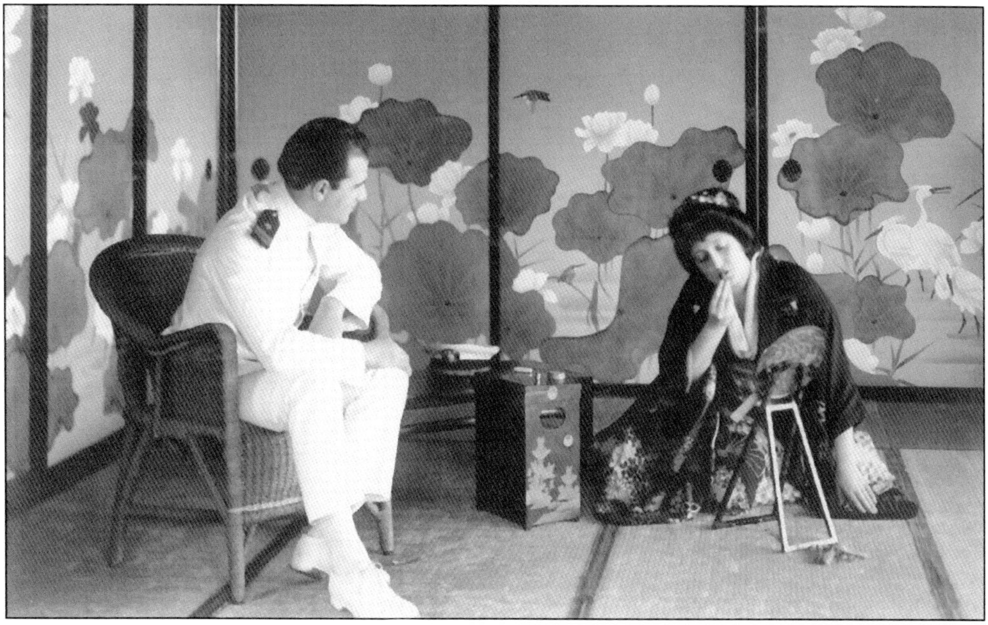

Isabel Stine was an active supporter of the new San Francisco Opera Company and Opera House, advising the director on the stage scenery for the 1924 San Francisco production of Puccini's *Madama Butterfly*. A year earlier, she held an exclusive performance of *Madama Butterfly* at Hakone. The singers, soprano Bianca Saroya as Cio-Cio-San (Butterfly) and Dimitri Onofrei as Lt. B.F. Pinkerton, pose in the Moon Viewing House. (Courtesy of Peter Stine.)

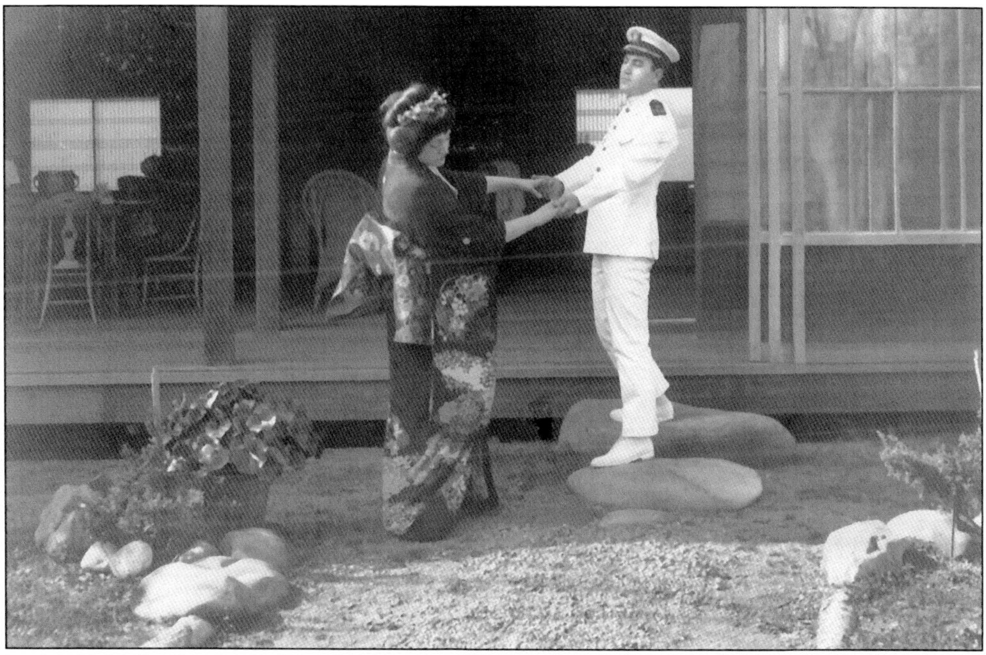

In 1923, the lead singers of *Madama Butterfly* re-enact a scene outside the Lower House, with Dimitri Onofrei as Lieutenant Pinkerton wooing Butterfly, played by Bianca Soraya. They are standing on the same stones still in use at Hakone today. The singers were a married couple who were well known in the opera world. (Courtesy of Peter Stine.)

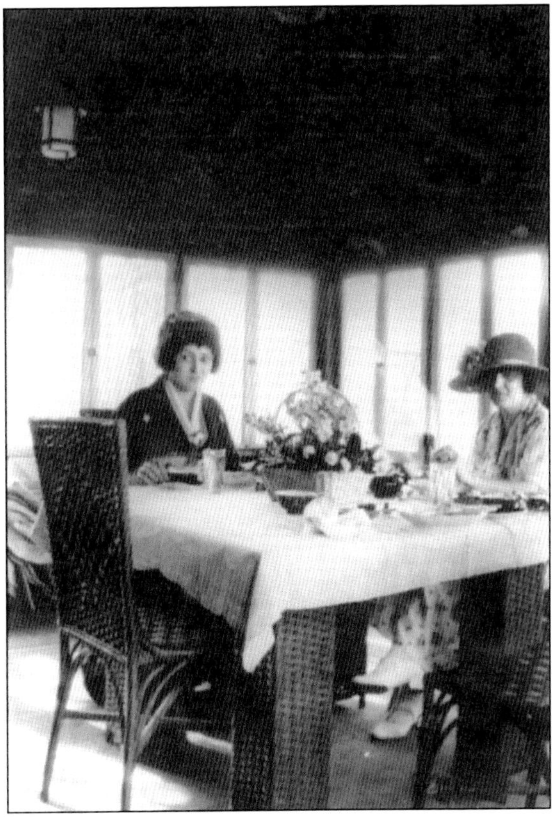

With Isabel Stine Leis's involvement, the San Francisco premiere of *Madama Butterfly* was a brilliant success. In the informal production at Hakone, Isabel played the role of Kate, the American wife of Lieutenant Pinkerton, who comes with him to Japan, causing Butterfly to commit suicide. Here Bianca Soraya, in her Cio-Cio-San costume, and Isabel, dressed as Kate Pinkerton, enjoy a break at Hakone's Lower House. (Courtesy of Peter Stine.)

In 1939, Joan Fontaine married Brian Ahern, with Isabel's sons as groomsmen. The bride's sister, Olivia de Havilland, is to the right of the bride, and the bride's mother, Lilian de Havilland, is to the left of the groom. John MacLeod Stine is at left in back, and Oliver Stine is second from the right. As children, the de Havilland sisters and Stine boys played together at Hakone. (Courtesy of Peter Stine.)

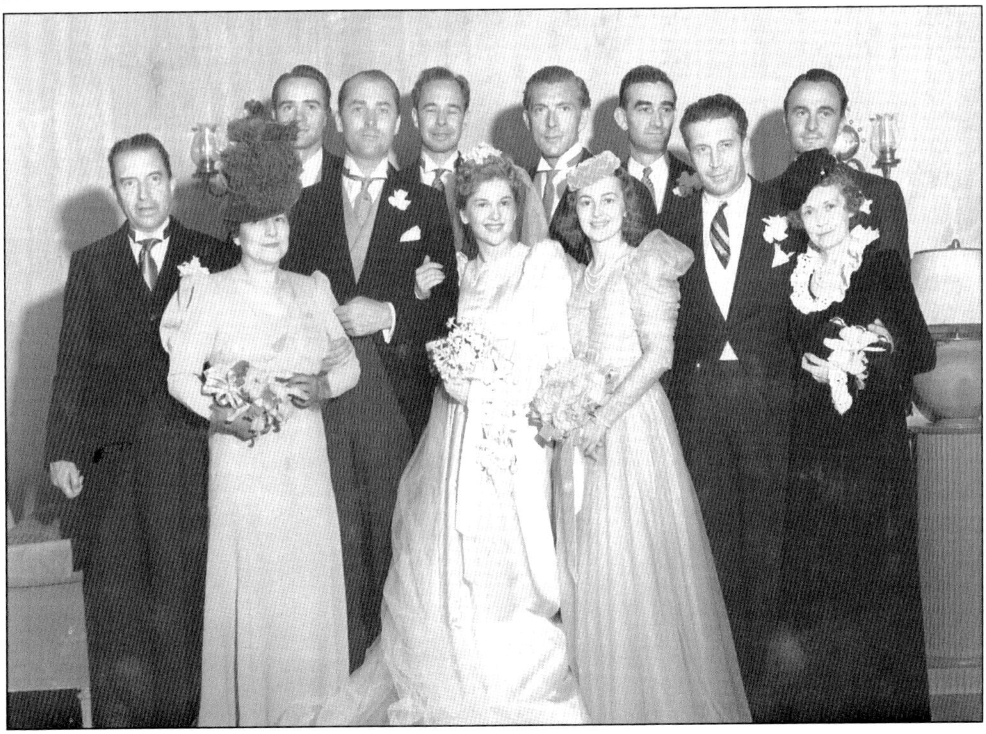

Two

The Tilden Era
Strength and Endurance in War and Peace

During the Depression, Isabel Stine Leis could no longer afford to own Hakone. Fortunately, someone she knew and respected, Charles Tilden, purchased it from her. Thus began the longest private ownership of Hakone, from 1932 to 1961.

Charles Lee Tilden (1857–1950) was an attorney, businessman, and financier. While in the National Guard, he married Lily Von Schmidt Mitchell, a widow with two little daughters, Alexine and Marion. A major in the 1st California Infantry, he served in the Philippines during the Spanish-American War. The couple had a son, Charles Tilden Jr. Major Tilden was a world traveler, visiting Japan several times. He was the president of the East Bay Regional Parks District, saving thousands of acres of land for public use, and Tilden Park is named in his honor.

Hakone was Tilden's retreat from his business and civic duties. He commissioned the building of the main gate, the Mon, by brothers Shinzaburo and Gentaro Nishura, devout Buddhists who constructed buildings for the Japanese community in San Jose. He hired a young agricultural worker, James Sasaki, born in Ketotori, Japan, as Hakone's gardener. James Sasaki was married to Shizue Takagi, born in Alviso, California, and they had a son, David. Three more children, Betty, Jane, and Kathy, were born after they moved to Hakone. James Sasaki worked continuously at Hakone for three decades, except for the three and a half years during World War II when he and his family were interned at Topaz, Utah, by Executive Order 9066. During this period, Japanese gardens throughout the United States were vandalized and destroyed, but Hakone, protected by Major Tilden, was unharmed. When the Sasakis were released after the war, Tilden's stepdaughter Marion met them at the train station to return them to Hakone. Resuming his position, James Sasaki brought Hakone to its greatest height of beauty.

When Tilden died in 1950, his stepdaughter Alexine Mitchell Gregory inherited Hakone. Upon her death in 1958, Hakone was passed to her son Michael Gregory. He and his wife, Ora, allowed outsiders to see the gardens, inviting the California Historical Society to use Hakone for a benefit.

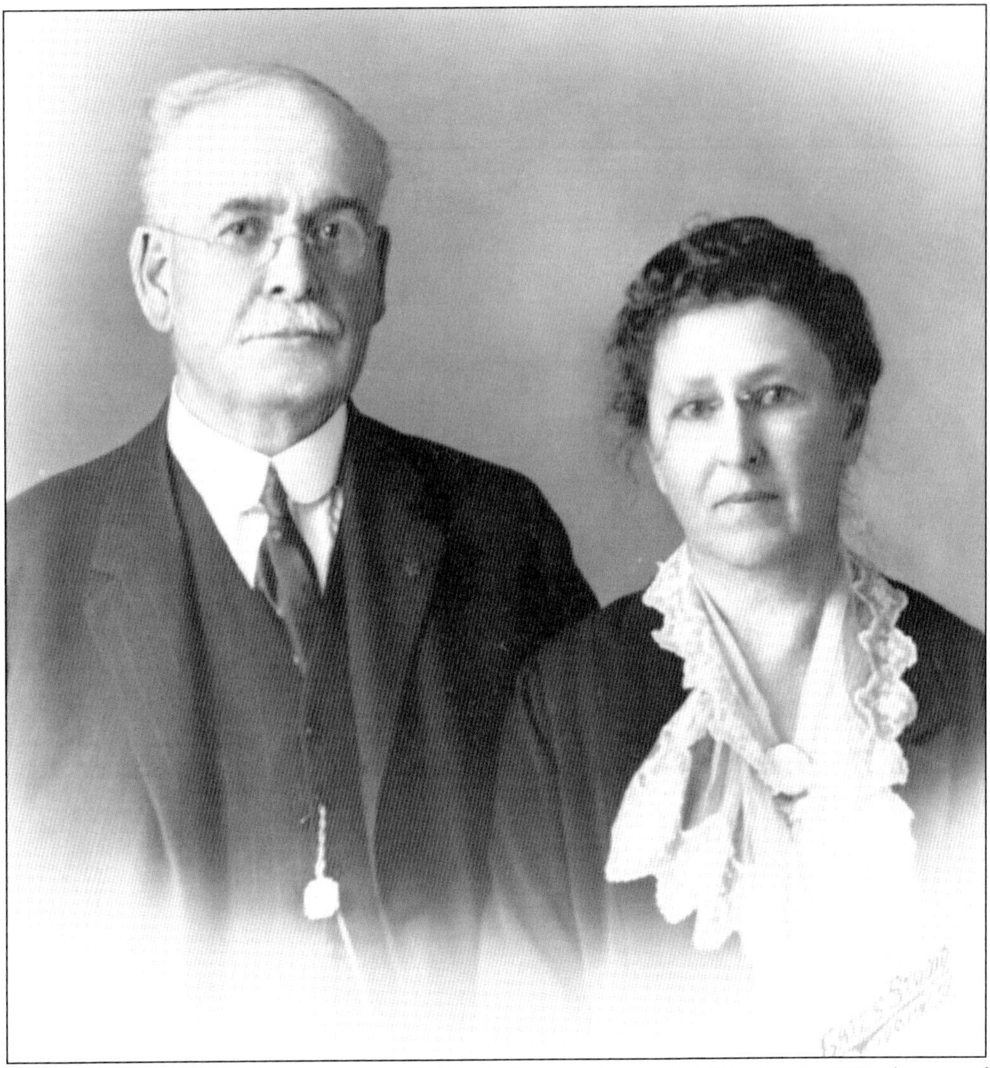

Charles Lee Tilden was born in Chile Gulch, Calaveras County, California, in 1857, the son of a judge. On June 4, 1892, he wed Lilian Francis Von Schmidt Mitchell, born in San Francisco in 1859. "Lily," as she was known, was a widow with two young daughters, Alexine and Marion. Two years later, they had a son, Charles Lee Tilden Jr. A businessman, attorney, and civic leader, Charles Tilden was a major in the infantry of the California National Guard, serving in the Philippines during the Spanish-American War in 1898. The Tildens, who resided in Alameda, California, enjoyed world travel, visiting Japan several times. This photograph shows the couple in their middle age, still years before they owned Hakone. (Courtesy of Tilden-Gregory Archives.)

This is a photograph of a youthful Lilian Francis von Schmidt. Her father was Alexis Waldemar von Schmidt, who came to California from Russia during the Gold Rush and became a prominent civil engineer. She was married to Harrison Whitman Mitchell, and they had two daughters. Mitchell died in 1886, and Lilian married Charles Lee Tilden in 1892. Two years later, they had a son. (Courtesy of Tilden-Gregory Archives.)

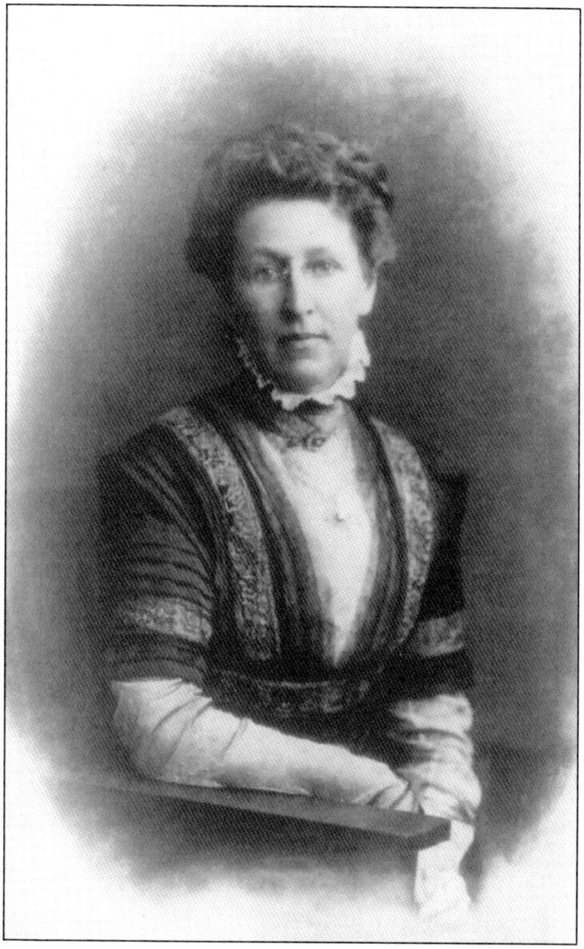

Maj. Charles Lee Tilden is seen on his 80th birthday at Hakone in 1937. A man of great accomplishments, he was a military man, an attorney, and a civic leader. He also had a lumber business in Richmond. When Major Tilden bought Hakone from Isabel Stine Leis in 1932, he was considered one of the richest men in the Bay Area. (Courtesy of Tilden-Gregory Archives.)

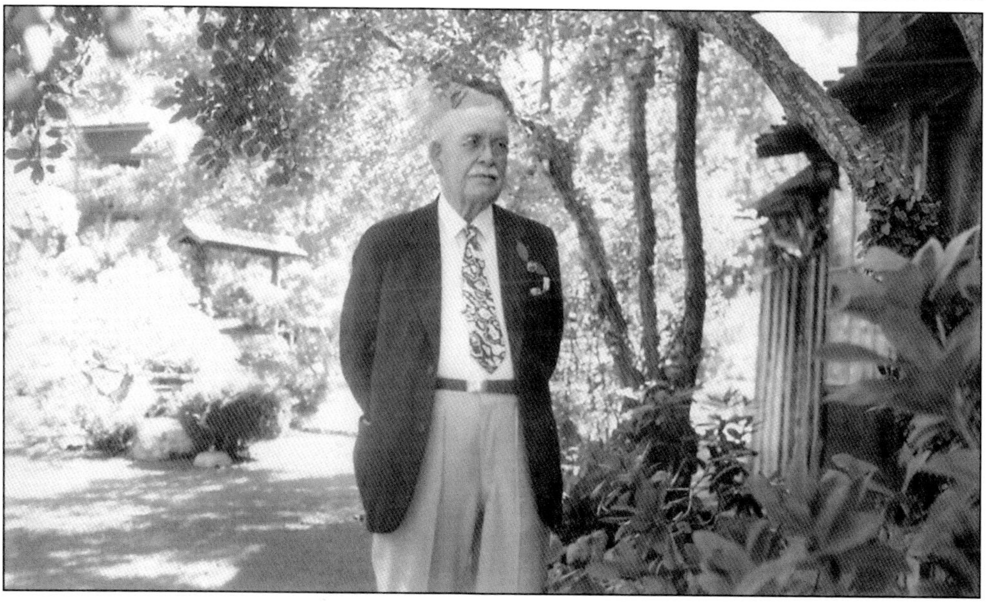

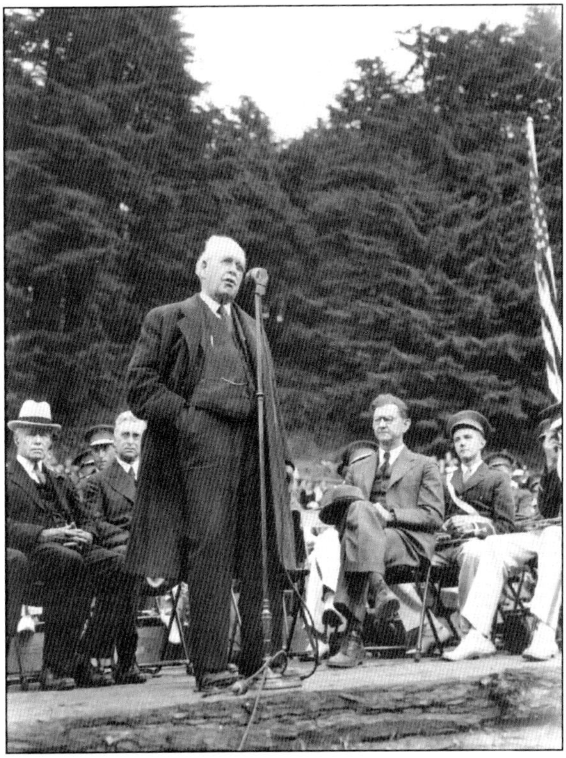

Major Tilden was a founder of the East Bay Regional Park District, which saved thousands of acres of land for public use. As president, he delivered the dedication speech at the opening of the first park for the district, Redwood Regional Park in Oakland, California, in 1935. The city of Berkeley's Tilden Park is named for him. (Courtesy of East Bay Regional Park District Archives.)

A successful attorney and wealthy businessman, Tilden was a dedicated civic leader, providing recreational land for public use in the Bay Area. On November 11, 1937, he gave the keynote speech at the opening of Tilden Park Golf Course, designed by architect William Park Bell and constructed by Works Progress Administration workers. (Courtesy of East Bay Regional Park District Archives.)

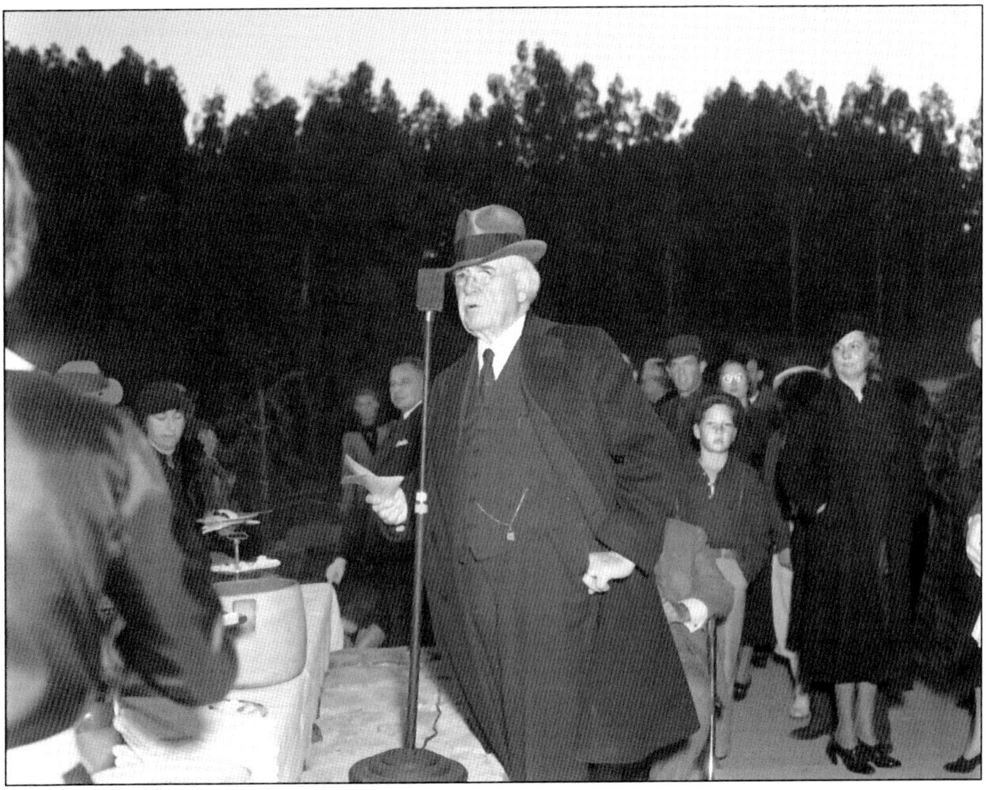

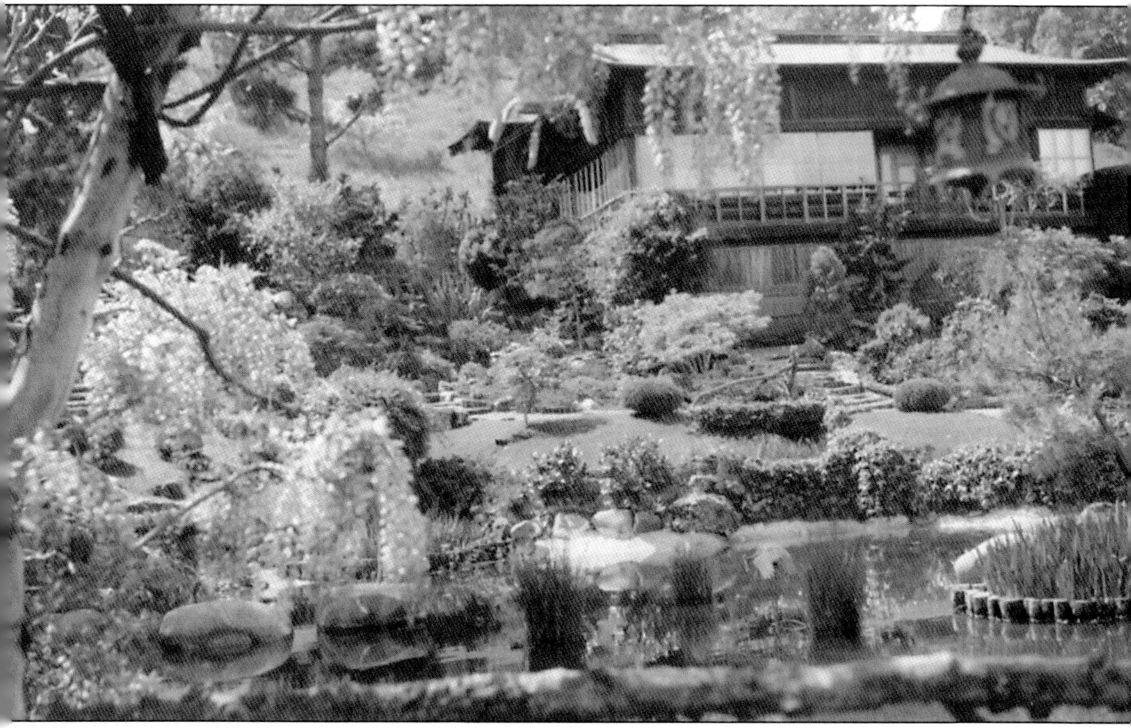

Hakone was Major Tilden's retreat from his professional life and civic duties. It was a summer home for all his family. Both Charles and Lily Tilden had a deep appreciation for traditional Japanese landscaping. The sisters Alexine Mitchell Gregory and Marion Mitchell loved Hakone and helped their parents manage the garden estate, organizing special family celebrations and cultural events for guests. Alexine took scenic photographs of Hakone such as this one she captioned "Paradise of Beauty." While keeping Hakone's original garden landscaping and design, Tilden added new features and enhancements, most notably the construction of the corridor leading to Hakone's entrance and the iconic main gate, the Mon. By employing James Sasaki as the live-in gardener, Tilden launched a new era of Hakone's garden artistry. (Courtesy of Tilden-Gregory Archives.)

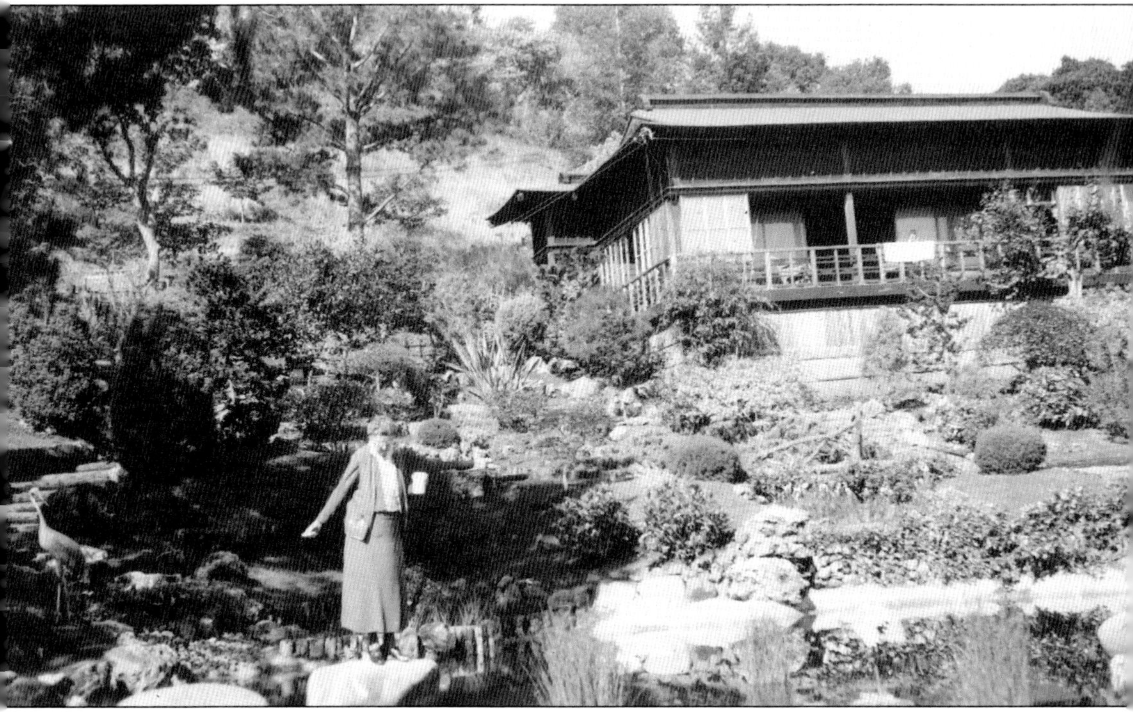

Lily Tilden is pictured feeding the koi on an idyllic summer day. Seen in the background at right is James Sasaki, the gardener who lived at Hakone in a cottage with his family. The Tildens stayed annually at Hakone from Memorial Day to Labor Day. It was their escape from busy city life and the chilly East Bay climate. Sasaki cultivated a variety of flowers by the orchard all spring for the floral arrangements the Tildens enjoyed throughout the summer. His wife, Shizue, was their cook. She accommodated their American tastes and had special recipes for baking cakes. Lily Tilden loved her cooking and presentation. (Courtesy of Tilden-Gregory Archives.)

This is a photograph from the Tilden family album of Lily, Charles, their son Charles Jr., and his three children, labeled "Our son and grandchildren." Charles Lee Tilden Jr., who lived with his family in Piedmont, was a member of the gold-medal US rugby team in the 1920 Summer Olympics. (Courtesy of Tilden-Gregory Archives.)

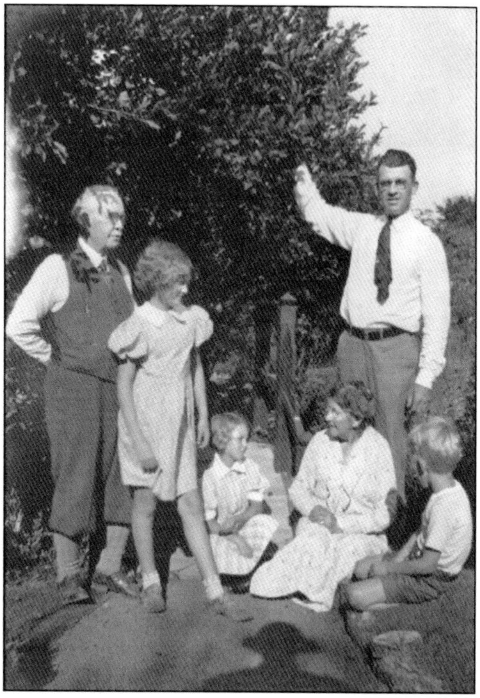

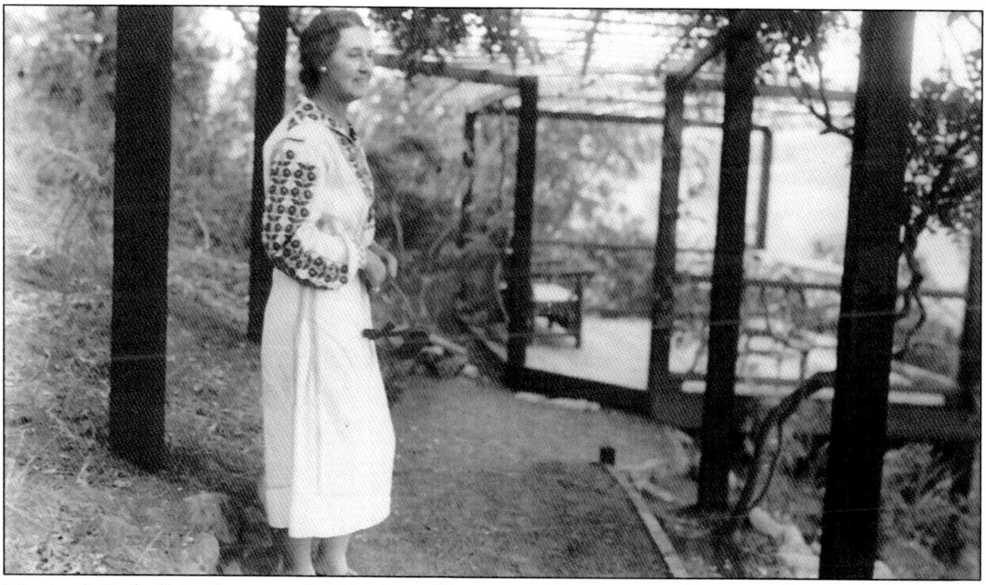

Marion Mitchell is photographed by her older sister Alexine at Hakone's trellis and labeled "Sir Boss." The sisters were bonded by the experience of volunteering to work for the Motor Services of the American Fund for the Wounded (AFFW) in World War I. They drove and repaired military supply vehicles and ambulances for the French. They delivered supplies and tended to the wounded, visiting field hospitals throughout Alsace-Lorraine on the Western Front. Marion, who never married, was a world traveler and loved the tranquility of Hakone. It was Marion, with a big car, who met James Sasaki and his family at the Oakland train station after they were released from incarceration during World War II and drove them home to Hakone. (Courtesy of Tilden-Gregory Archives.)

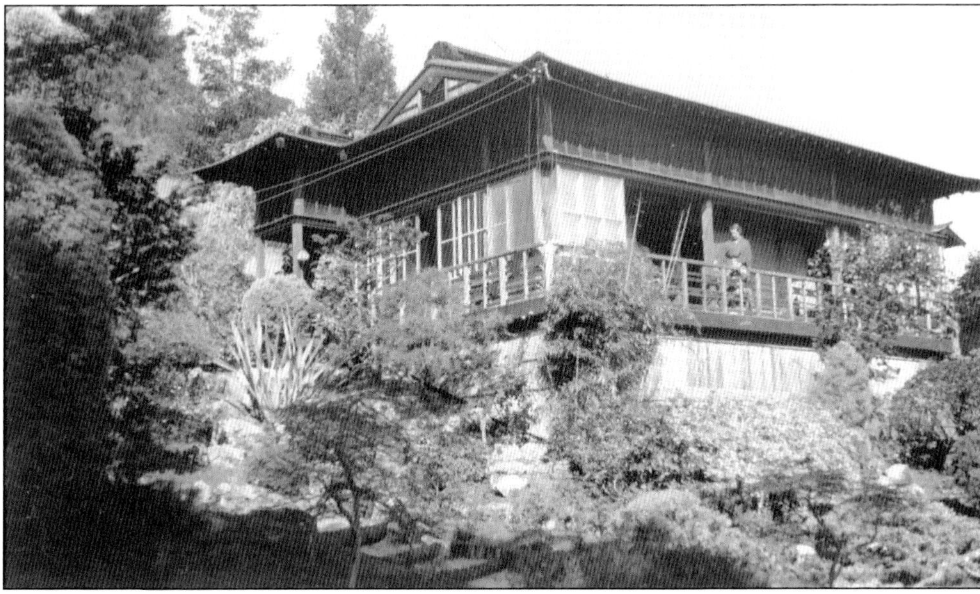

Marion, in Hakone's Upper House, enjoys a lofty view of the pond and landscape below. She was very devoted to Hakone, but it was Alexine, the older of the two, who would inherit the Japanese garden estate; Marion inherited the family home in Alameda. (Courtesy of Tilden-Gregory Archives.)

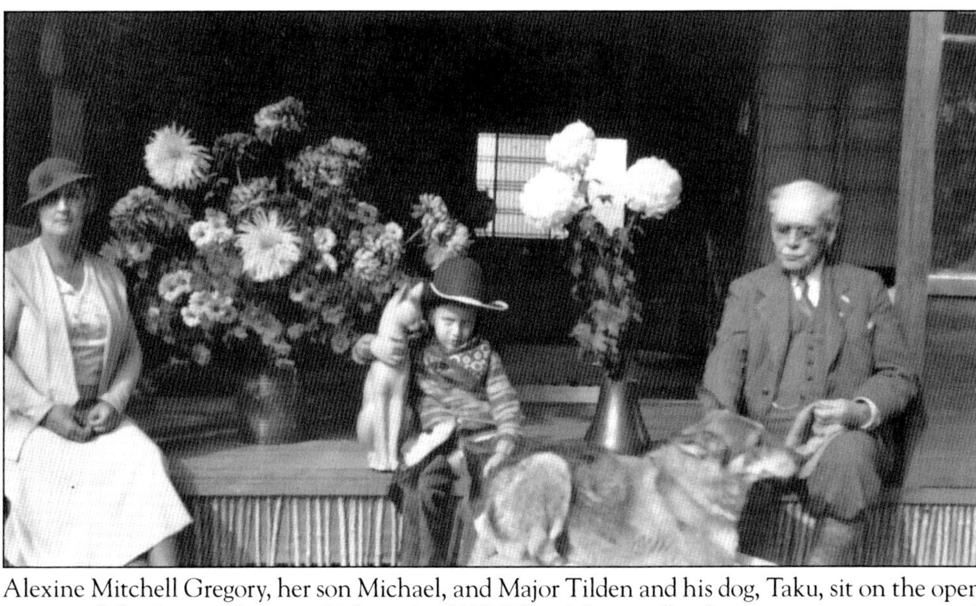

Alexine Mitchell Gregory, her son Michael, and Major Tilden and his dog, Taku, sit on the open terrace of the Lower House at Hakone in 1937. The elaborate floral arrangement was created by James Sasaki with blooms he grew on a field outside the formal gardens. Major Tilden willed Hakone to his stepdaughter Alexine, and after she passed away in 1958, her son Michael Gregory inherited the estate. (Courtesy of Tilden-Gregory Archives.)

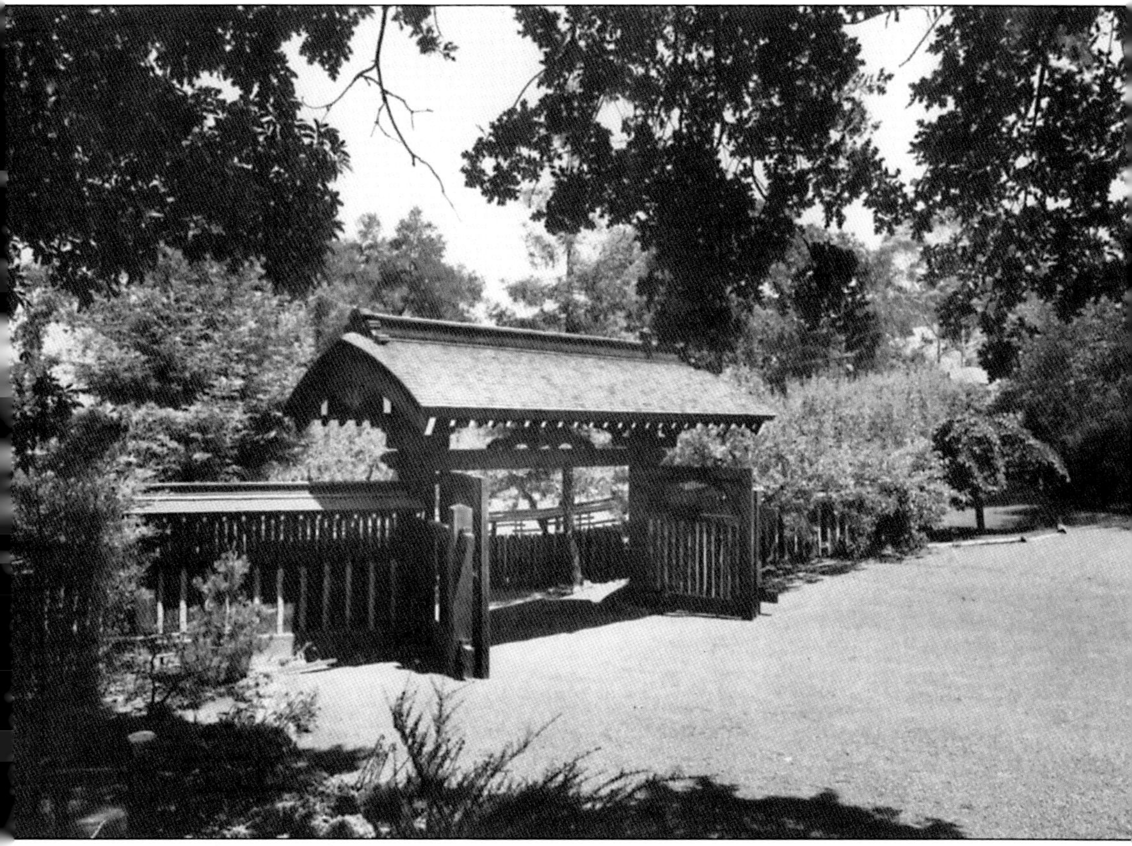

The main gate, known as the Mon, was Major Tilden's spectacular addition to Hakone. Sixteen feet high and 20 feet wide, it has 12 layers of handmade shingles on the roof, large double doors with split bamboo decorations, and hand-forged hinges. Made of select California redwood and imported long-jointed bamboo, it was built by brothers Shinzaburo and Gentaro Nishiura, devout Buddhists who constructed landmark buildings for the Japanese community, notably the Buddhist Church in San Jose. Work on the corridor leading to the entrance and the Mon was supervised by Tilden, who altered the Nishiuras' dimensions so cars could be accommodated. The Nishiura brothers, adhering to traditional design measurements and the religious character of their work, were not pleased and stopped working for a couple months, but they eventually came to an agreement with Tilden. (Courtesy of Tilden-Gregory Archives.)

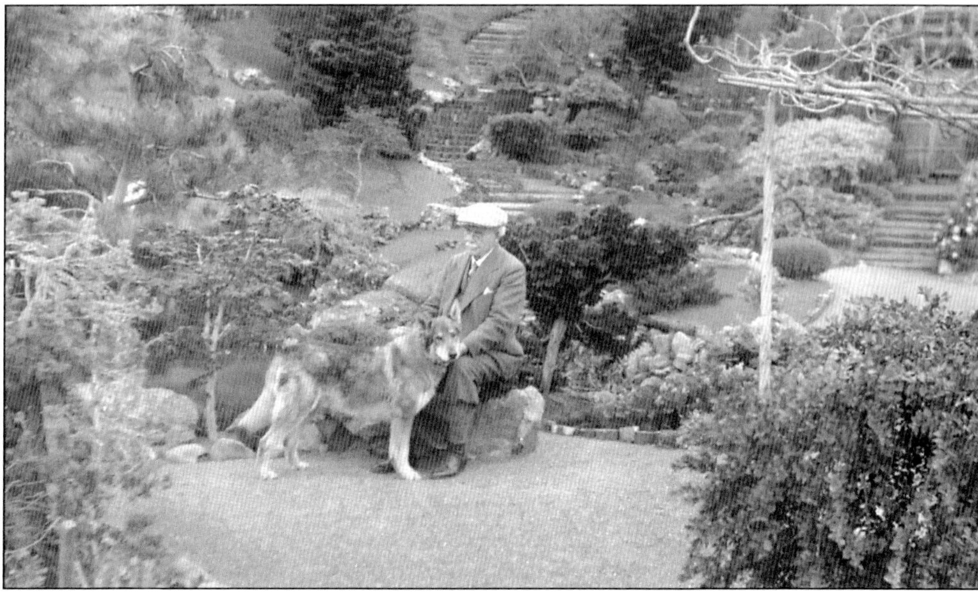

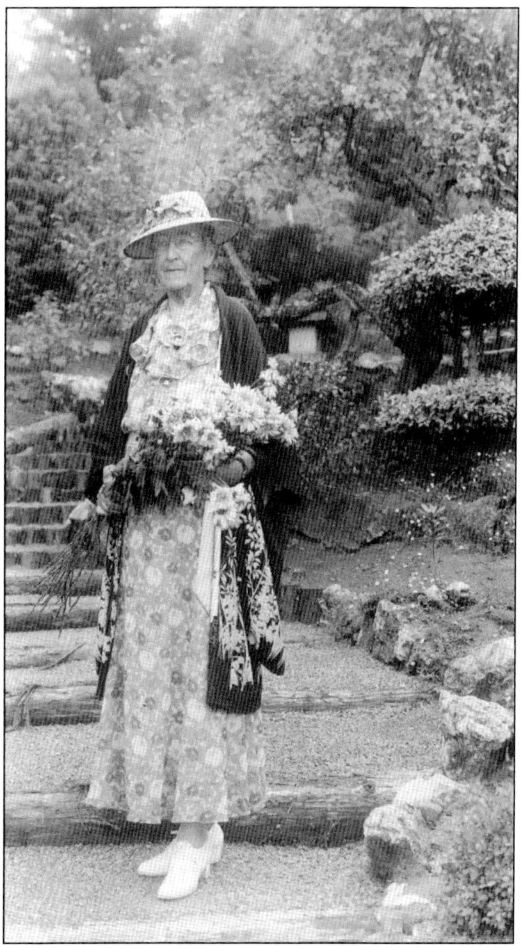

Major Tilden is photographed by Alexine with Taku, his loyal, well-trained German shepherd. He made daily strolls through Hakone, with Taku always by his side. (Courtesy of Tilden-Gregory Archives.)

Lily Tilden holds a bouquet of summer blooms standing on the steps by Hakone's pond. James Sasaki grew these flowers outside the formal garden in the orchard, where the parking lot is now. (Courtesy of Tilden-Gregory Archives.)

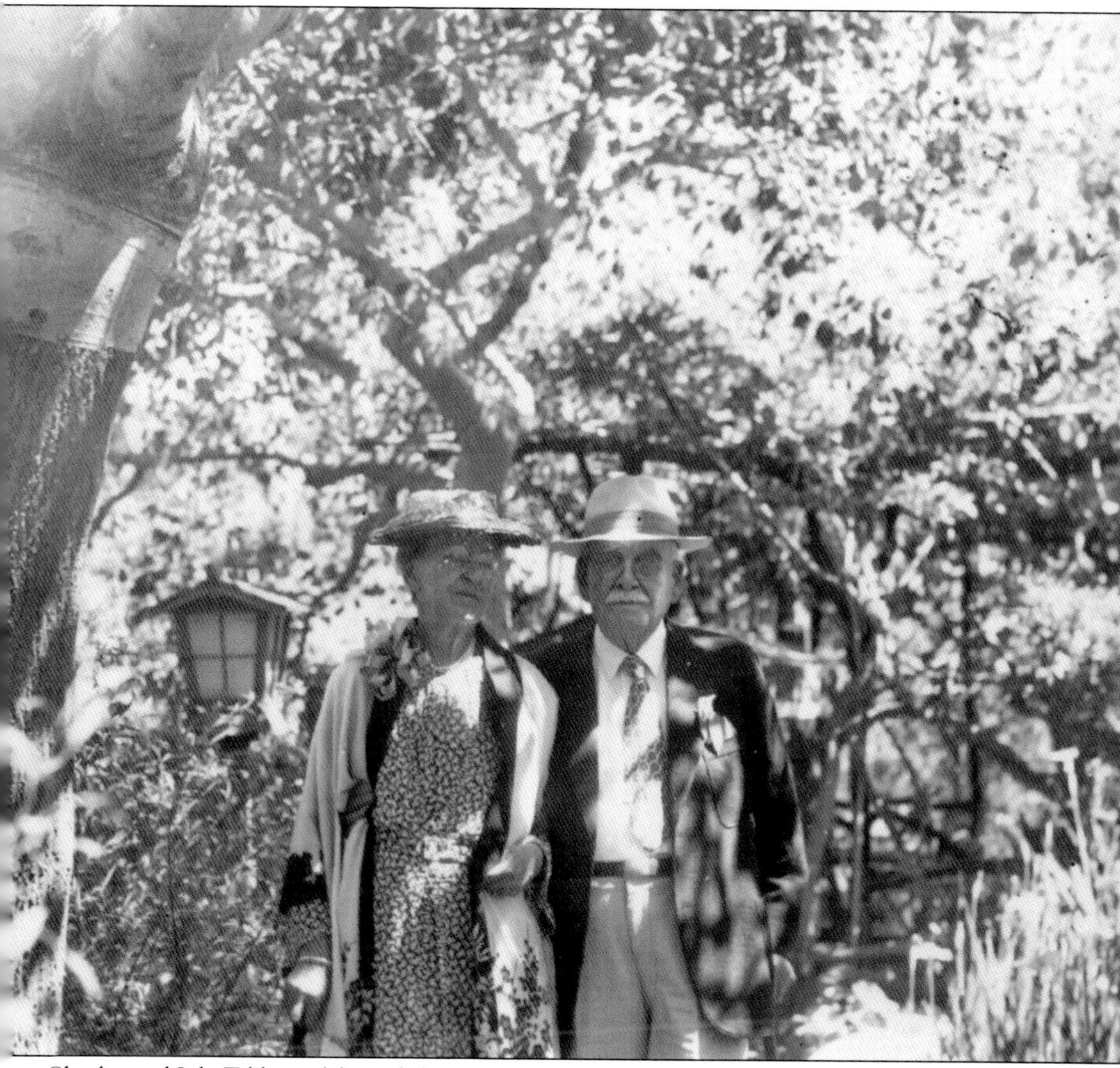

Charles and Lily Tilden celebrated their 50th anniversary at Hakone. It was a long and happy marriage of 56 years. They raised a wonderful family and traveled extensively around the world. In their retirement years, Hakone was their beautiful garden paradise, where they spent every summer. Lily died in 1946 and Charles in 1950. (Courtesy of Tilden-Gregory Archives.)

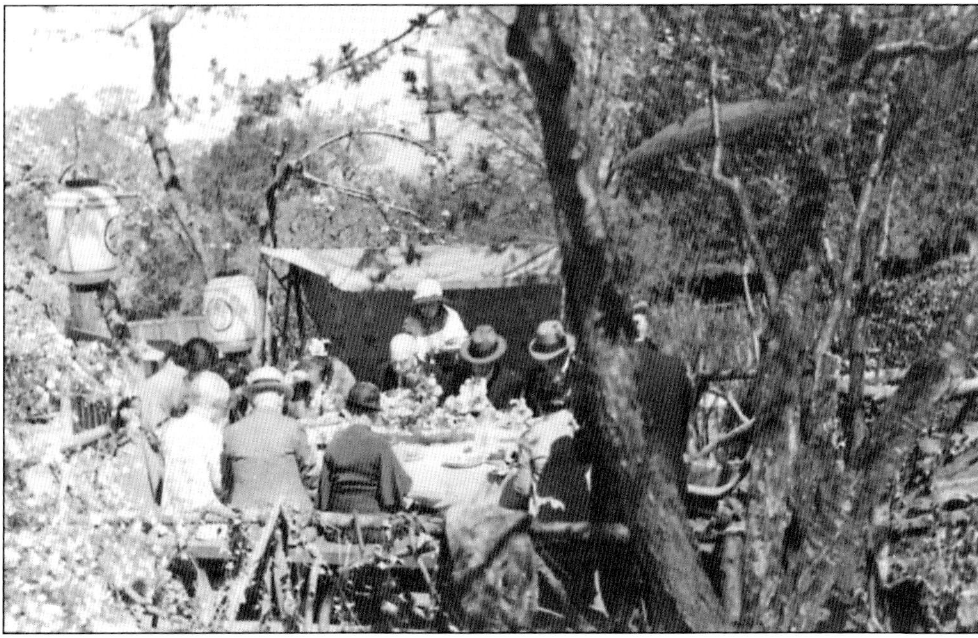

The Tildens invited their friends to enjoy the cherry blossoms at Hakone in the springtime. Here the "Blossom Party," as labeled in this photograph by Alexine Mitchell, features festive outdoor dining in front of the Lower House, decorated with lanterns and flowers. The California oak tree completes the setting. (Courtesy of Tilden-Gregory Archives.)

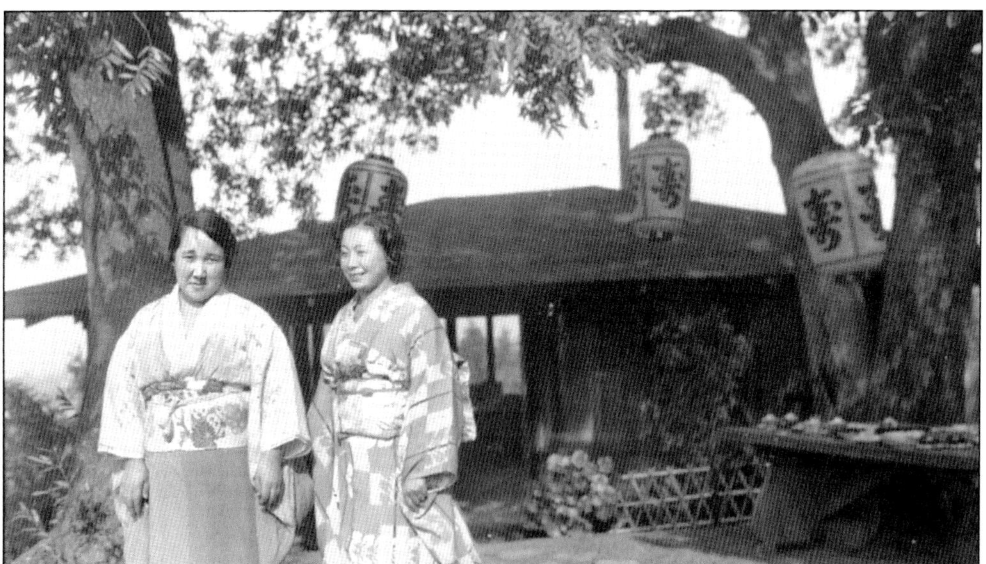

Dressed in their lovely Japanese kimonos, Shizue Sasaki (left) and Hama serve the guests at the festivities of the Blossom Party in 1933. For large parties, the Tildens would bring their cook, Hama, from their home in Alameda, across the bay from San Francisco, to assist Shizue with the cooking and table preparations. (Courtesy of Tilden-Gregory Archives.)

During the Depression, people went fishing to catch food to feed their families, not for trophy hunting. A neighbor of Hakone who owned a boat invited James Sasaki on a fishing expedition to Half Moon Bay, nearby on the Pacific coast. Here, Sasaki proudly shows off his catch of a huge salmon before it was prepared for consumption by his family. (Courtesy of Jane Sasaki Abdalla.)

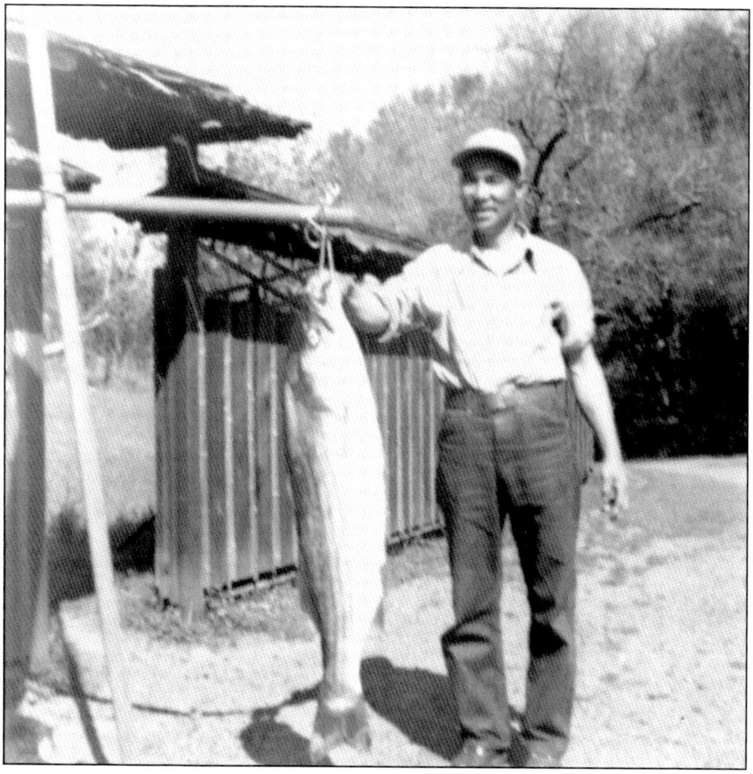

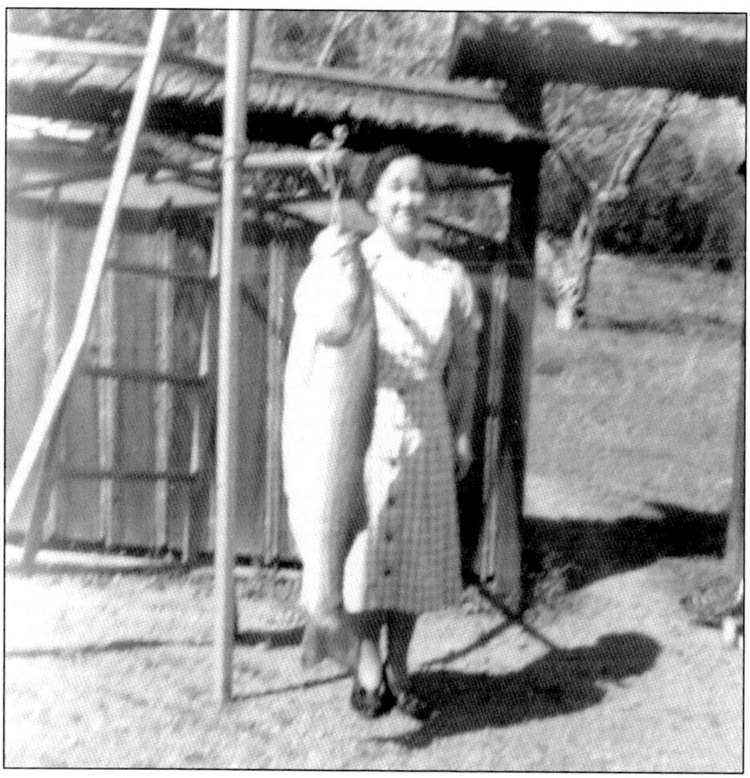

Shizue Takagi Sasaki poses with her husband's amazing catch. She was a marvelous cook, and this fish would provide quite a few meals for their family. At this time, they had three children, David, Betty, and Jane. (Courtesy of Jane Sasaki Abdalla.)

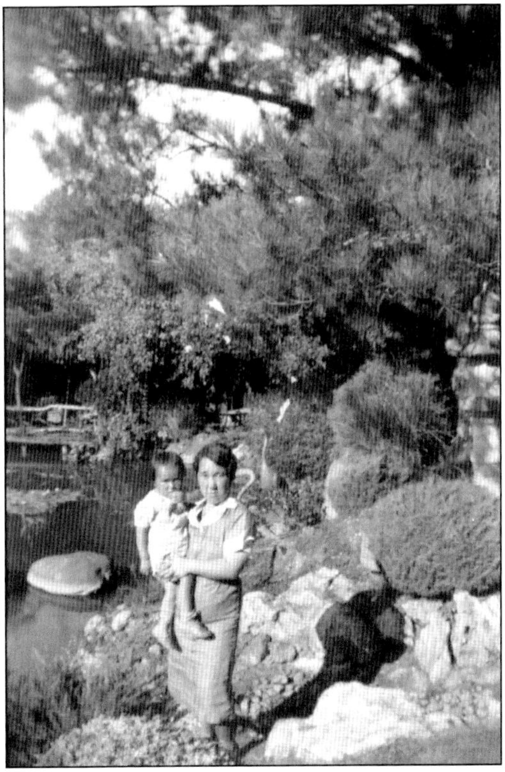

Shizue Takagi Sasaki stands in front of Hakone's pond in 1939 holding her third child, Jane, age two. A fourth child, Kathy, would be born in November 1941. Betty recalls her mother as extremely capable, raising a family and working at Hakone. She was a thoughtful, kind mother, comforting her children when they had to leave for a relocation camp, saying "you may each bring one toy." (Courtesy of Jane Sasaki Abdalla.)

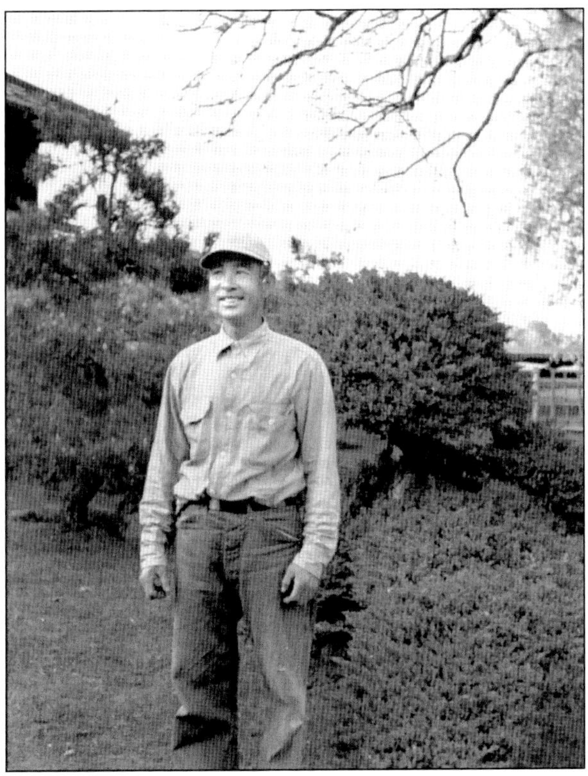

James Sasaki, in a 1939 photograph, was Hakone's gardener for 30 years, except for the three and a half years during World War II. Born in Japan, he thought Executive Order 9066 was meant for him but not his American-born wife and children. He said to his wife, "Shizue, I will have to go, but not you or the children." But the whole family was incarcerated. (Courtesy of Jane Sasaki Abdalla.)

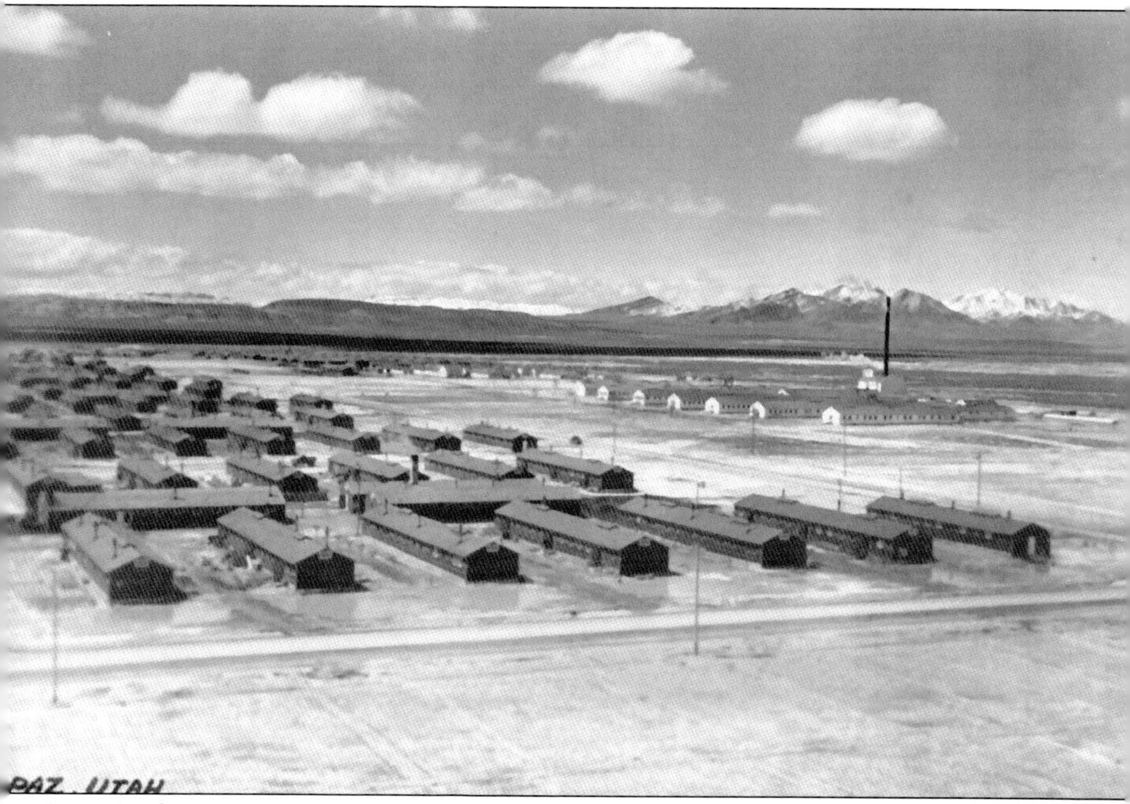

Topaz, Utah, was one of the 10 relocation camps in remote areas that Japanese Americans were forced into by Executive Order 9066. James Sasaki and his family were held there for three and a half years. They should have been incarcerated at Heart Mountain, Wyoming, designated for Japanese from Santa Clara County, but Shizue wanted to leave with her brother and other relatives, who lived in Alameda County. So the Sasakis departed for camp from an assembly center in the East Bay and took a train to Topaz, bringing only what they could carry. Before leaving Hakone, James built a bonfire in the orchard and burned all their Japanese possessions. Charles Tilden kept in touch with the Sasakis and protected Hakone during the wartime hysteria, when Japanese gardens were destroyed throughout the United States. (Courtesy of Bancroft Library.)

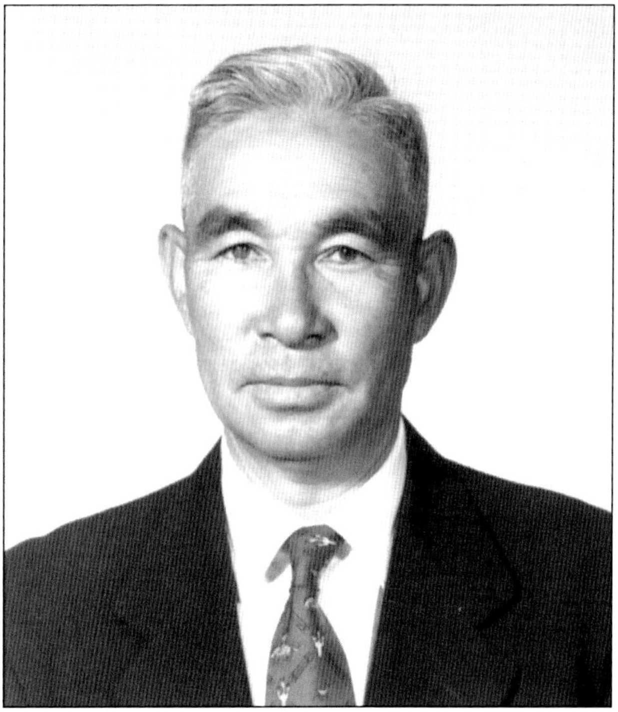

In Sasaki's absence, the Tildens hired a white gardener. After three and a half years at Topaz, James Sasaki and family returned to Hakone, and in the years following, he brought the garden to its ultimate beauty. Without horticulture training, he possessed natural talent and a keen sense of the Japanese aesthetic. "How my father loved Hakone," his daughter, Betty Sasaki Furuta recalls. "I heard it said that James Sasaki had four children and the fifth was Hakone." (Courtesy of Jane Sasaki Abdalla.)

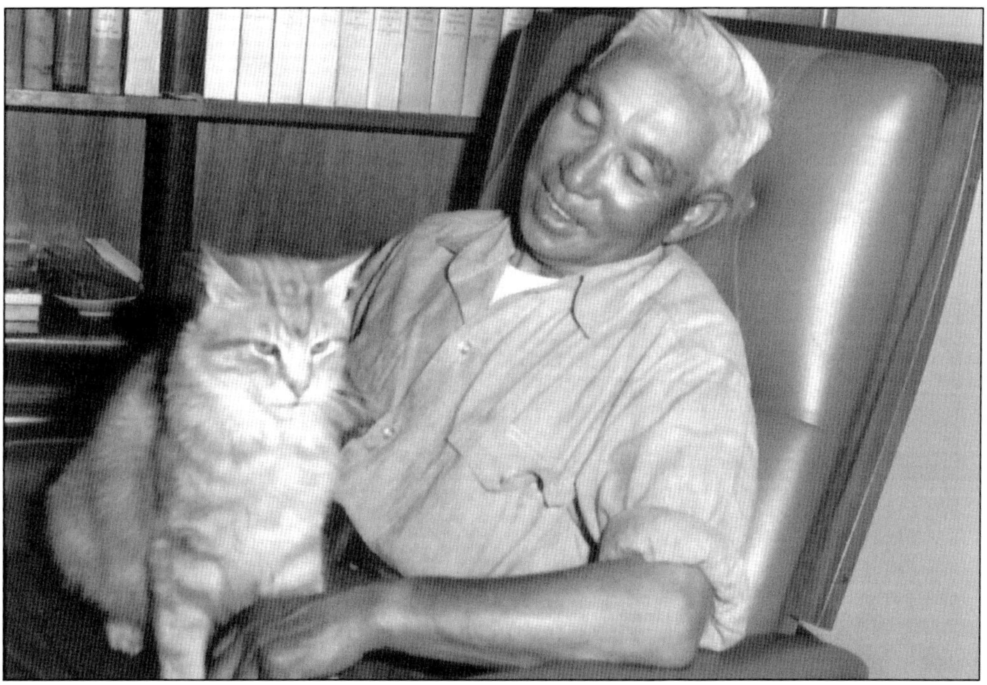

In retirement, James Sasaki and his wife, Shizue, lived in Campbell, next to Saratoga. He is pictured here at home with a cat named Penny, who also resided at Hakone for many years. The first cat the Sasaki family owned at Hakone was a lovable calico named Kitty, who greeted them jubilantly upon their return from the Topaz relocation camp with loud, prolonged meowing. (Courtesy of Hakone Foundation.)

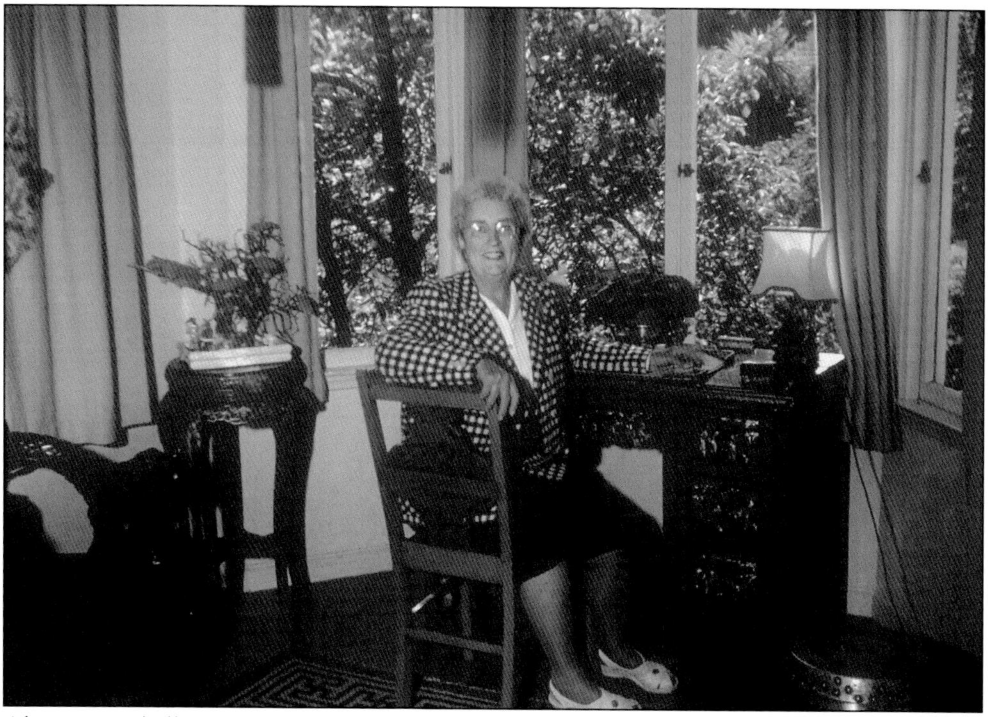

Alexine Mitchell Gregory is pictured here in her home in Berkeley. After she inherited Hakone from her stepfather, Charles Lee Tilden, she welcomed groups to use the gardens for benefit events. As a young woman, she was a courageous adventurer who went to France to aid wounded soldiers before America entered the Great War. Later, she taught French at Bowdoin College and the University of California at Berkeley. (Courtesy of Tilden-Gregory Archives.)

Ora Gregory, wife of Michael Gregory, is pictured with her young daughter Alexa in 1956. When her husband inherited Hakone in 1958, Ora continued Alexine Mitchell Gregory's legacy of sharing Hakone Gardens. She made it possible for the California Historical Society to hold a benefit garden tour at Hakone. Alexa Gregory is the family historian, having inherited the trunk of her great-aunt Marion Mitchell containing scrapbooks, memorabilia, and letters of her worldwide travels. (Courtesy of Alexa Gregory.)

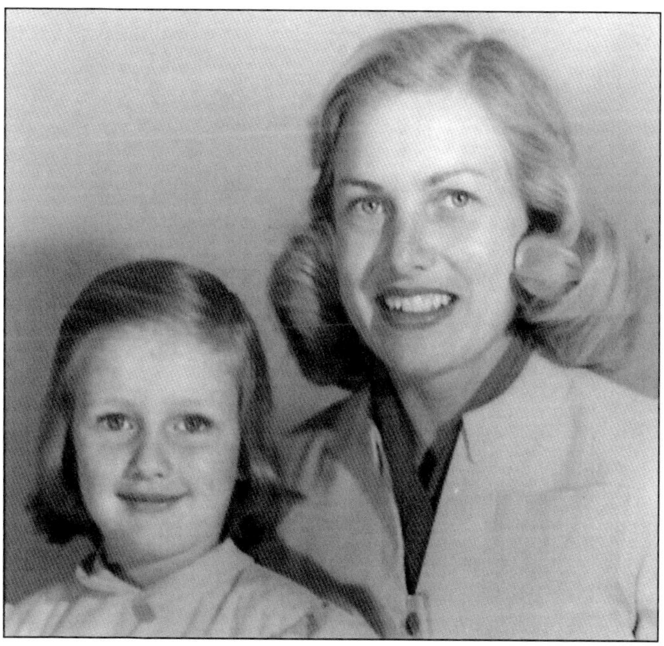

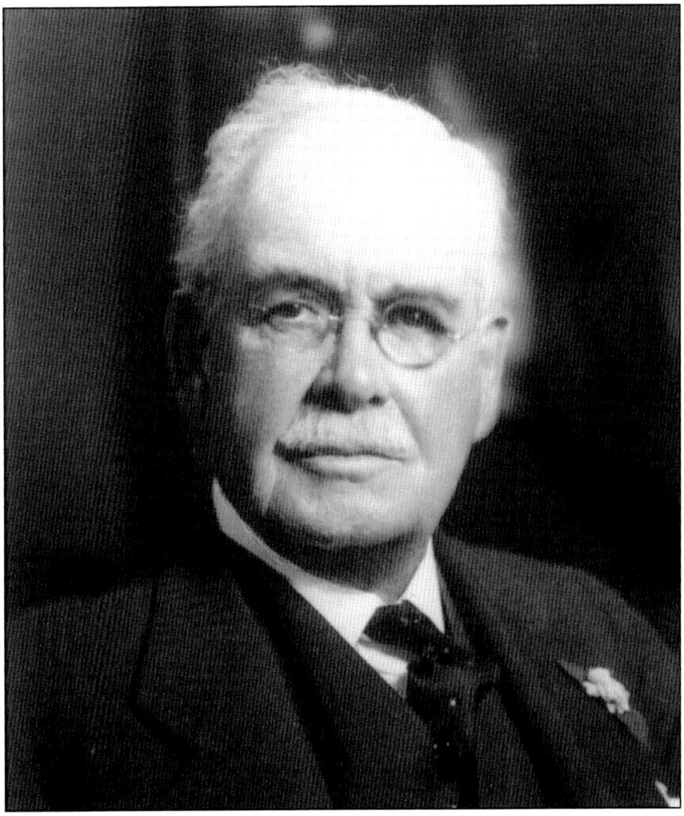

This is a formal portrait of Charles Lee Tilden when he was president of the East Bay Regional Parks District. His skill and foresight in planning for public use of open space left a great, lasting legacy for the Bay Area. (Courtesy of Tilden-Gregory Archives.)

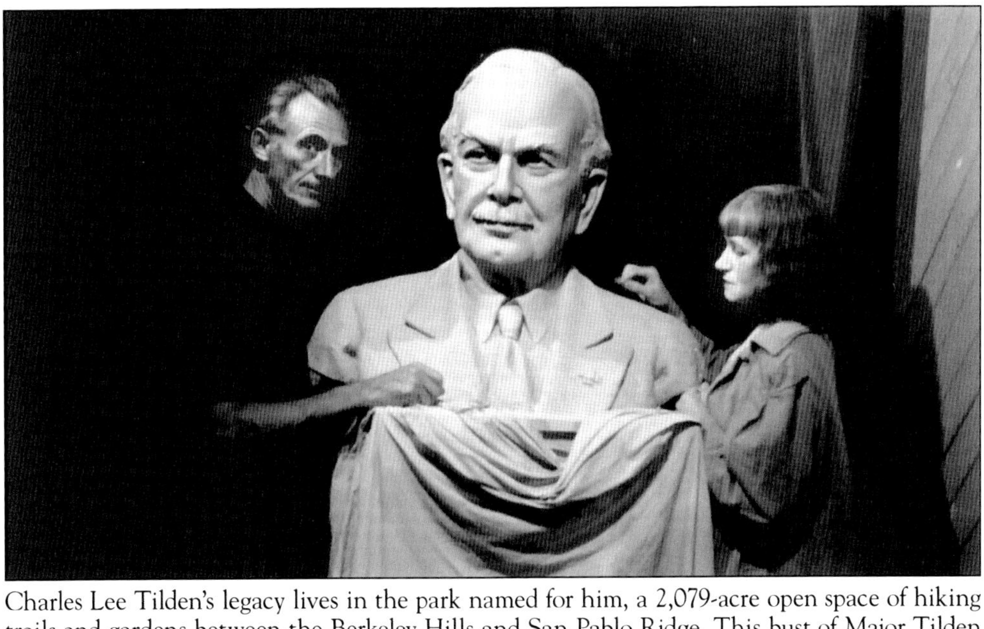

Charles Lee Tilden's legacy lives in the park named for him, a 2,079-acre open space of hiking trails and gardens between the Berkeley Hills and San Pablo Ridge. This bust of Major Tilden resides in the Brazilian Room at Tilden Park. Used for events, the room was built of recycled wood from the Brazil exhibit at San Francisco's 1939 World's Fair Golden Gate International Exposition, held on Treasure Island. (Courtesy Tilden-Gregory Archives.)

Three

Hall, Kan, Lee, Young, Gresham, and Gresham

Hakone's Last Private Owners

In 1961, a partnership of six couples changed the destiny of Hakone Gardens. They bought it for $96,500 from Michael Gregory, an English professor living in Berkeley, who inherited Hakone upon the death of his mother, Alexine Mitchell Gregory, stepdaughter of Charles L. Tilden.

The partnership originated at Ming's of Palo Alto. It was the favorite restaurant of Joe and Clara Gresham, who lived in Saratoga across the road from Hakone. The Greshams became good friends of Dan Lee, the manager of Ming's, and his wife, June. Gresham, a general contractor, approached the Lees about forming a partnership to purchase the 15-acre property. Dan Lee invited his friends and business partners, Johnny Kan, George Hall, and John Young. Joe brought in his son Eldon and daughter-in-law Deon. It was the most congenial of partnerships. Marie Lee Hall and Mary Lee Young were sisters. Their husbands, George Hall and John C. Young, were president and vice president, respectively, of Wing Nien Longevity Brand Soy Sauce Company. Johnny Kan was a famed restaurateur, and Hall and Young were partners in Kan's Restaurant. The brothers-in-law were also partners in Ming's Restaurant of Palo Alto, the principal owner and manager being Dan Lee. The new owners faced suspicion and hostility as they worked to restore Hakone. They hired an African American man, Charley Ray, as their live-in caretaker and gardener. Rumors circulated that the new owners were planning on building a Chinese restaurant at Hakone.

After five years, the partners decided it was impractical to keep Hakone as a private retreat. However, they feared that if Hakone left their hands, it would be subdivided into lots, as Saratoga was becoming a highly desirable residential area. They would only sell Hakone to the City of Saratoga. Joseph Gresham brought the proposal to the city council and was initially turned down, but Mayor Bill Glennon made a strong case for acquiring Hakone as a public park. The rest is history. This chapter is about the last private owners, remarkable individuals who loved and cared for Hakone and insured its future.

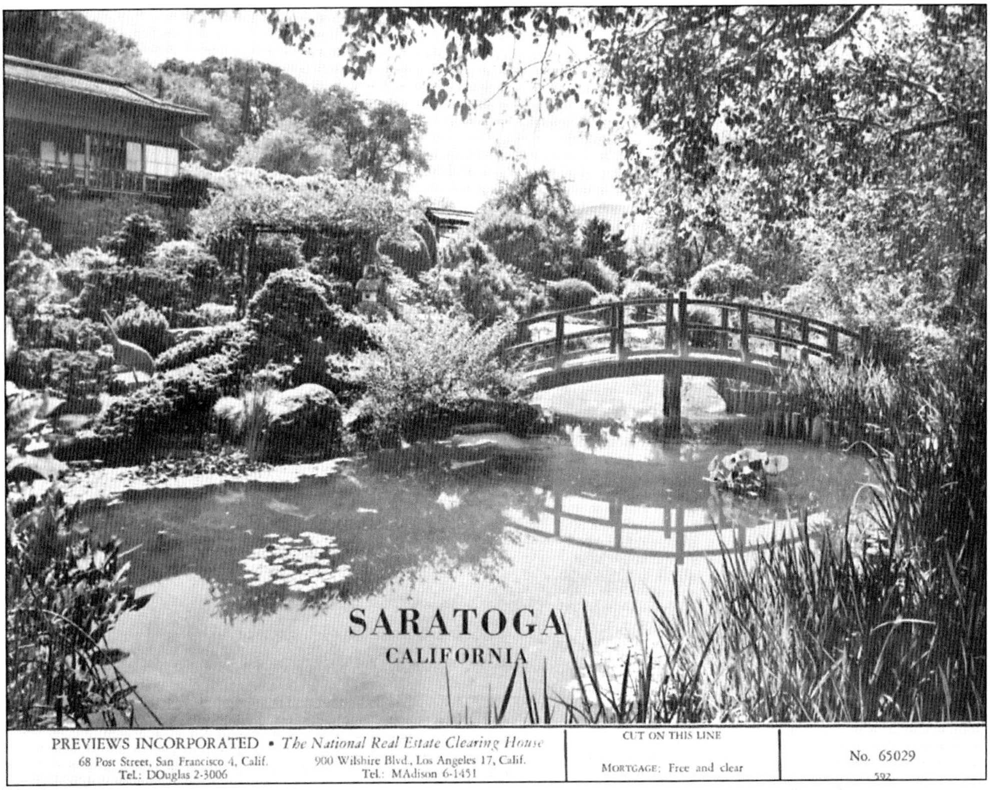

Previews Inc. advertised Hakone as a "unique property" with excellent potential for real estate development. The brochure states: "Consisting of a little over 17 acres, it is secluded yet readily accessible from the Saratoga-Skyline Boulevard Highway. Although in the past it has been used exclusively as a residence, it is so zoned that it offers a variety of other possible uses, including hotel, motel or restaurant." (Courtesy of Hakone Foundation.)

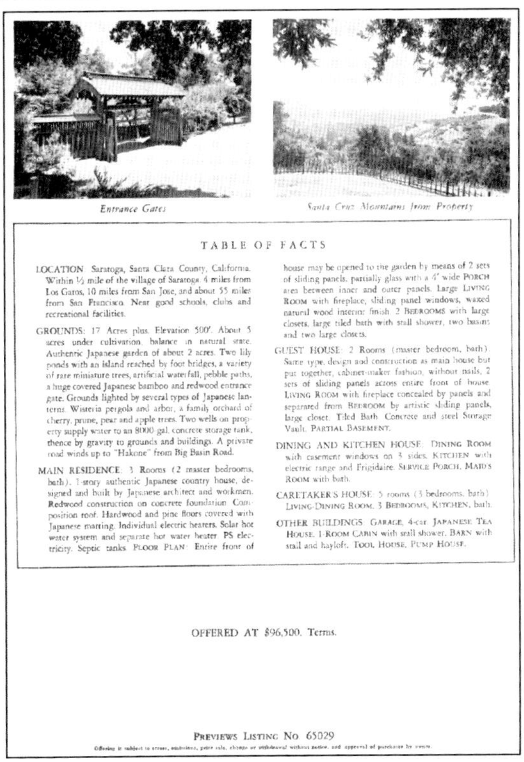

Entrance Gates

Santa Cruz Mountains from Property

TABLE OF FACTS

LOCATION: Saratoga, Santa Clara County, California. Within ½ mile of the village of Saratoga. 4 miles from Los Gatos, 10 miles from San Jose, and about 55 miles from San Francisco. Near good schools, clubs and recreational facilities.

GROUNDS: 17 Acres plus. Elevation 500′. About 5 acres under cultivation, balance in natural state. Authentic Japanese garden of about 2 acres. Two lily ponds with an island reached by foot bridges, a variety of rare miniature trees, artificial waterfall, pebble paths, a huge covered Japanese bamboo and redwood entrance gate. Grounds lighted by several types of Japanese lanterns. Wisteria pergola and arbor, a family orchard of cherry, prune, pear and apple trees. Two wells on property supply water to an 8000-gal. concrete storage tank, thence by gravity to grounds and buildings. A private road winds up to "Hakone" from Big Basin Road.

MAIN RESIDENCE: 3 Rooms (2 master bedrooms, bath). 1-story authentic Japanese country house, designed and built by Japanese architect and workmen. Redwood construction on concrete foundation. Composition roof. Hardwood and pine floors covered with Japanese matting. Individual electric heaters. Solar hot water system and separate hot water heater. PS electricity. Septic tanks. FLOOR PLAN: Entire front of house may be opened to the garden by means of 2 sets of sliding panels, partially glass with a 4′ wide PORCH area between inner and outer panels. Large LIVING ROOM with fireplace, sliding panel windows, waxed natural wood interior finish. 2 BEDROOMS with large closets, large tiled bath with stall shower, two basins and two large closets.

GUEST HOUSE: 2 Rooms (master bedroom, bath). Same type, design and construction as main house but put together, cabinet-maker fashion, without nails. 2 sets of sliding panels across entire front of house. LIVING ROOM with fireplace concealed by panels and separated from BEDROOM by artistic sliding panels, large closet. Tiled Bath. Concrete and steel Storage Vault. PARTIAL BASEMENT.

DINING AND KITCHEN HOUSE: DINING ROOM with casement windows on 3 sides. KITCHEN with electric range and Frigidaire. SERVICE PORCH. MAID'S ROOM with bath.

CARETAKER'S HOUSE: 5 rooms (3 bedrooms, bath). LIVING-DINING ROOM, 3 BEDROOMS, KITCHEN, bath.

OTHER BUILDINGS: GARAGE, 4-car. JAPANESE TEA HOUSE. 1-ROOM CABIN with stall shower. BARN with stall and hayloft. TOOL HOUSE. PUMP HOUSE.

OFFERED AT $96,500. Terms.

PREVIEWS LISTING NO 65029

The back page of the real estate brochure announced the sale of the Japanese estate and gardens for $96,500. The seller, Michael Gregory, an English professor residing in Berkeley, inherited Hakone upon the death in 1958 of his mother, Alexine Mitchell Gregory, stepdaughter of Major Charles L. Tilden. The advertisement caused neighbors to worry that the garden would turn into a housing development. (Courtesy of Hakone Foundation.)

In 1961, six couples purchased Hakone: Joseph and Clara Gresham, Eldon and Deon Gresham, George Hall and Marie Lee Hall, Johnny and Helen Kan, Dan and June Lee, and John and Mary Lee Young. A partial gathering of the partnership took place in 1965. From left to right are John C. Young, Mary Lee Young, Joseph Gresham, Helen Kan, Johnny Kan, and Eldon Gresham. (Courtesy of Young family collection.)

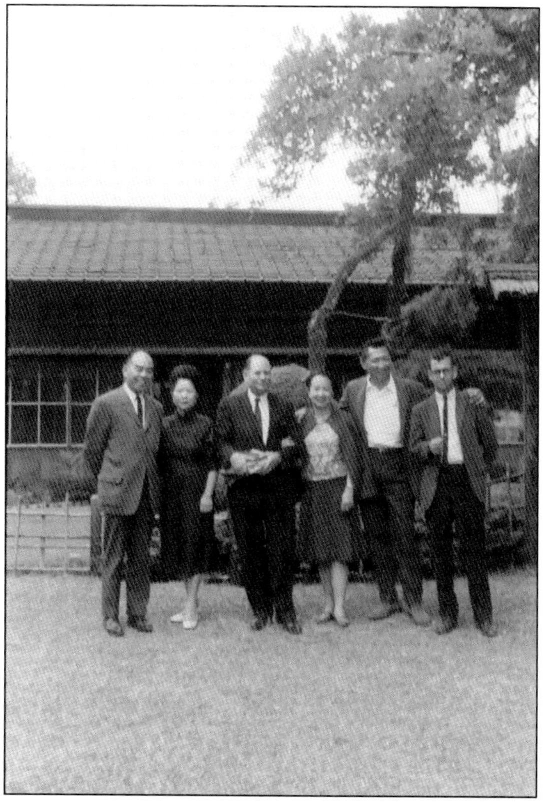

Johnny Kan takes over as photographer so Dan Lee can be in the picture. The partners stand in front of Hakone's Lower House. All the partners were in mutual agreement on maintaining and enhancing Hakone and sharing it as a personal retreat. Rumors, however, circulated in the community about the partners planning to destroy the gardens in order to build a Chinese restaurant. (Courtesy of Young family collection.)

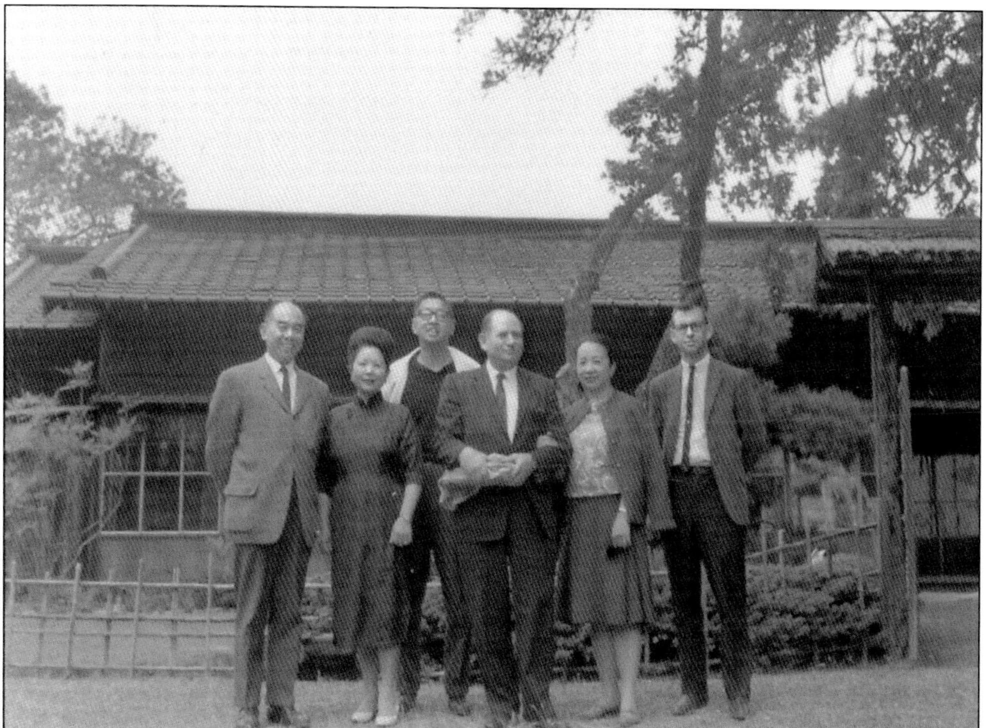

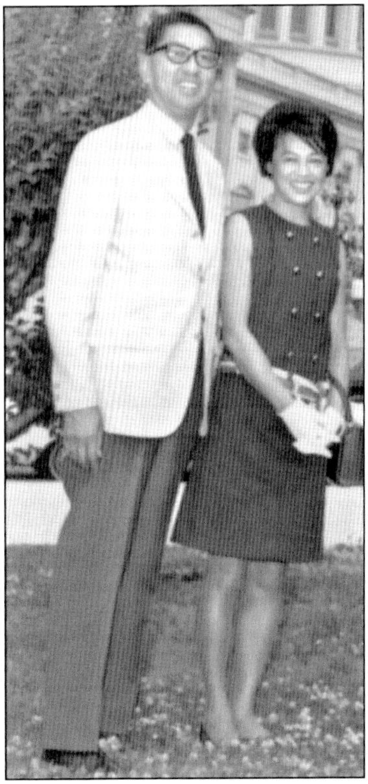

Dan Lee was from Stockton, and June Lee was from Seattle. Dan designed for Kan's Restaurant and met June when she was working at Gump's in San Francisco. They settled in Palo Alto with their two children when Dan became the proprietor of Ming's Restaurant, which he opened in 1956 on El Camino Real in Palo Alto with George Chow, George Hall, and John C. Young. (Courtesy of Debbie Lee.)

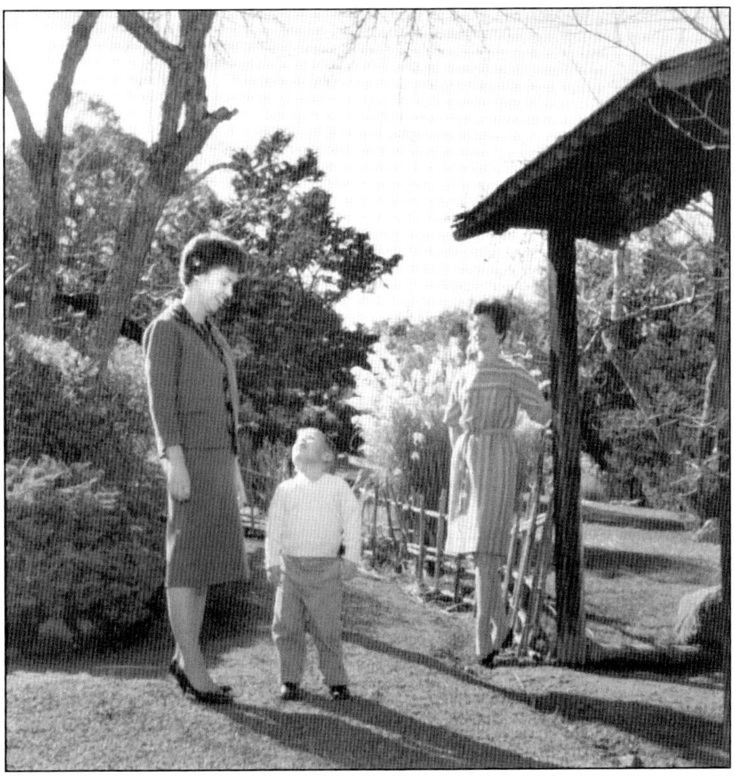

In the spring of 1962, Deon Gresham was asked by the *San Jose Mercury News* to be in a photo shoot at Hakone with her family. Deon was a teacher in San Jose's Alum Rock School District. She obligingly stands with her son Mark as sister-in-law Darlene Gresham Harms, daughter of Joseph and Clara Gresham, poses by Hakone's wooden gate called the "small mon." (Courtesy of Deon Gresham.)

George and Marie Hall lived in San Francisco, where they raised four children. George established Wing Nien Longevity Brand Soy Sauce Company after World War II and was president of US Enterprise Corporation, with the soy sauce company as a subsidiary. The corporation was in the import and export business and property redevelopment. George, a director of the Chinese Chamber of Commerce, was active in Chinatown community improvement. (Courtesy of Effie Hall Dilworth.)

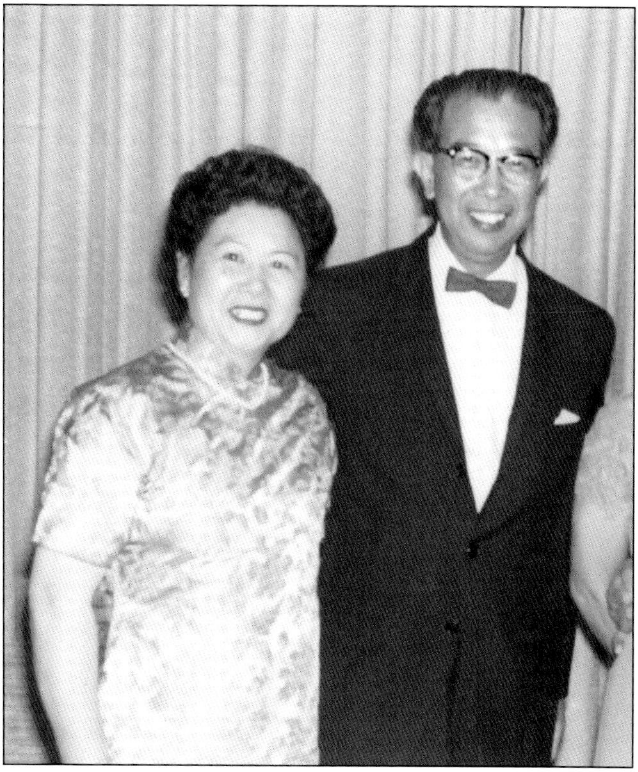

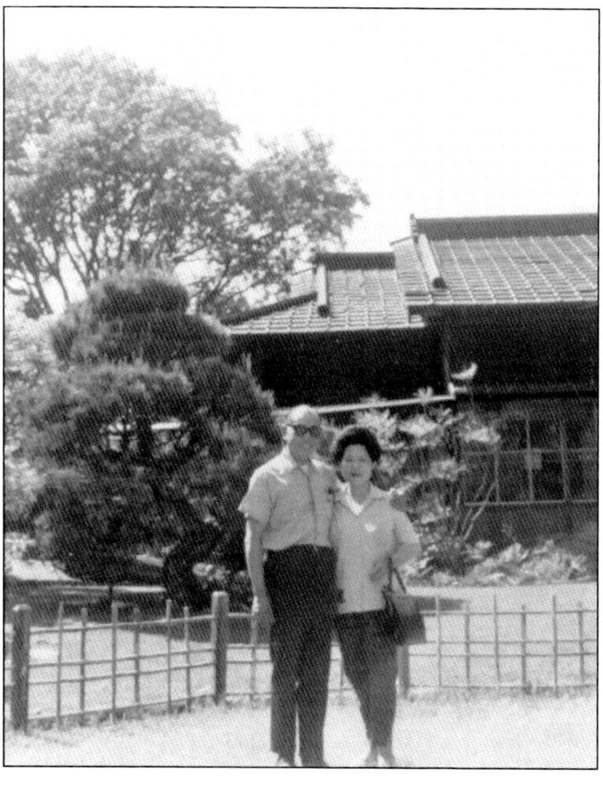

John and Mary Young stand in front of Hakone's Lower House. Born in San Jose, John was George Hall's brother-in-law and vice president of US Enterprise Corporation. He served in the China-Burma-India theater during World War II and was a colonel in the US Army Reserves. John and Mary were collectors of Chinese art but admired Hakone's Japanese authenticity and never brought any Chinese elements to the garden. (Courtesy of Young family collection.)

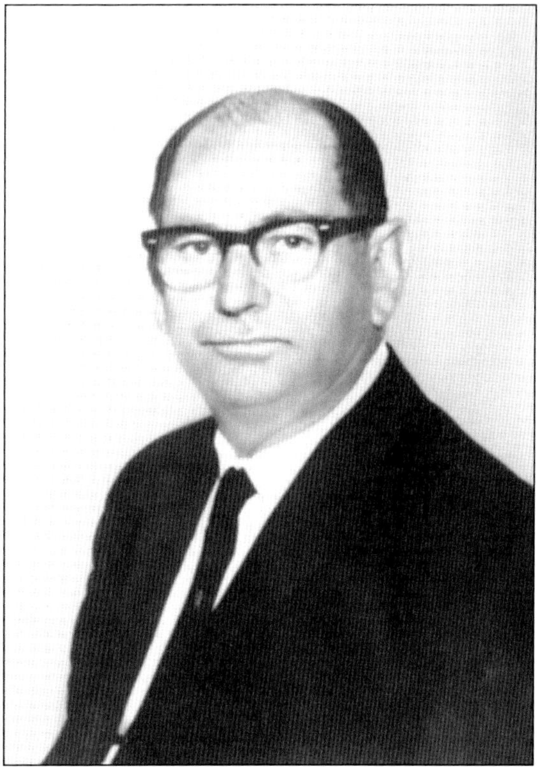

Joseph "Joe" Gresham was born in Kansas in 1907, and his family relocated to Southern California. Living in Pomona, Joe met Clara Coppersmith, also from Kansas. They married and had five children. The family moved to Mountain View, where they temporarily lived in a trailer and a tent, when Joe was employed as a construction supervisor for an airplane hangar at Moffett Field. They then resided in Sunnyvale, where Joe became a real estate developer. Joe, Clara, and their five children settled in a large home in Saratoga. They had other property near Big Basin Road across the street from Hakone Gardens, and the couple lived there after their children were grown. Clara was active in the community activities of Saratoga Federated Church and as a member of the Foothill Club. (Both, courtesy of Deon Gresham.)

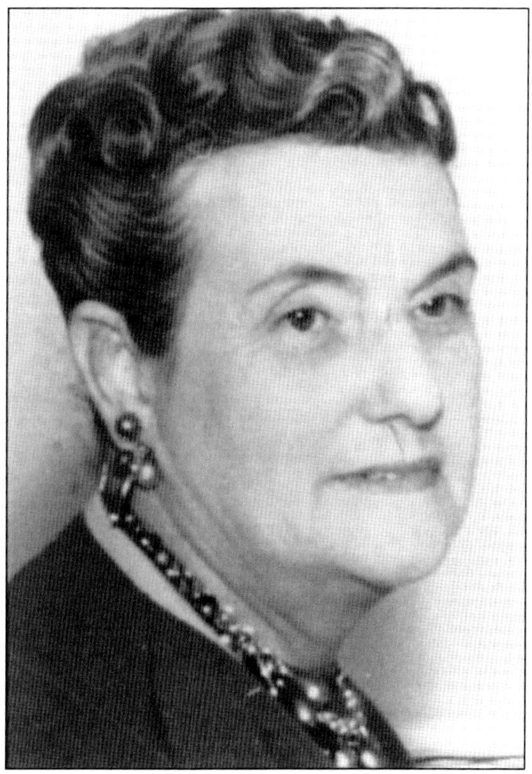

On January 21, 1962, an unusual weather phenomenon occurred in Santa Clara Valley: it snowed. Eldon Gresham got out his camera and took pictures of Hakone looking for one day like an enchanted winter garden in Japan. This view was taken from above the pond and near the Upper or Moon Viewing House. (Courtesy of Deon Gresham.)

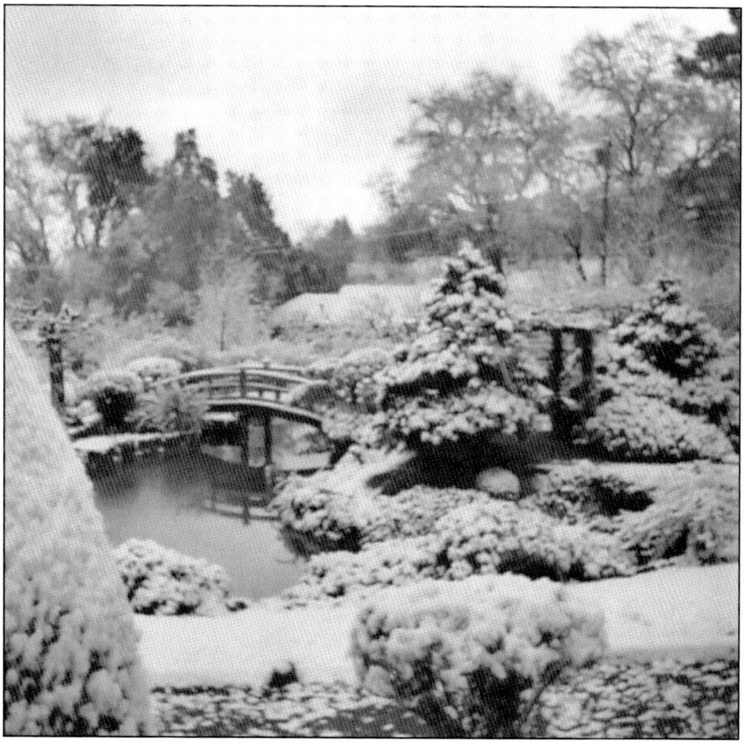

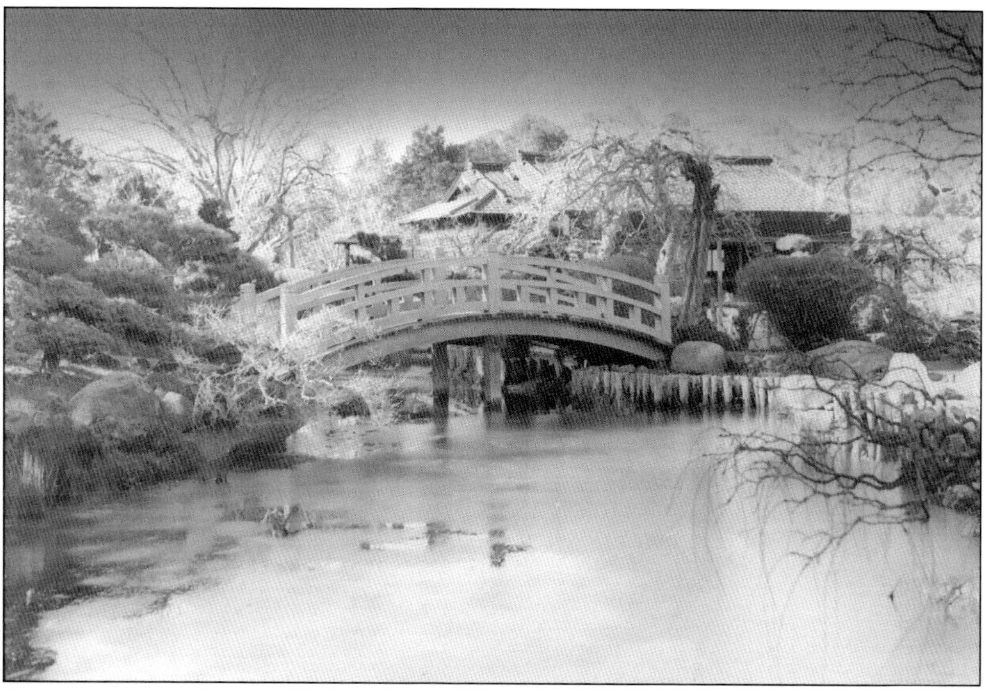

An exquisite, surreal scene of Hakone during the same 1962 snowfall in Saratoga was also captured by photographer Emil Edgren, on assignment for the *San Jose Mercury News*. The photographer took the picture from the edge of the pond, with the Lower House in the background past the Moon Bridge. Note the icicles under the bridge, a rarity in the Bay Area. (Courtesy of Deon Gresham.)

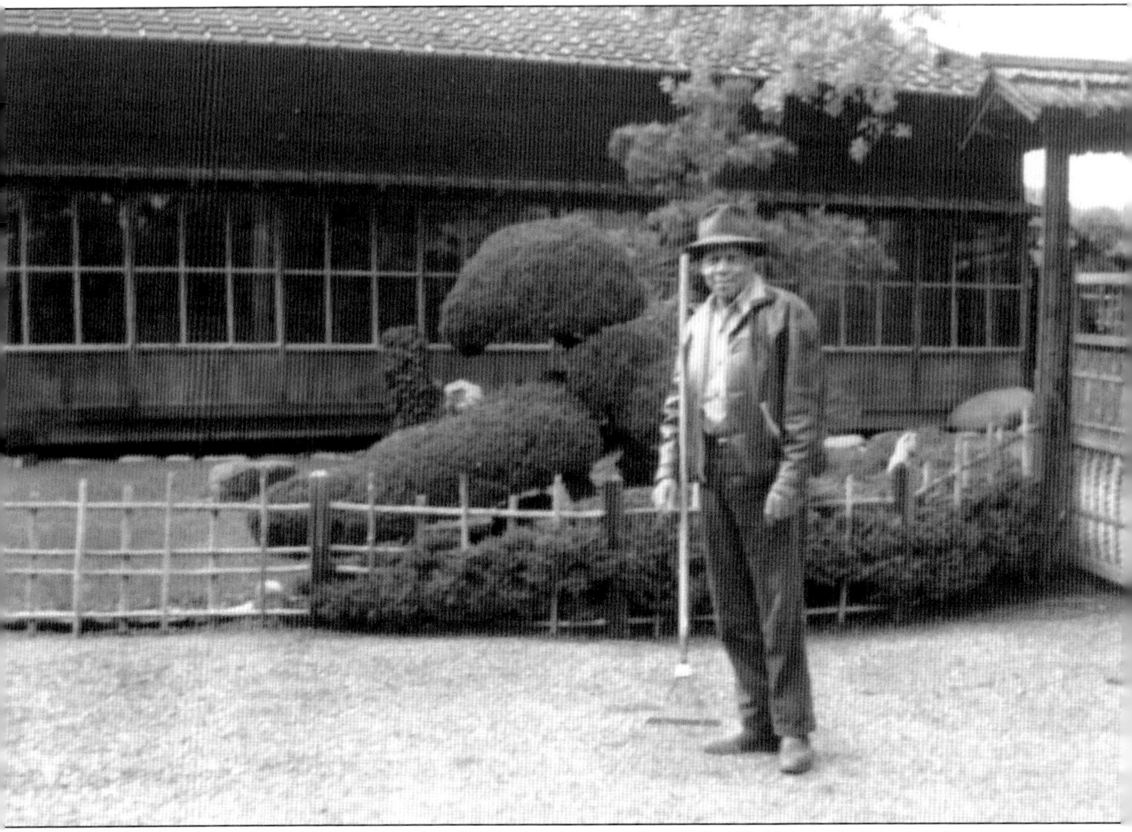

In 1961, Charlie Ray was hired by the partners as gardener for Hakone, settling in the cottage on the grounds. That he was the only African American resident of Saratoga caused consternation among neighbors. They assumed that he could not take care of a Japanese garden and that the partners were going to raze Hakone so they could build a Chinese restaurant. Ray, however, was a capable gardener and took to the job of caring for Hakone with dedication. He protected the property, kept the landscaping pristine, and tended the orchard of pear trees, now Hakone's parking lot. A single man, he felt the partnership was family and Hakone was home. After the partners sold Hakone to the City of Saratoga, Ray was employed by Dan Lee to work at Ming's Restaurant at its new location on Embarcadero Road in East Palo Alto. (Courtesy of Young family collection.)

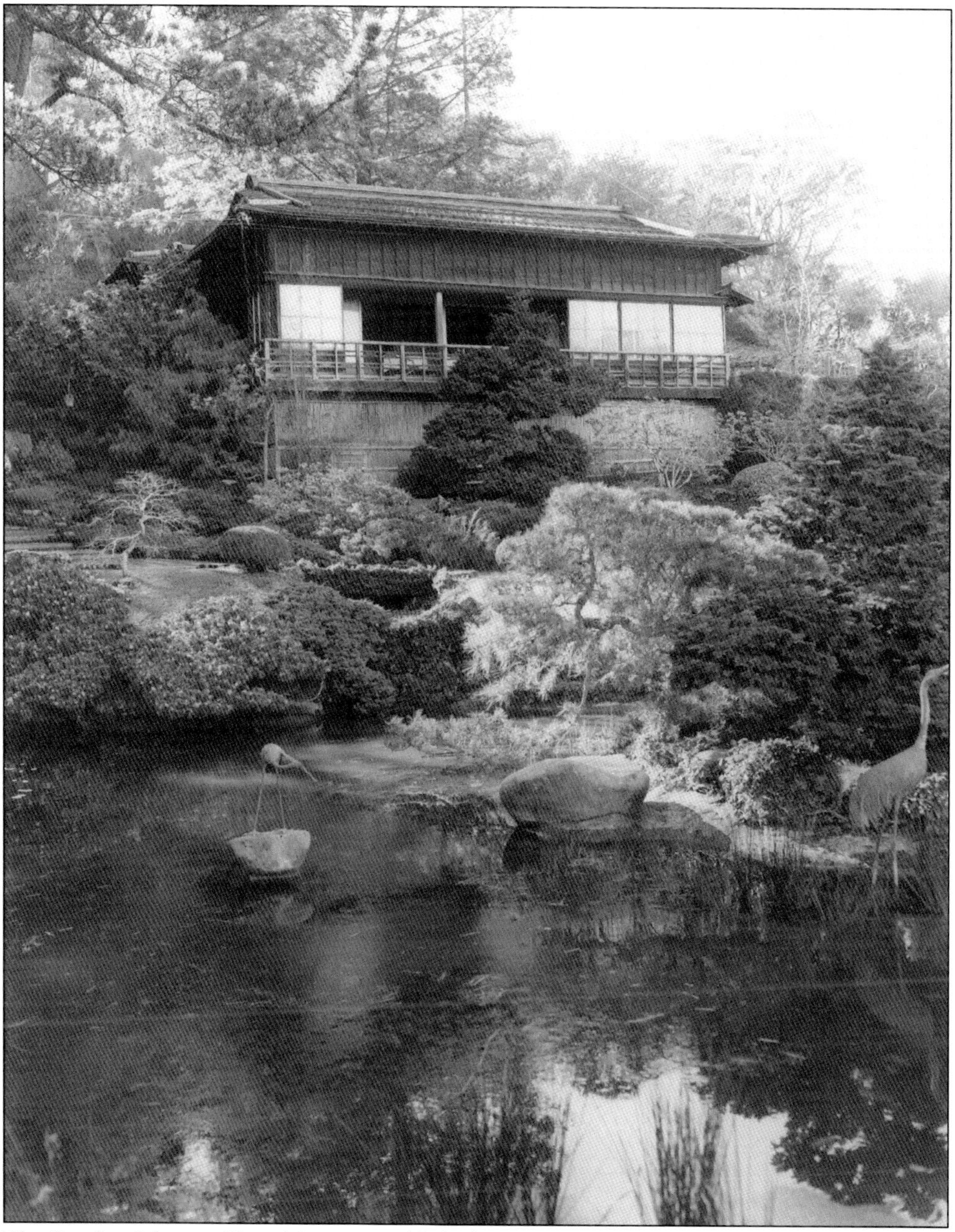

The *San Jose Mercury News Magazine* published a story on Hakone titled "17 Acres of Japanese Tradition" on March 14, 1962. Gorgeous shots of the garden estate were featured, including this iconic picture of the Upper House. Built in 1917 and intended as a place of quiet retreat, it was called the Moon Viewing House by Isabel Stine. The interior was designed after a Zen monastery, with the large study room belonging to the head priest. In the 1960s, it was carefully used by the owners, who never allowed food in the Upper House. As a student at Mills College in Oakland, Connie Young, daughter of the Youngs, used the Upper House during exam times with three classmates, all sitting on the tatami mats while studying. Major Tilden, in an earlier era, was a trustee of Mills. (Courtesy of Deon Gresham.)

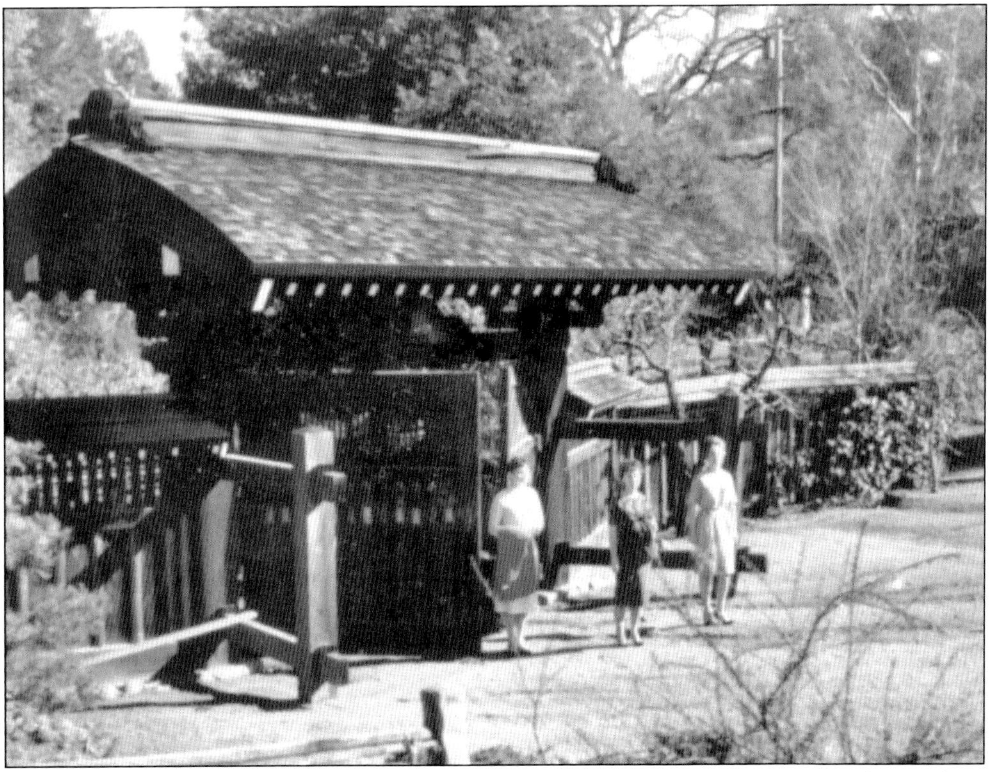

Deon Gresham (center) poses at the Mon with her friend Mickey Dench and sister-in-law Darlene Gresham Harms. Note the large double doors that impressively hang on massive hand-forged iron hinges. This was one of the many photographs taken but not featured in the story of Hakone for the *San Jose Mercury News Magazine* on March 14, 1962. (Courtesy of Deon Gresham.)

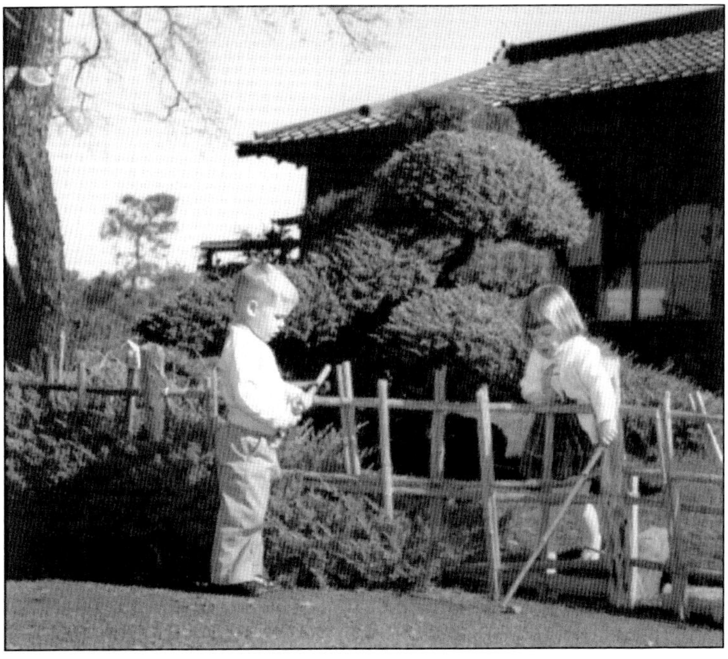

Hakone was designed as a strolling garden, but it was also a magical place for children to frolic without disturbing the landscape. Here the Greshams held annual Easter egg hunts and birthday parties for their children and friends. Playing by the fence of long-jointed bamboo designed by Naoharu Aihara for Isabel Stine are Mark, son of Eldon and Deon Gresham, and his cousin Melissa Gresham. (Courtesy of Deon Gresham.)

Mary Lee Young (second from left) and her sister Marie Lee Hall (far right) host friends from San Francisco at Hakone. They were born in San Francisco, as was their father, Lee Yoke Suey, who was an importer and exporter. Their grandfather Lee Wong Sang came to California from a Cantonese village in 1866 to be a worker on the first transcontinental railroad. (Courtesy of Young family collection.)

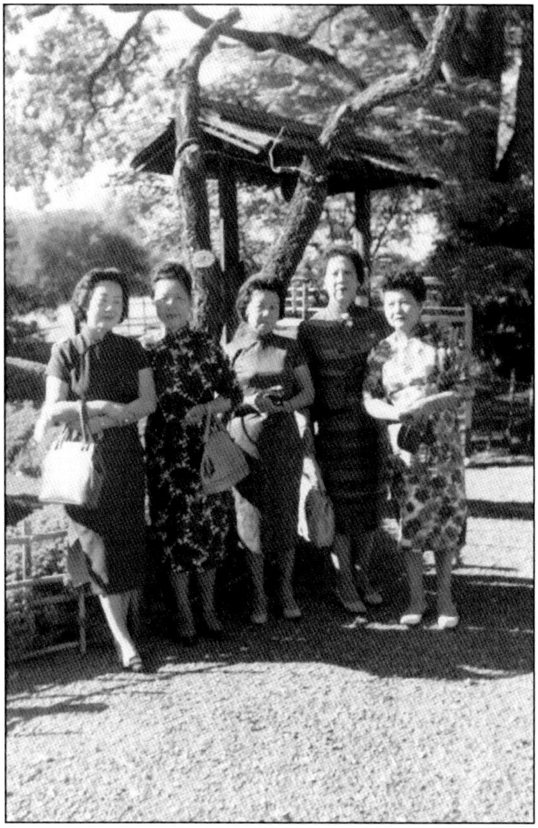

Jeung Hing Tong, widow of Lee Yoke Suey and mother of Hakone partners Mary Lee Young and Marie Lee Hall, stands at Hakone's Mon, the word for "door" in both Chinese and Japanese. In 1924, she was detained for 15 months on Angel Island because of the Chinese Exclusion Law, her story told in *Detained at Liberty's Door*, a film by Barre Fong. (Courtesy of Young family collection.)

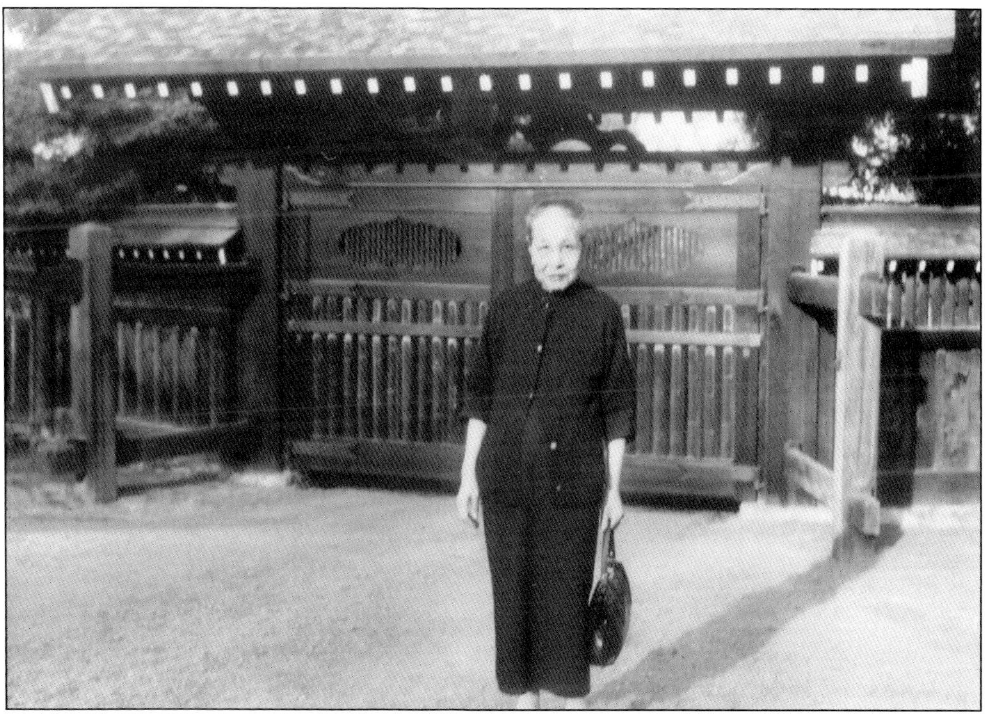

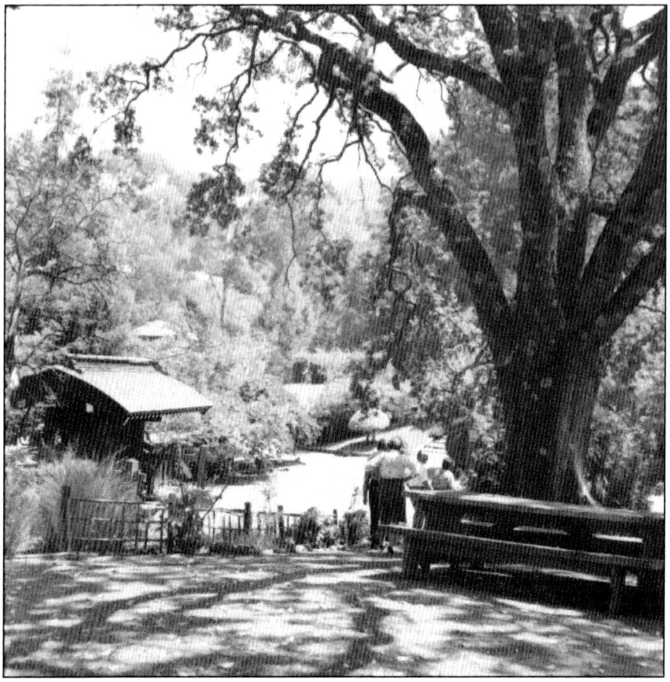

The picnic tables were constructed during the Tilden era. Nearby was the building known as "the cook house." Deon Gresham recalls making lunches there with her children and cleaning the kitchen. The partnership families chose to not allow dining in the Upper and Lower Houses. Following Japanese tradition, the partnership families always took their shoes off when they entered the Upper and Lower Houses. (Courtesy of Young family collection.)

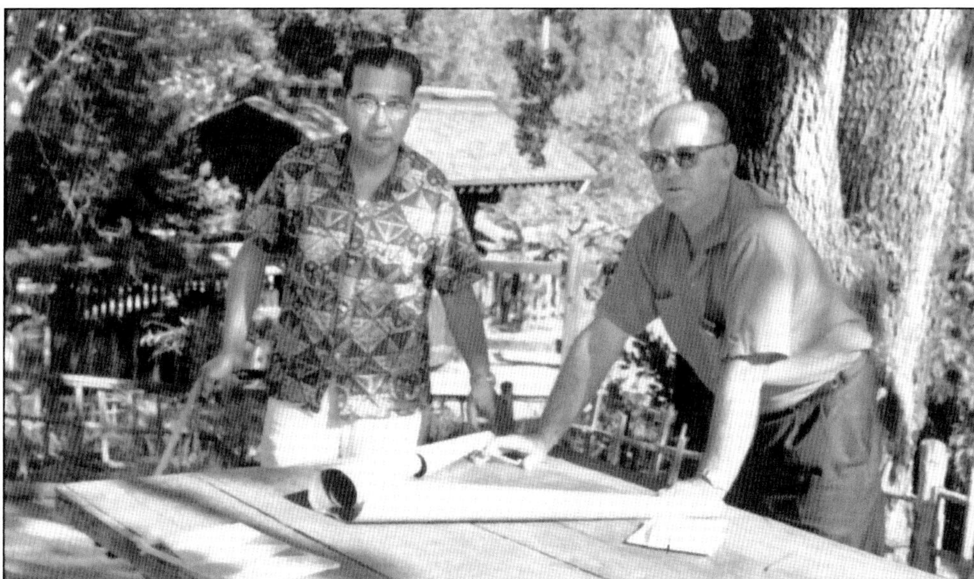

In 1961, George Hall (left) and Joe Gresham review Hakone's blueprints. George was a civil engineer and soy sauce manufacturer, and Joe was a general contractor with his firm, Gresham Construction Company. His son Eldon, a realtor and investor, joined his father's business. The partners pitched in to handle problems caused by nature, the first being the removal of the poison oak that within one season had invaded Hakone, climbing into the trees. Deon Gresham, Eldon's wife, recalls Dan Lee standing knee-deep in the koi pond with a net, clearing out the frog eggs that thickened the water. There were challenges by the city, according to Deon, to the partners' desire to replace Hakone's narrow gravel road with a wider paved road. But they prevailed and built a new access road still in use today. (Courtesy of Mel Hall.)

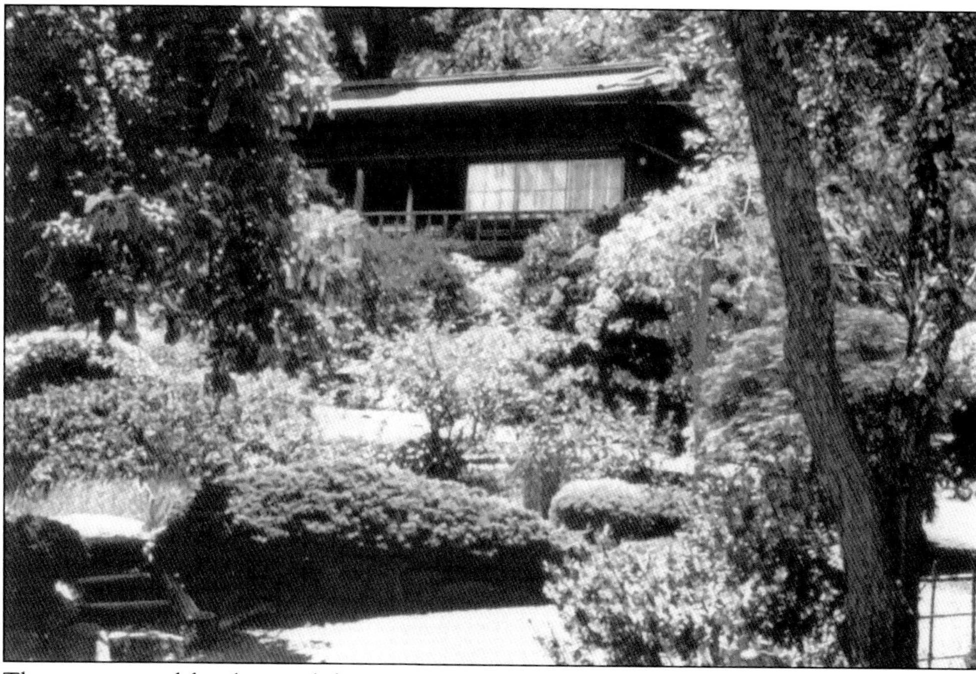

The partners and families used the Upper or Moon Viewing House as a special place for viewing the garden below during the daytime as well as the moon in the evening. It was also lovely to see over the beautifully landscaped foliage, as photographed by John Young. Note the trimmed juniper bushes in the foreground, still there today. The stone steps have been moved. (Courtesy of Young family collection.)

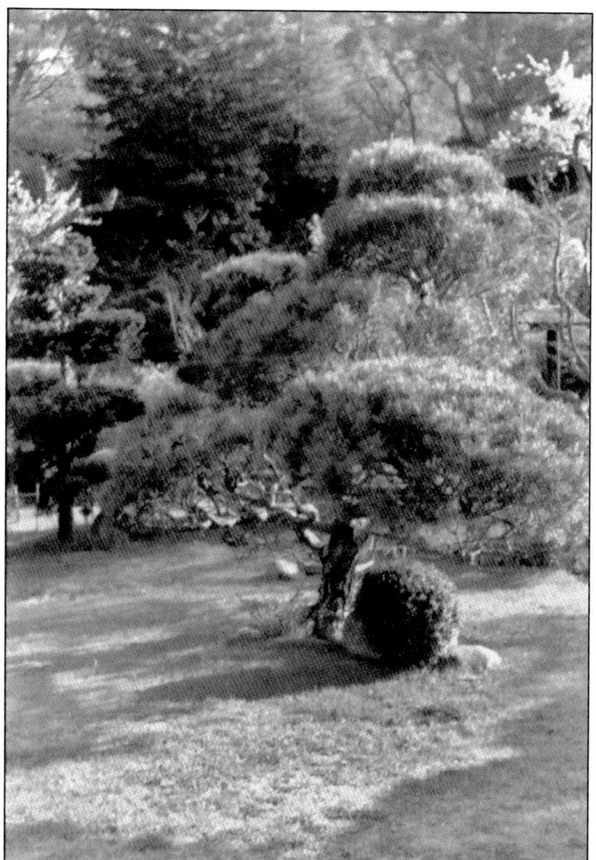

John Young photographed this scene of three elegantly sculpted Japanese black pine trees in front of the Lower House. As originally designed by Naoharu Aihara, cultivated by James Sasaki, and maintained by Charlie Ray, Hakone continued to exemplify Japanese garden art for educating western visitors. (Courtesy of Young family collection.)

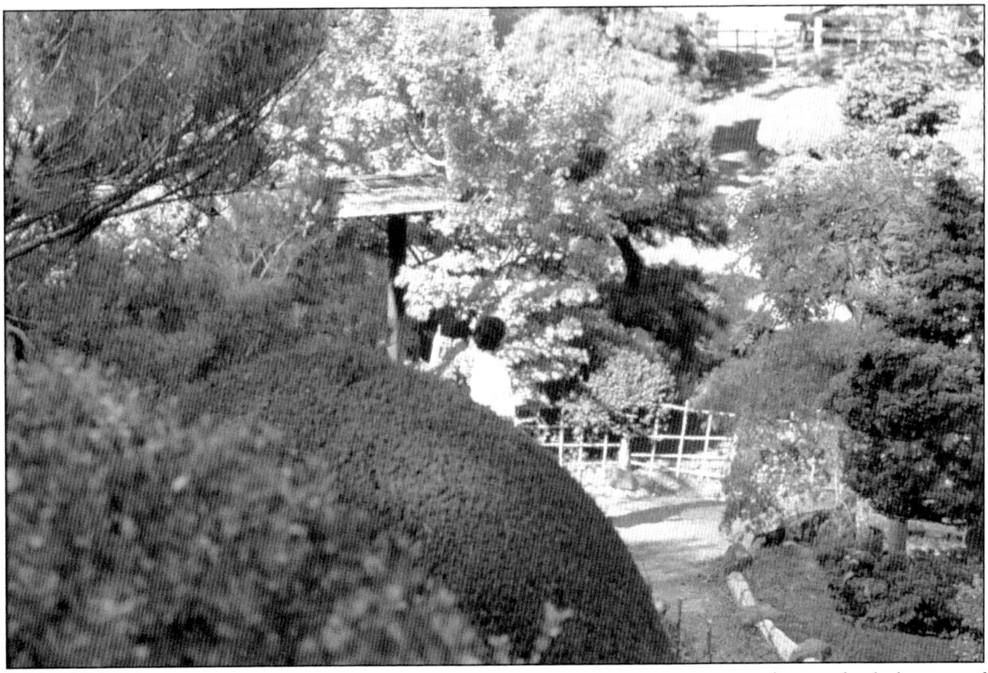

June Lee had a special interest in the Japanese aesthetics of Hakone, as she studied the art of *ikebana*, Japanese flower arranging, and consulted on the garden with James Sasaki, now retired and living in nearby Campbell. She is seen walking along a Hakone path past the small mon gate near the pond. It is a warm fall day, with the landscape beginning to change color. (Courtesy of Carina Chiang.)

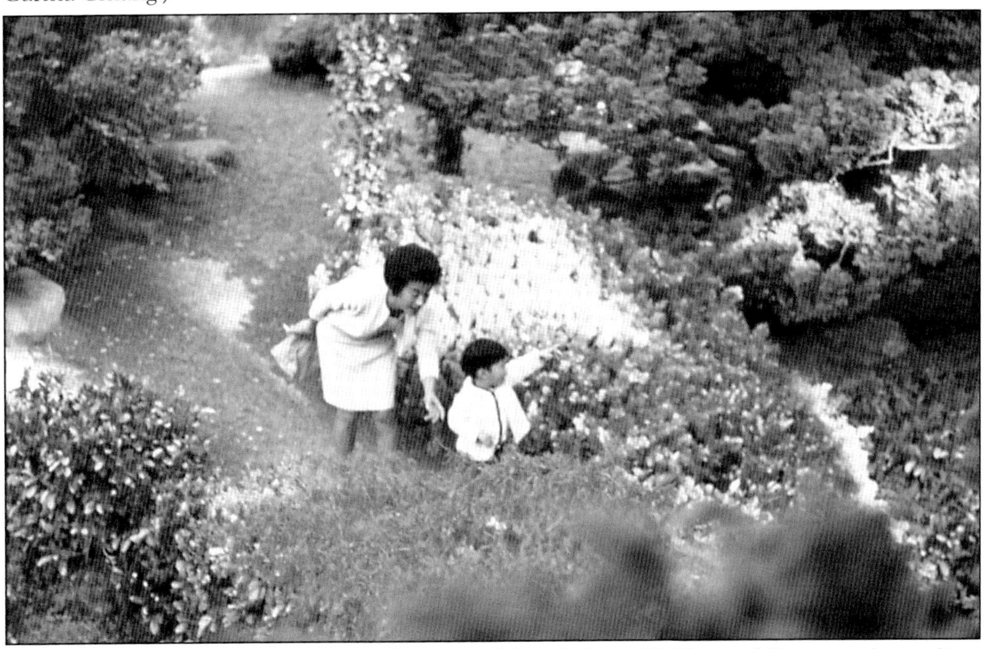

June came regularly to Hakone from Palo Alto with her children, Debbie and Stuart, to do weeding, trim the shrubbery, and tend the Japanese maple trees. Here she is helping young Stuart explore the pathways winding through the landscape. (Courtesy of Carina Chiang.)

June Lee hosted the Chiang family on a warm fall day at Hakone. From left to right, Debbie Lee and friend Dawn Chiang cool their feet in the pond as June, son Stuart, and friend Carina stand on the rocks. On the right is Julia Lau Chiang, Dawn and Carina's mother. These lovely scenes of Hakone were photographed by Julia's husband, Franklin Chiang. (Courtesy of Carina Chiang.)

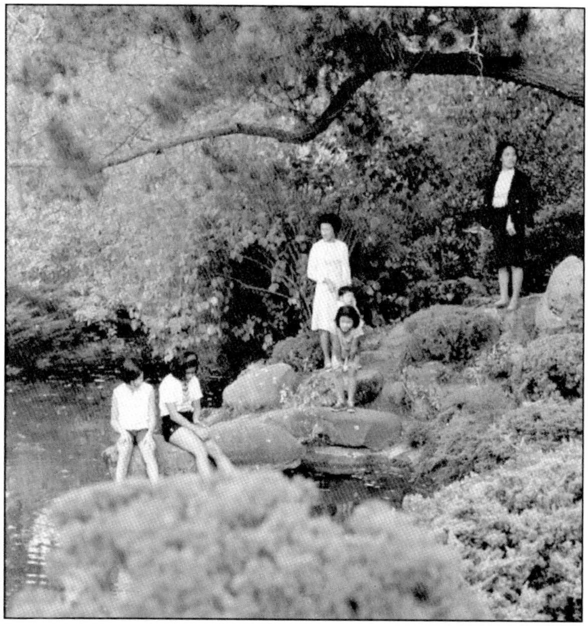

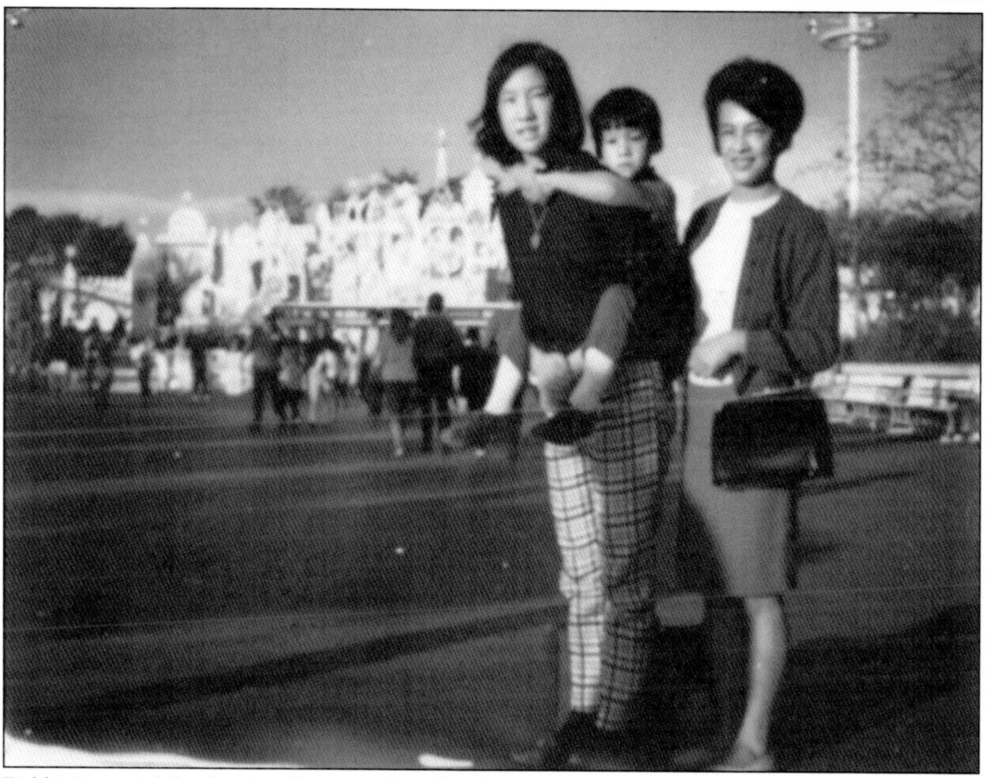

Debbie Lee, with her brother Stuart and mother, June Lee, enjoy New Year's Eve 1967 at Disneyland. Debbie recalls happy memories at Hakone with her Girl Scout troop and extended family gathering. Her mother remained close friends with Clara Gresham after the sale of Hakone. Debbie was glad she would still see her friend Charlie Ray, whom her dad hired to work at Ming's Restaurant. (Courtesy of Debbie Lee.)

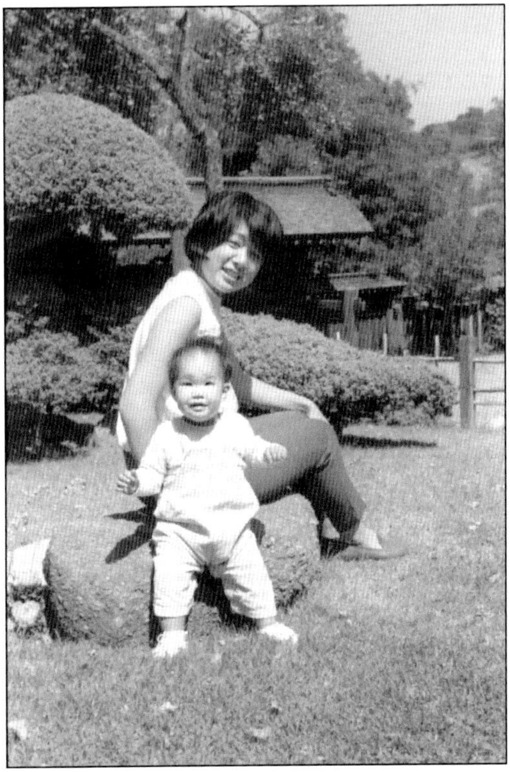

Three generations of Halls spend a summer's day at Hakone. Marie Hall snapped this photograph of her daughter Effie Hall and little Susan Jue, the child of her daughter Isabelle. Effie sits on the flat "seat stone" outside the Lower House. It is one of Hakone's "eternal" stones that continue to be appreciated today. The Mon can be seen in the background. (Courtesy Young family collection.)

This is a view of the Lower House photographed by John Young, who admired Japanese architectural design. Inside were the comfortable furnishings, bamboo settees, and cushioned chairs that Charles Tilden had custom-made in Oakland decades earlier and antique Japanese chests of the Stine era. The partners were grateful that Michael Gregory, the previous owner, left the interior furnishings in both houses for them to enjoy. (Courtesy of Young family collection.)

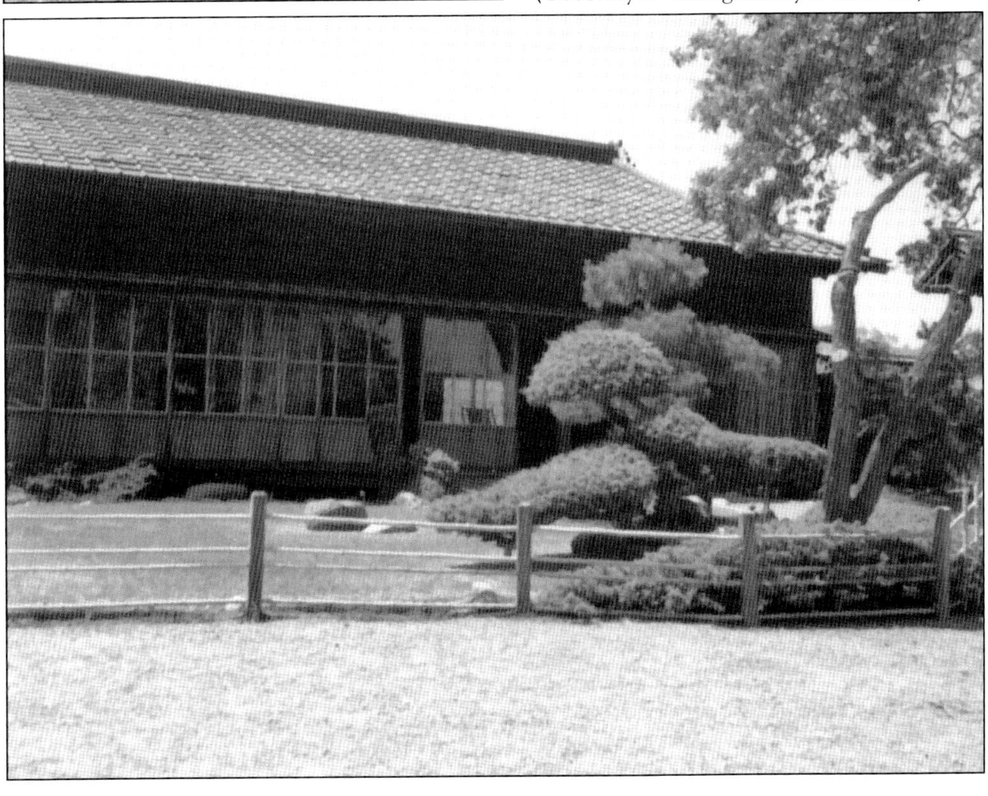

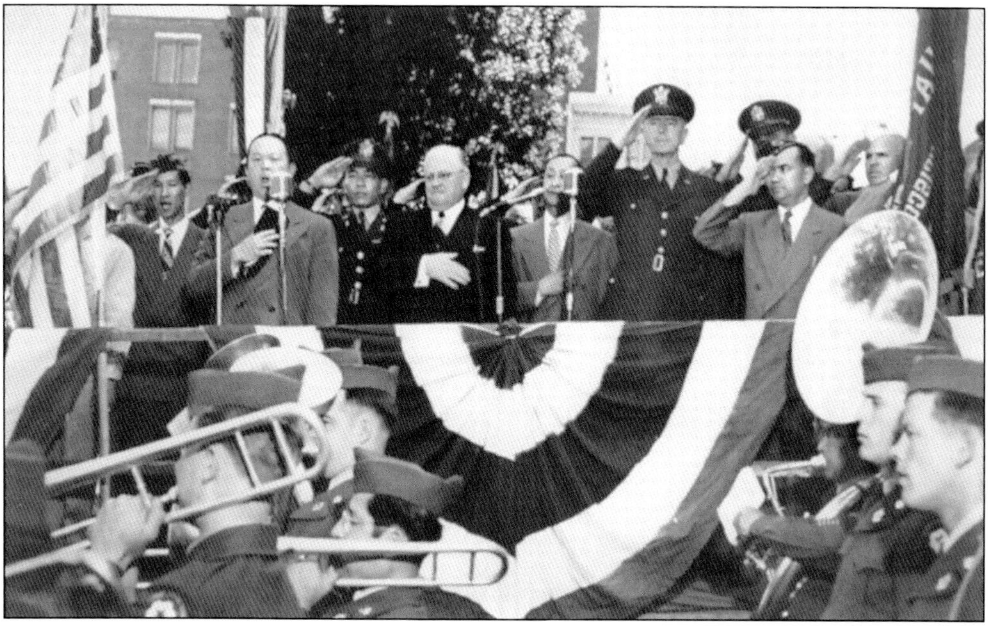

The memorial honoring Chinese American military killed in both world wars was dedicated on May 31, 1951, at St. Mary's Square in San Francisco. Standing at the ceremony are, from left to right, (first row) Patrick Sun, consul general, Republic of China; Mayor Elmer Robinson; Gen. Albert Wedemeyer; and Lim P. Lee; (second row) James H. Wong and Lt. Col. John C. Young, one of Hakone's owners. (Courtesy of Young family collection.)

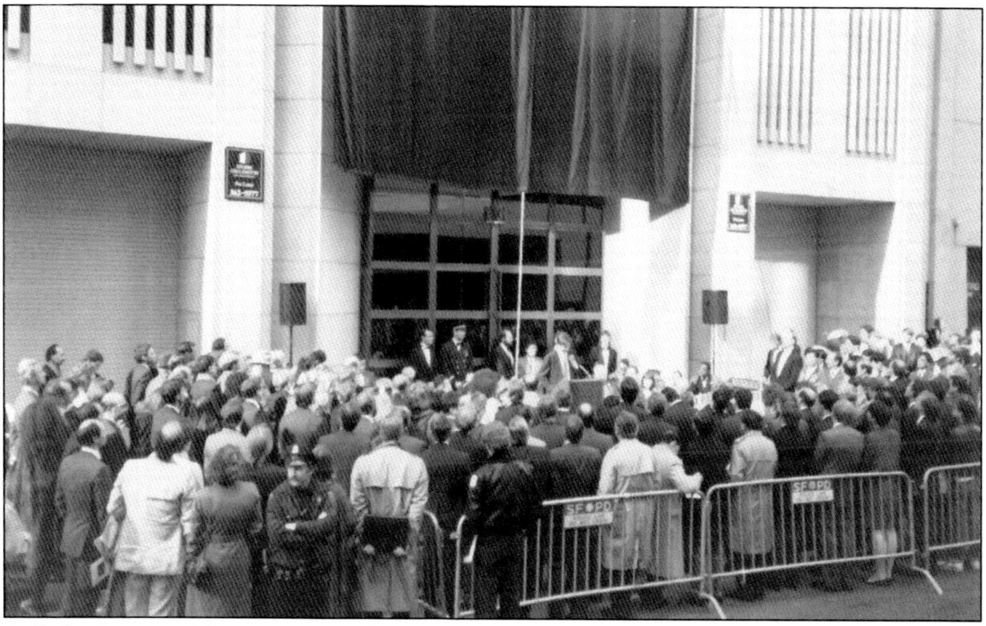

Called to Rise, at 235 Pine Street and dedicated in January 1991, is a series of 20 relief sculptures, each portraying an individual from San Francisco history, heroic in stature, who contributed significantly to the city. The image of John C. Young is on the right, fourth from the top. He is recognized for improving the infrastructure of Chinatown and establishing the war memorial at St Mary's Square. (Courtesy of Young family collection.)

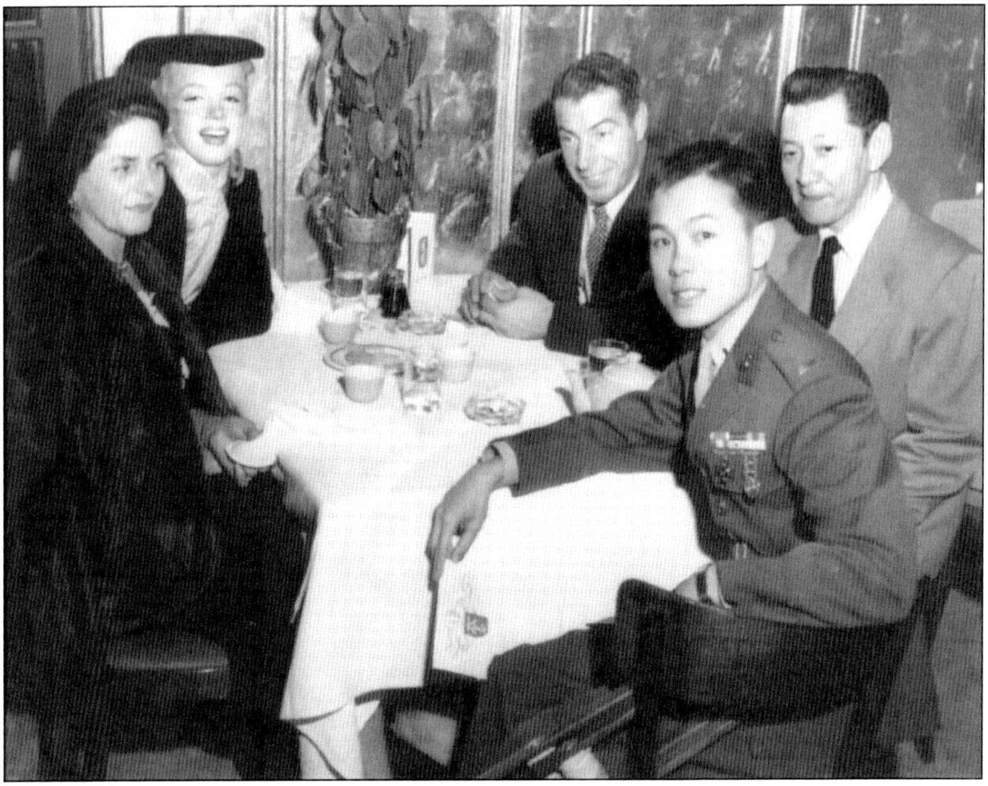

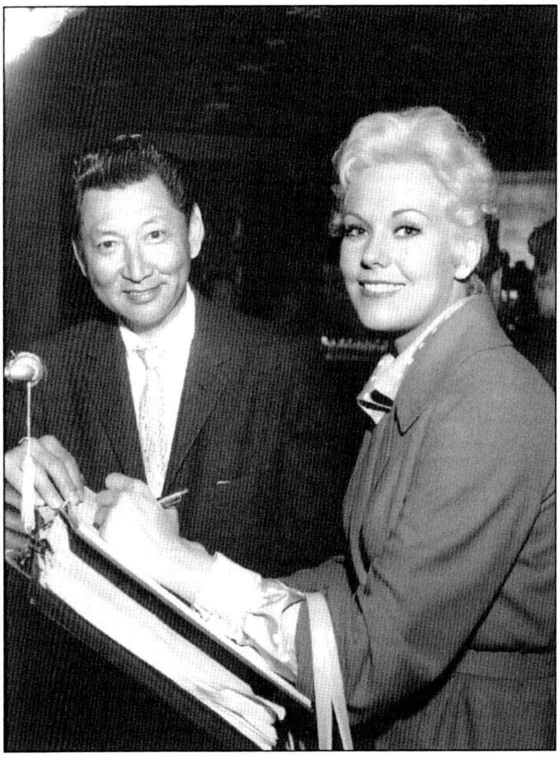

Soon after opening on Grant Avenue, Kan's became a popular restaurant among celebrities and dignitaries. In October 1953, Johnny Kan (right) hosted Marilyn Monroe (second from left), Joe DiMaggio (center), and Lt. Thomas Lee (second from right), wounded in Korea and recipient of a Purple Heart. In the following years, Kan's reputation grew nationally and internationally and was regularly on the top-ten lists of San Francisco restaurants. (Courtesy of Chinese Historical Society of America.)

The 1957 movie *Pal Joey* was set in San Francisco. The stars, Frank Sinatra and Kim Novak, dined at Kan's Restaurant after filming at the palatial Spreckels Mansion on Nob Hill. Here, Kim Novak signs Kan's impressive guest book with restaurateur Johnny Kan looking on. Kan was also an owner of Hakone. (Courtesy of Young family collection.)

Danny Kaye, comedian, movie star, and UNICEF ambassador, loved Chinese cuisine and was a fan of Kan's Restaurant. He was serious in his quest to learn the art of Chinese cooking from Kan's master chef, Ming Jang. Proudly wearing chef's attire, he poses with John C. Young, Johnny Kan's restaurant partner and also his partner in Hakone's ownership. (Courtesy of Young family collection.)

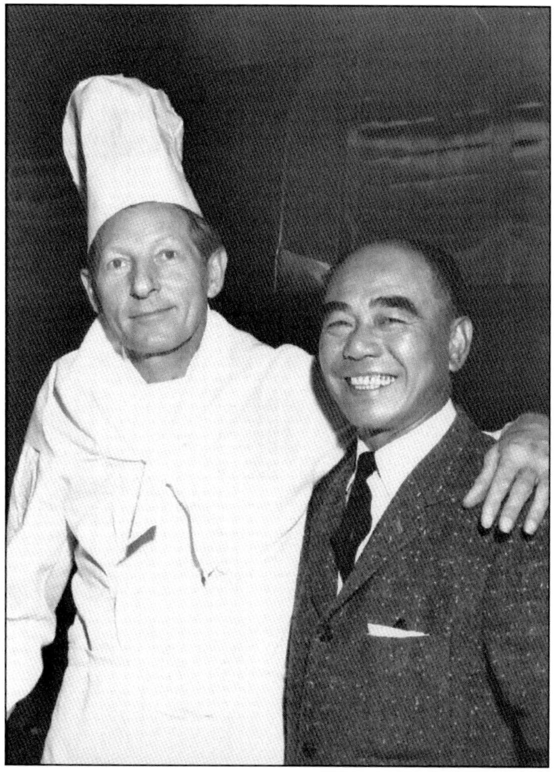

Singer Robert Goulet (right), performing in San Francisco in 1964, is hosted at Kan's Restaurant by Johnny Kan (center) and joined by Dan Lee, owner of Ming's Restaurant. Johnny Kan had published *Eight Immortal Flavors*, the first popular cookbook written by a Chinese American. Lee was a personal friend of Goulet, who loved Chinese cuisine and dined at Ming's and the Lee home in Palo Alto. (Courtesy of Chinese Historical Society of America.)

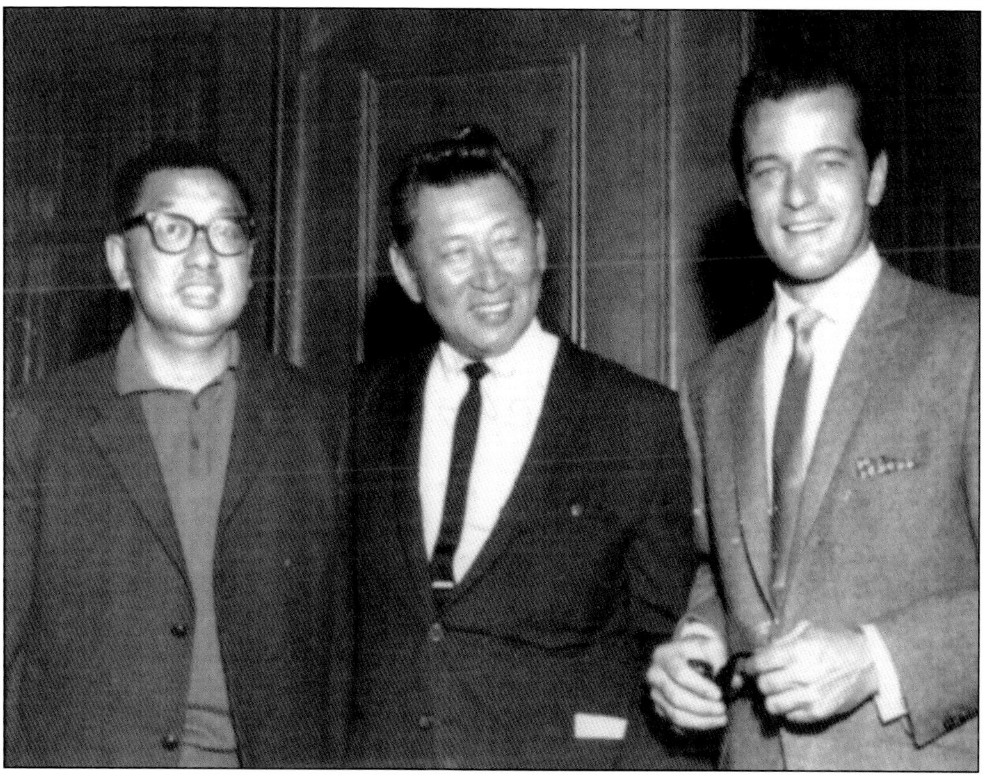

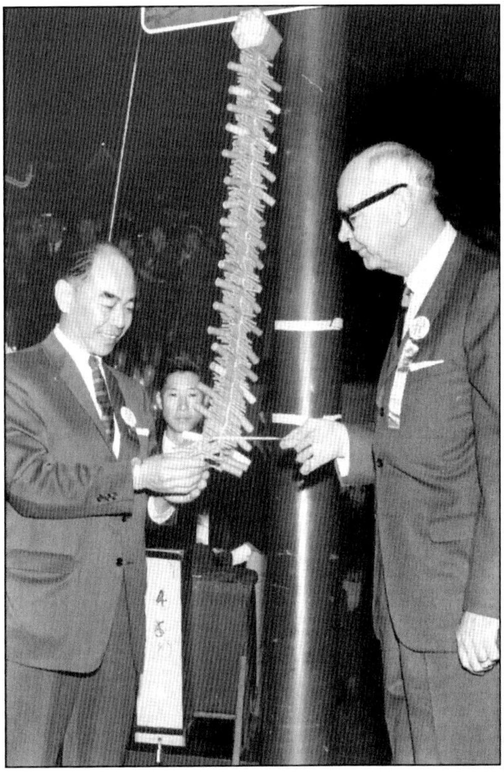

John Young, with Mayor John Shelley, officially opens the 1963 Chinese New Year's celebration in San Francisco. Known as "the Colonel" because of his rank in the US Army Reserves, Young was chairman of the annual Lunar New Year Parade in San Francisco, a position he held for 20 years. (Courtesy of Young family collection.)

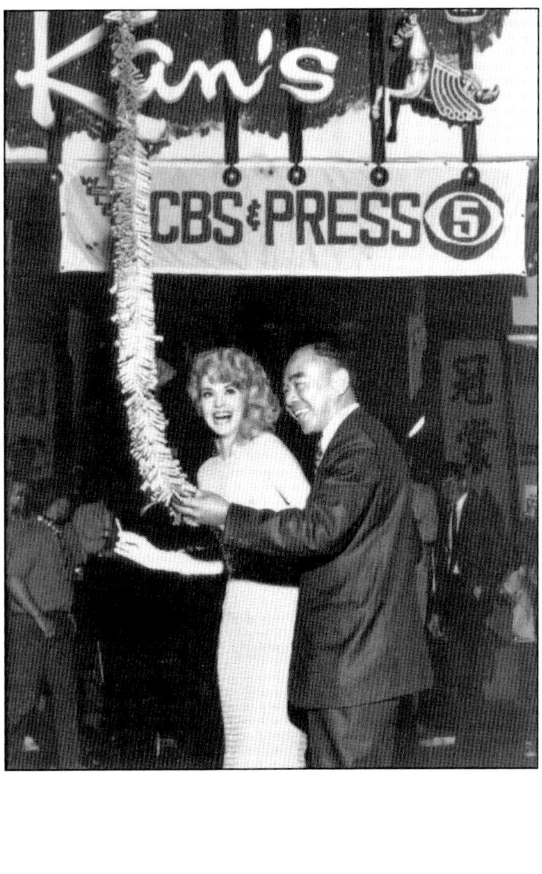

CBS publicized its fall television series in San Francisco's Chinatown on May 27, 1966, with the lighting of firecrackers in front of Kan's Restaurant on Grant Avenue. Donna Douglas, "Ella Mae" in the *Beverley Hillbillies* TV show, does the lighting honors assisted by John Young, representing the Chinese Chamber of Commerce. Both Johnny Kan and John Young were part of the partnership owning Hakone. (Courtesy of Young family collection.)

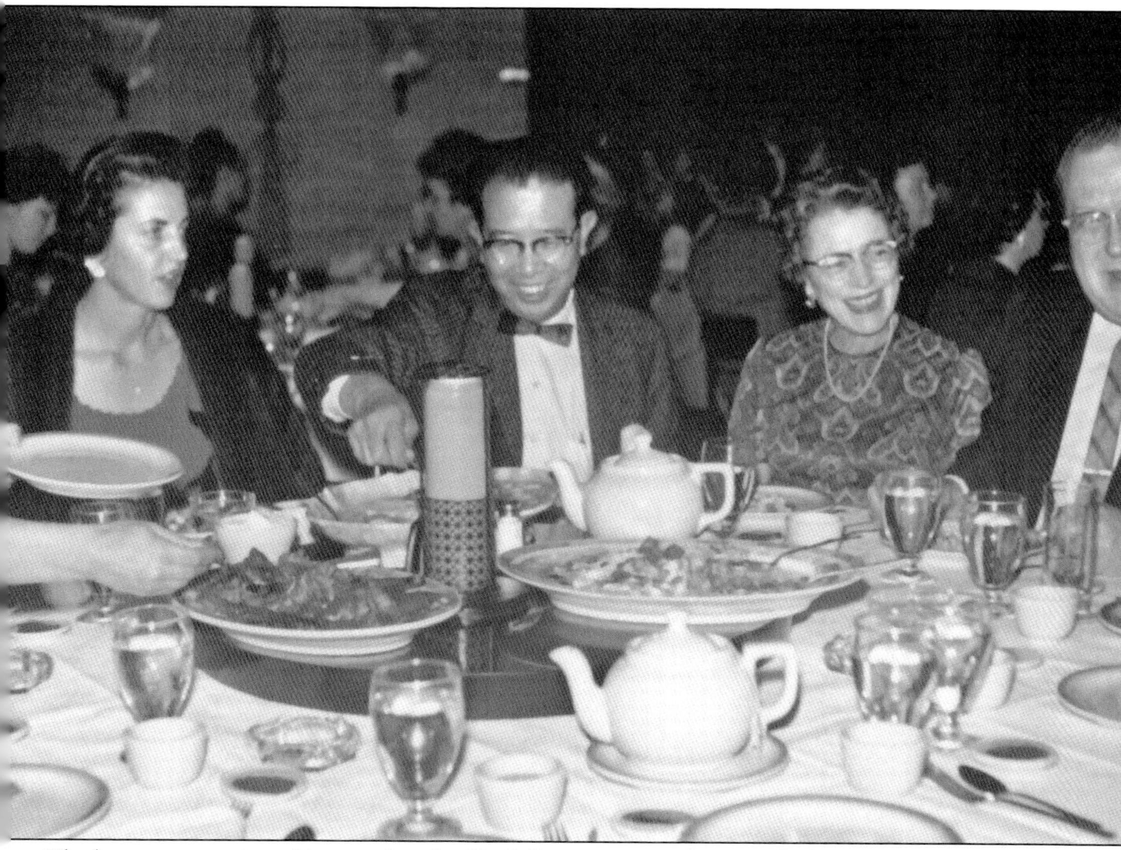

The lazy susan serving table introduced at Kan's Restaurant revolutionized Chinese dining around the world. In the early 1950s, George Hall, tinkering in his basement with wood rounds and ball bearings, designed a revolving tabletop for Kan's. It became a permanent feature in the restaurant banquet room and was quickly copied by other restaurants in Chinatown. In this photograph, George (center) hosts a party for friends at Kan's in 1962, enjoying his marvelous invention. (Courtesy Effie Hall Dilworth.)

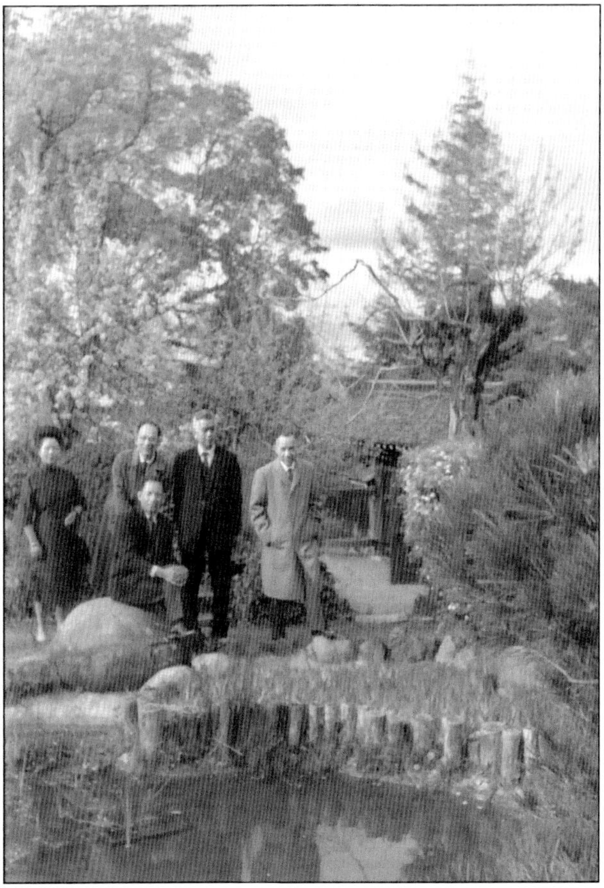

A group of prominent Chinese artists are guided through Hakone by Mary Lee Young, who studied and learned from their works. Second from right is the master painter Xheng Yue-Bo of San Jose, renowned for his paintings of horses. Hakone's unusual beauty has drawn many artists over the years to paint its landscape, which changes with the seasons. (Courtesy of Young family collection.)

Connie Young, daughter of John and Mary Young, visits Hakone in 1963 with Pai-Vuong Yu, her future mother-in-law, of Manila, Philippines. They are photographed in front of the koi pond by Connie's fiancé, Dr. John K.P. Yu. It is spring at Hakone, as evidenced by the blossoming wisteria. (Courtesy of Young family collection.)

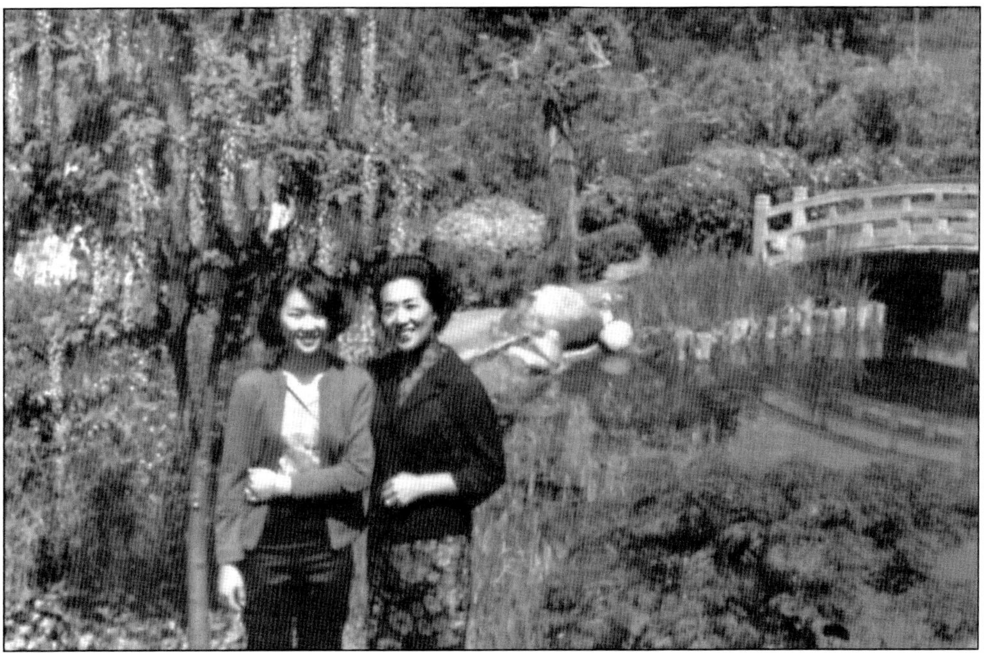

A dream came true for Eldon and Deon Gresham when their daughter was married at Hakone Gardens on June 10, 1989. Mari Gresham, in a wedding dress made by her mother, is escorted down the stone steps by her father. The wedding took place long after Hakone's sale to the City of Saratoga. Eldon and Deon, the former owners, retained their sentimental connection to the beautiful garden. (Courtesy of Deon Gresham.)

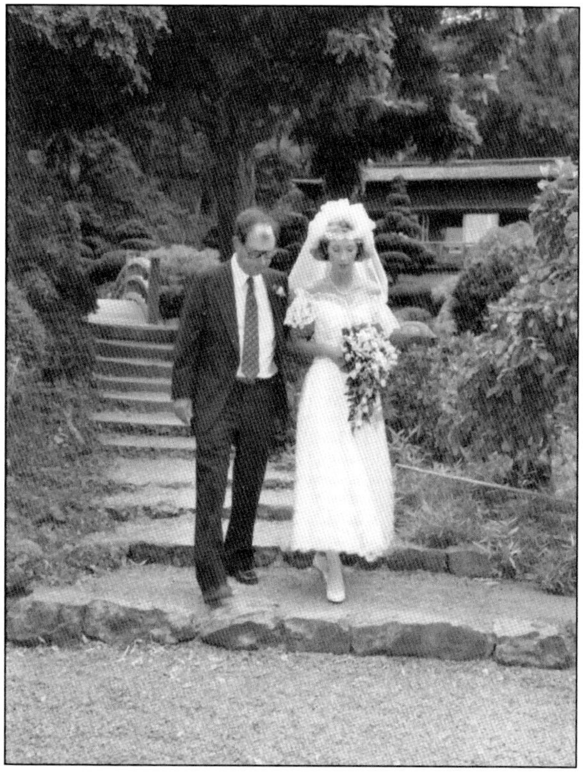

The bride, Mari Gresham, the daughter of Deon and Eldon Gresham, poses in Hakone's idyllic garden setting with her groom, Forrest Gingold, and grandmother Clara Gresham. Hakone continues to be a favorite wedding venue up to the present. (Courtesy of Deon Gresham.)

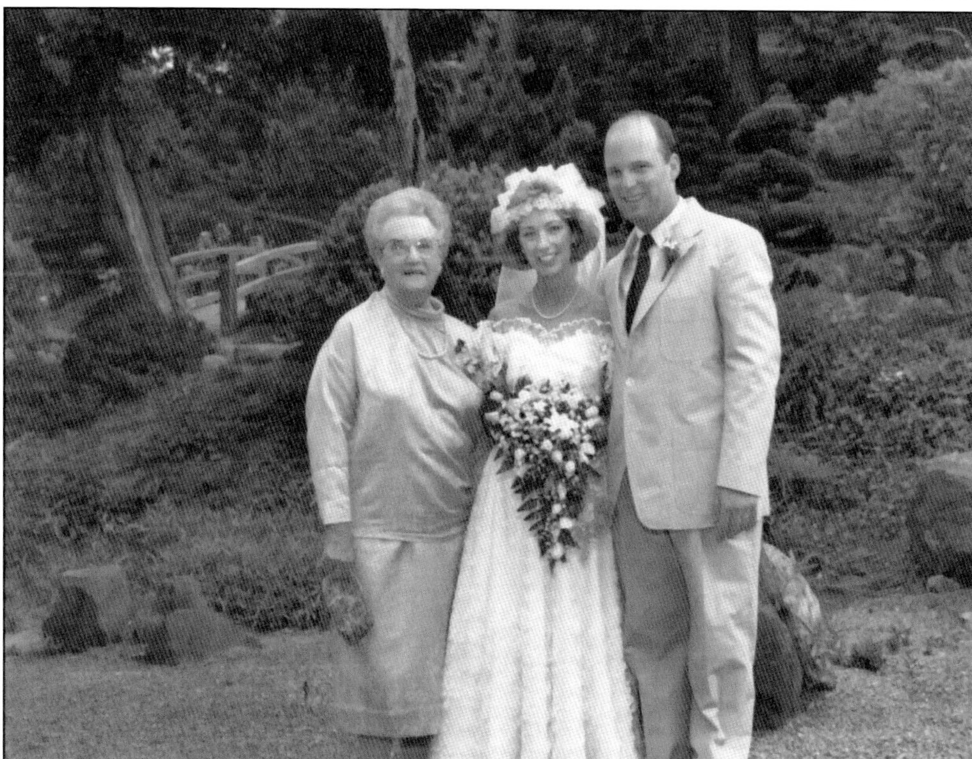

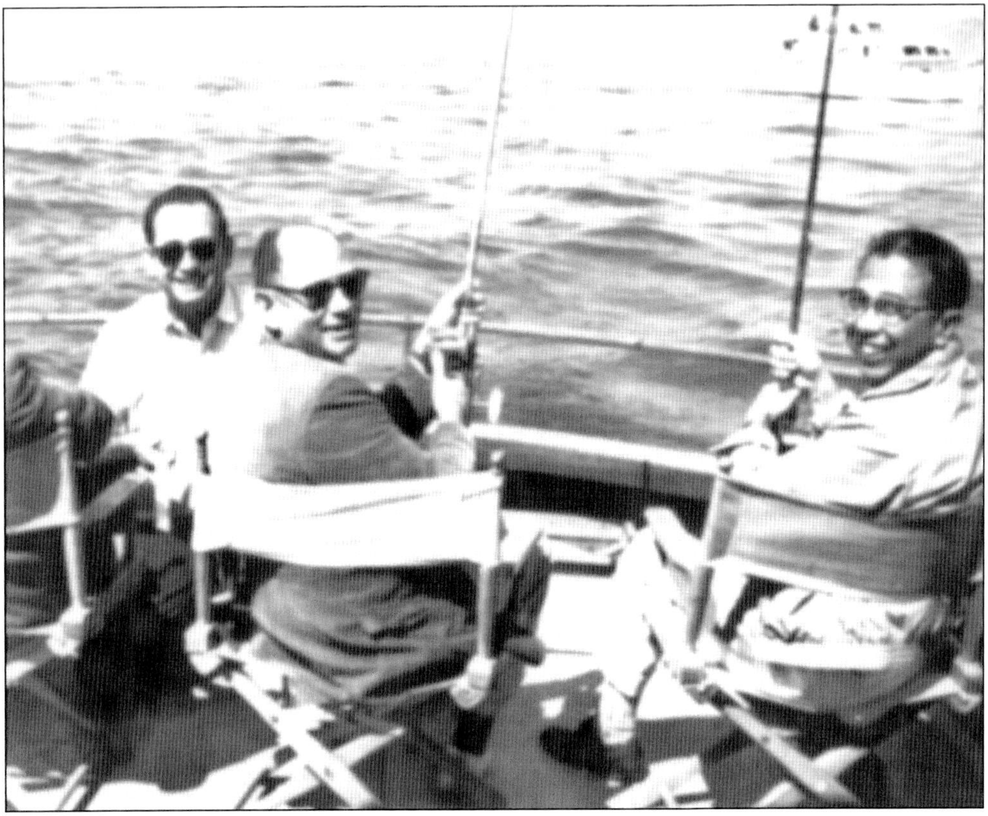

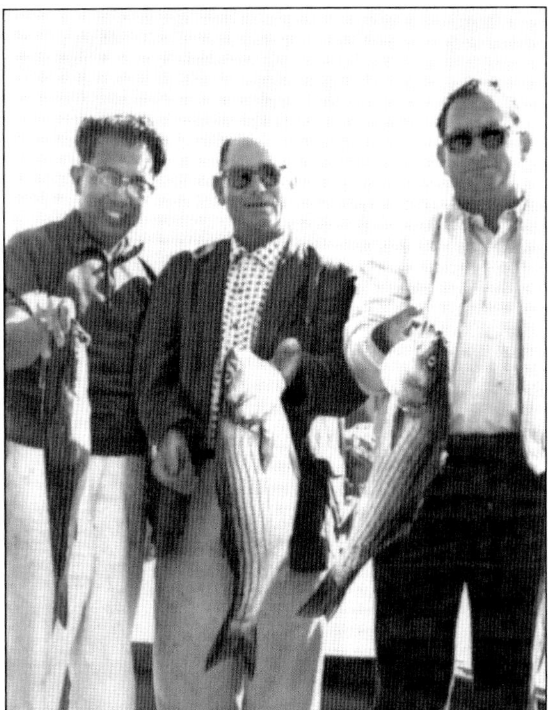

It was a most congenial partnership that owned Hakone. They were friends who enjoyed each other's company, especially on fishing trips on San Francisco Bay catching striped bass. Joe Gresham is pictured here at center with his son Conrad (left) and George Hall. Johnny Kan, also on the fishing boat, took the photograph. (Courtesy of Deon Gresham.)

Joe Gresham, the leader of the partnership, negotiated the sale of Hakone Gardens to the City of Saratoga in 1966 despite the initial reluctance of the city council. He died a few months later of a sudden heart attack on December 26, 1966, at the age of 59. Joe's friend and partner George Hall died from cancer two months earlier at the age of 58. (Courtesy of Deon Gresham.)

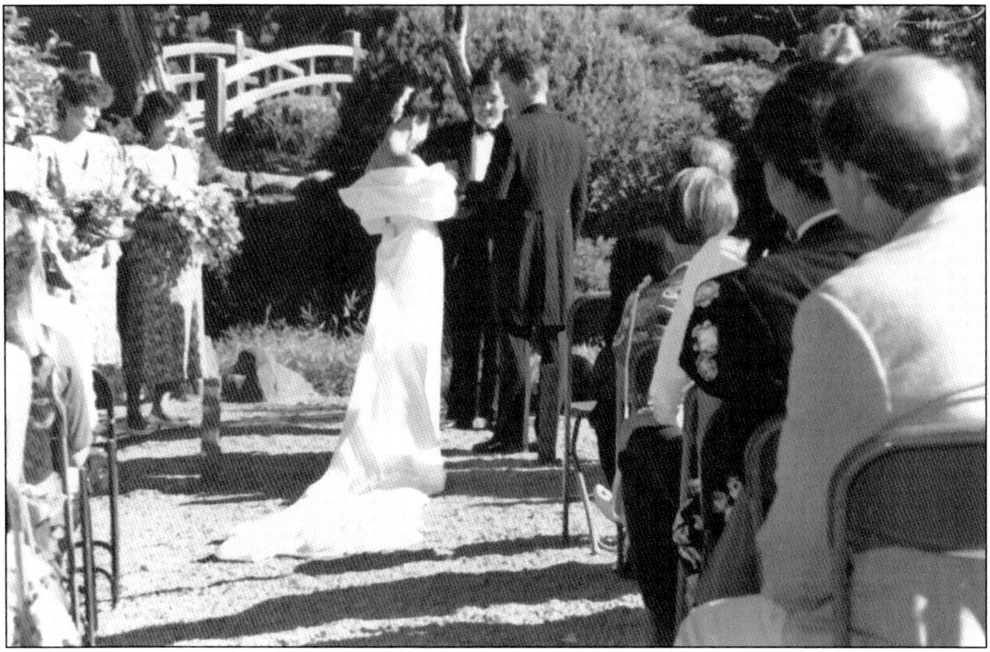

The wedding of Jessica Yu and Mark Salzman took place at Hakone Gardens on August 13, 1989, officiated by Jessica's uncle Al Young, son of John and Mary Young. Hakone partners Mary Lee Young (Jessica's grandmother) and June Lee were present. As former owners, it was a special sentimental moment for them, savoring Hakone's enduring beauty. (Courtesy of Yu family.)

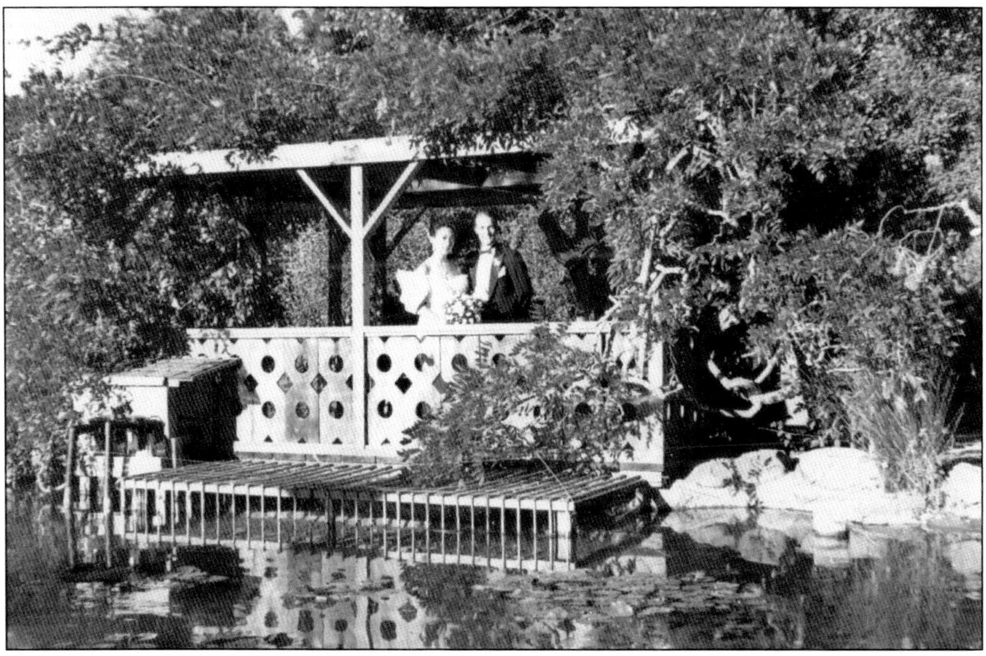

Hakone, with its unique, exquisite setting, was becoming one of the most popular places for weddings in the region in the 1980s, and Jessica Yu and Mark Salzman were drawn to it by the Young family history at the gardens. The wedding couple pose at the lovely wisteria pavilion by the pond once owned by the bride's grandparents. (Courtesy of Yu family.)

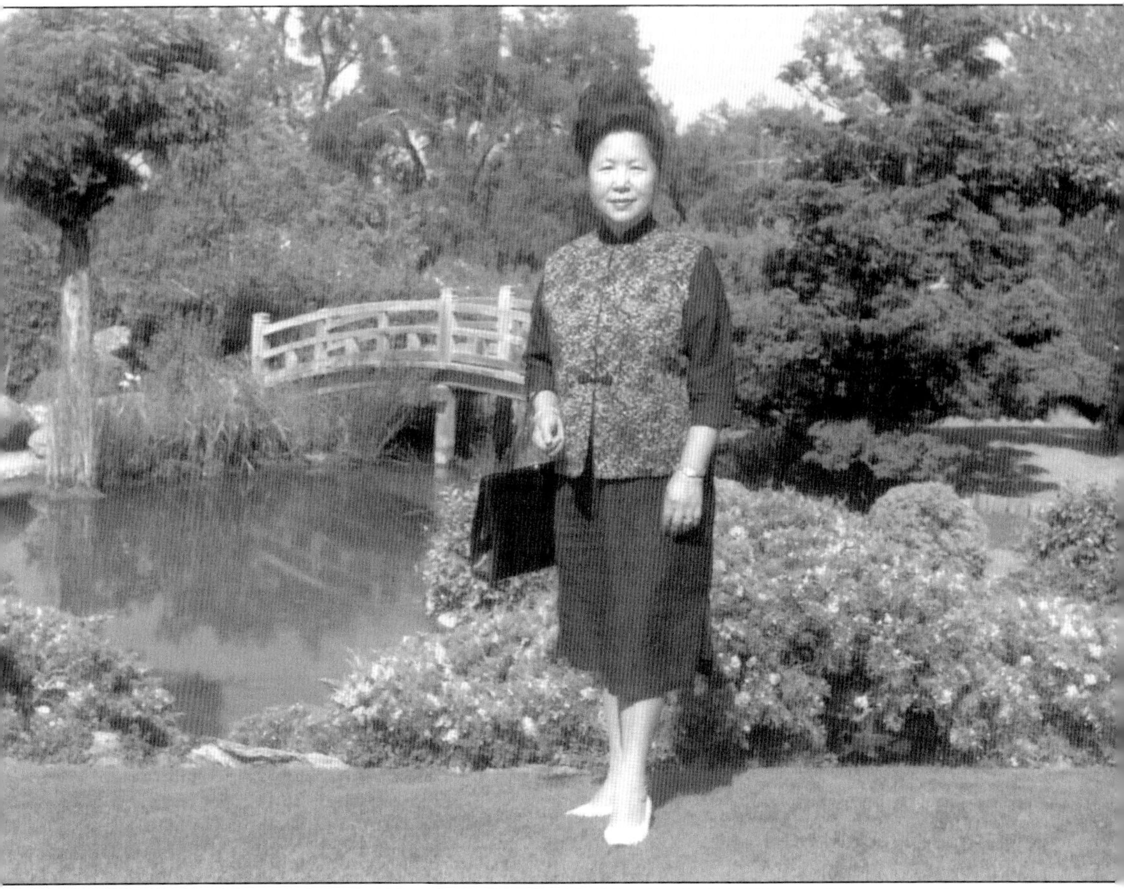

Mary Lee Young wrote to her daughter Connie on May 21, 1966: "We finally gave up the ownership of Hakone. I think it is very wise to sell it to the City of Saratoga as the City can afford to build up the garden, preserve the historic value, and take care of the rare trees a lot better than 6 partners. We didn't make much money instead of selling to other people for bigger profit. I feel the place is so beautiful and unique and should be open for the public to enjoy. I am sure you miss the garden, but the city people told me that we can go there anytime we want, even before it opens to the public." (Courtesy of Young family collection.)

Four

Saratoga's Purchase

Hakone Garden Becomes a Public Park

The city council of Saratoga purchased Hakone Gardens as a public park in 1966. Saratoga itself was newly incorporated as a city, yet the council had the foresight to purchase what would become a priceless cultural asset. Mayor Bill Glennon saw Hakone's timeless beauty and understood its potential value to the Bay Area's growing diverse and multicultural population.

By 1982, however, the city had discovered how difficult it was to manage an old Japanese garden with historic buildings. The city council reached out to its citizens for volunteer help. Many Saratogans and other citizens heartily responded. Contrarily, there was some pushback against having a Japanese garden. In addition to the persistent undercurrent of anti-Asian feeling in California, there were increasing anti-Mexican and Latino incidents. Mayor Glennon himself had responded to the racism by changing his name from Guillermo Gonzalez to William Glennon when he moved from St. Louis, Missouri, to California after his service in World War II.

With all of the enthusiastic citizen volunteerism for the garden, ultimately a formal sister city relationship was established with Muko, Japan, along with the Saratoga Bamboo Society. Also, the city established a nonprofit foundation in 1985 to meet the need for more specialized oversight of the garden. All the volunteer groups supported the garden by producing events, weekly tea ceremonies, art and cultural classes, and gardening alongside the two professional gardeners. For 20 years, the volunteer groups helped the city develop its special Japanese garden. It was an era of unprecedented financial growth in Japan and an increase in Japanese travel to America. Such Japanese outreach helped to develop the beautiful features of Hakone.

In the 55 years after World War II, the peninsula of the Bay Area was changing from a rural, sparsely populated region into a burgeoning urban/suburban area humming with technology companies. Santa Clara Valley acquired a new identity—Silicon Valley—with Saratoga right in its midst. The city, with an expanding agenda, needed a new organization for managing Hakone beyond the original group of volunteers and established the new Hakone Foundation, focused on raising funds.

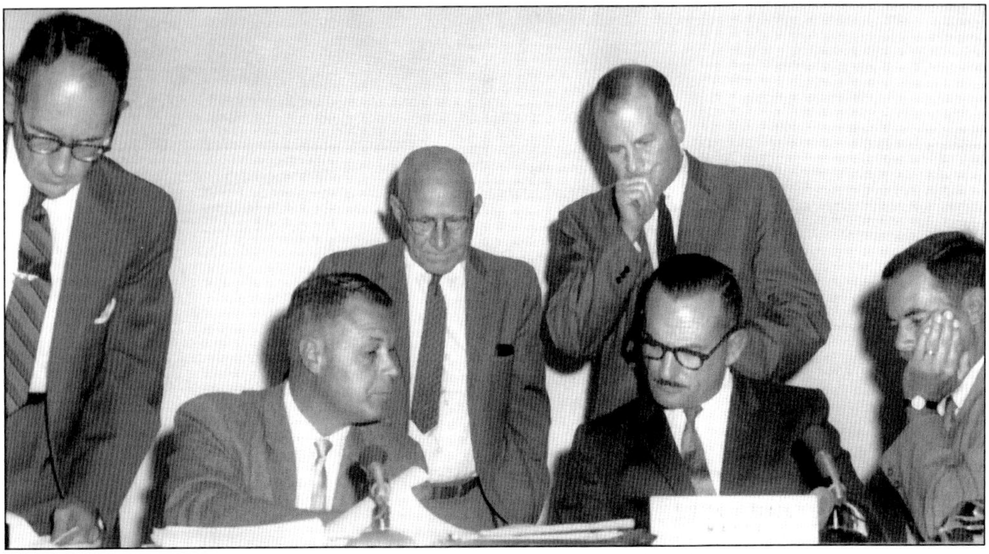

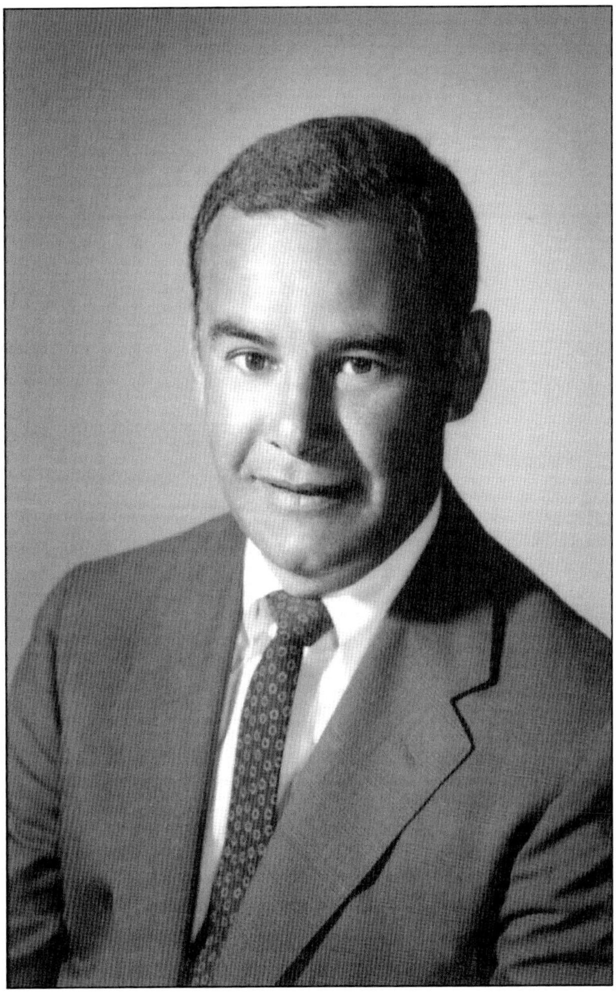

In 1956, rural Saratoga was incorporated, with few housing developments and a historic village. The new city council and small city staff built a new government, including zoning rules, buying park lands, and designing streets. From left to right are (seated) Kenneth Hartman, Mayor Burton Brazil, and Bill Glennon; (standing) Richard Drake, city manager Gordon Howe, and Frank Langwill. (Courtesy of City of Saratoga.)

Mayor Glennon and city council members Samuel Tyler, Ralph Burry, Richard Drake, and Kenneth Hartman approved the purchase of Hakone for $145,000. The city had to annex the property in order to purchase it, the land being just outside city limits. In his memoir, Glennon stated that he considered the purchase of Hakone Garden "my greatest contribution while I was Mayor." (Courtesy of City of Saratoga.)

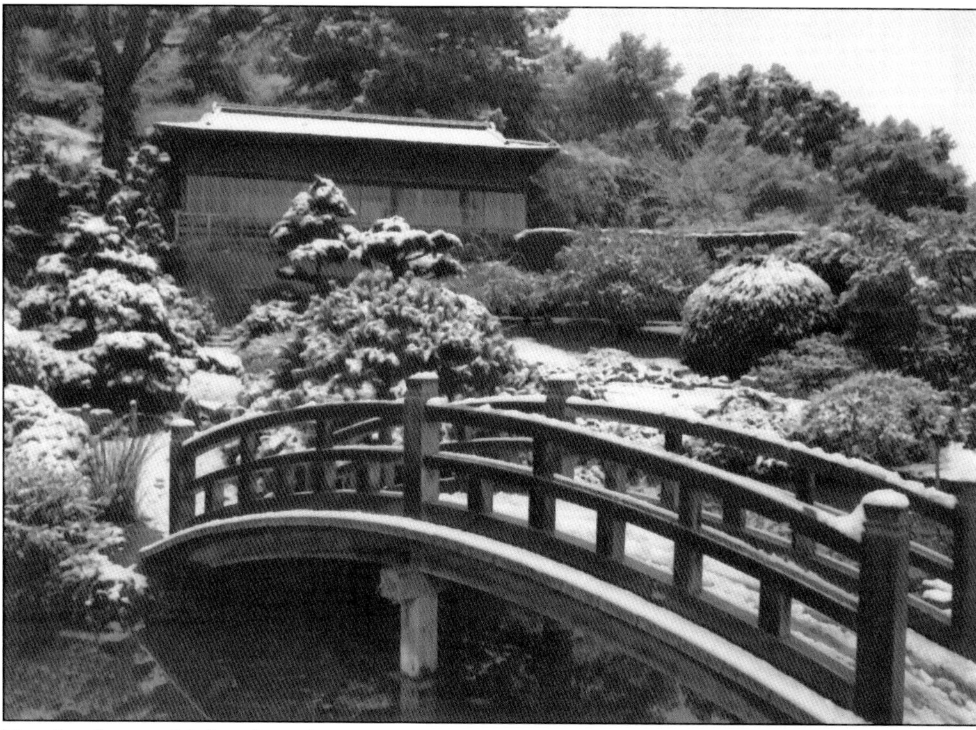

Despite the usual "chamber of commerce" year-round temperate weather, Mother Nature sometimes deals surprises. Hakone was briefly covered in snow during the winter of 1975, a very unusual sight. The bridge with the Upper House in the background has its beauty enhanced with the snow dusting. The charm of the new city park drew community volunteers to care for it. (Photograph by Bob Hall, courtesy of Elaine Salter.)

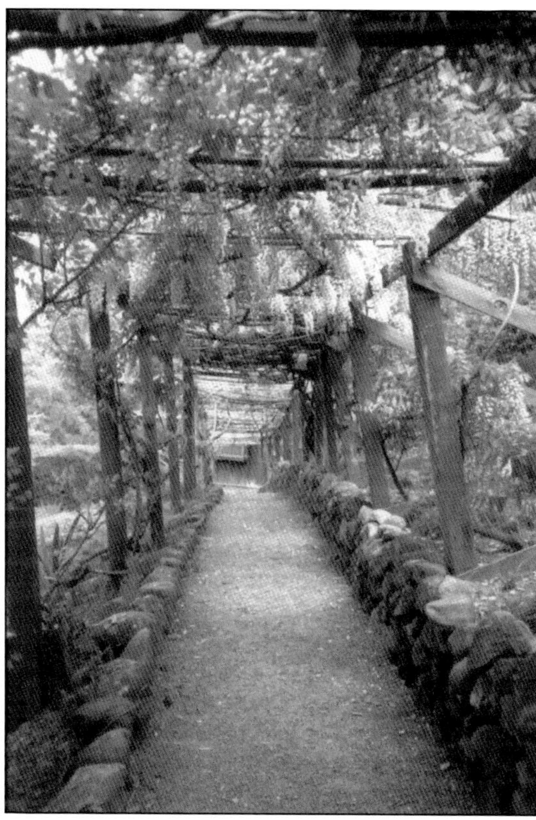

The wisteria arbor path next to the Upper House was lush with old wisteria vines, but by 1986, the redwood arbor was beginning to sag under the weight. Also, the arbor was too low for wedding couples to walk under for romantic photographs after a marriage ceremony. Years later, it was finally rebuilt and lifted to a new height. (Courtesy of Peter Marra.)

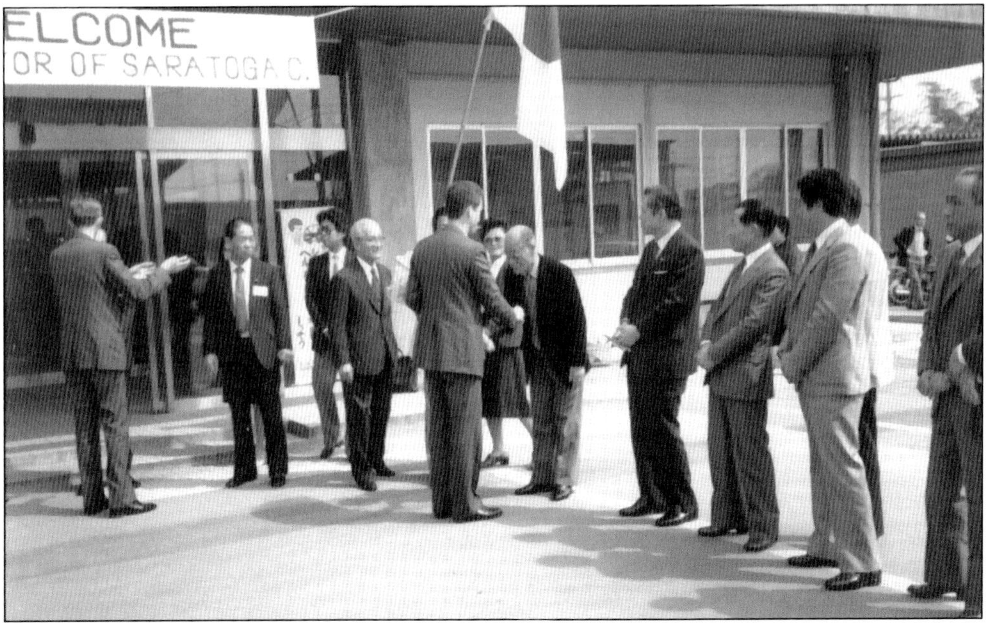

Saratogans visited Muko, Japan, in 1983 to negotiate a sister city relationship between the two cities. Sister city organizations are legal or social agreements between cities or counties to promote cultural understanding, friendship, and trade. David Moyles, mayor of Saratoga (center, back to camera), is shaking hands with Muko's mayor, Norio Tamiaki. To the left of Mayor Moyles is Muko sister city president Dr. Keiichiro Shimada introducing the mayors. (Courtesy of David Moyles.)

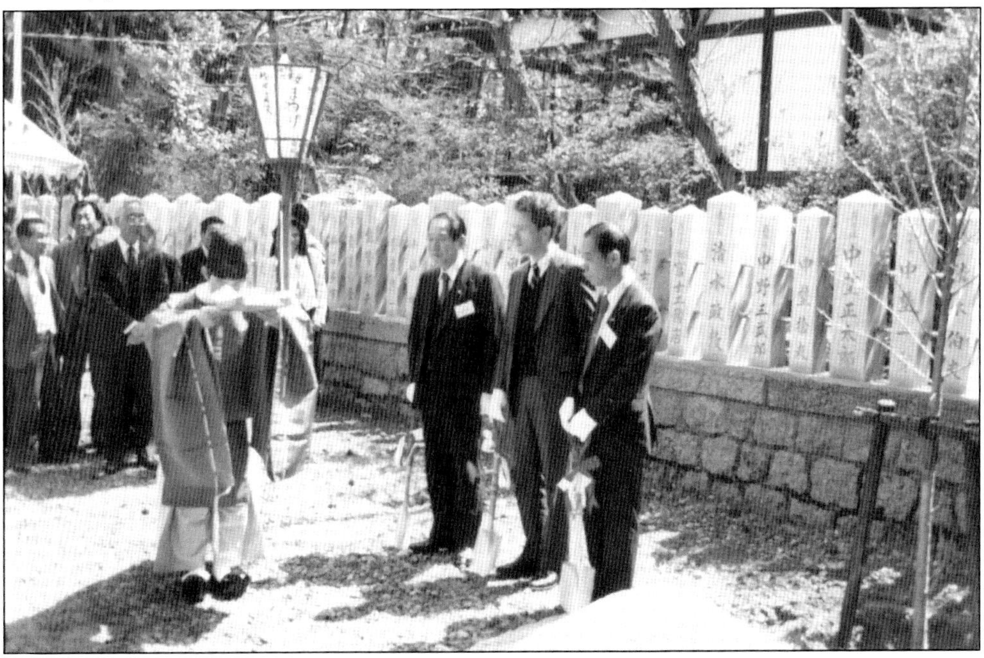

At the 1984 sister city agreement signing, a Muko Shinto priest performed a welcome ceremony. Mayor David Moyles is seen here flanked by two representatives of Muko. They are holding shovels preparing to plant a tree at the Shinto shrine in honor of the signing. The Saratoga-Muko sister city arrangement was to support the development of Hakone Gardens. (Courtesy of David Moyles.)

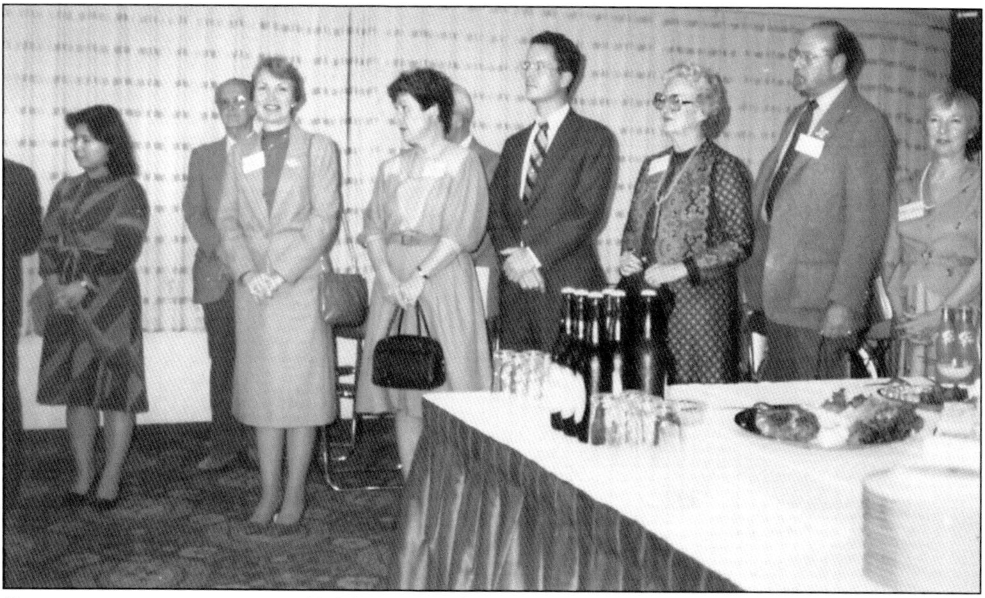

Saratoga representatives visited Muko to sign the sister city agreement in 1984. After the ceremony, there was a celebration. From left to right are unidentified; Bud Card; Saratoga mayor Virginia Fannelli; Saratoga City Council member Marti Clevenger; Saratoga Sister City member and translator John Tauchi (behind Clevenger); Saratoga City Council member David Moyles; Saratoga Sister City member Marion Card; Don Fannelli, husband of the mayor; and Marilyn White, Saratoga Sister City member. (Courtesy of David Moyles.)

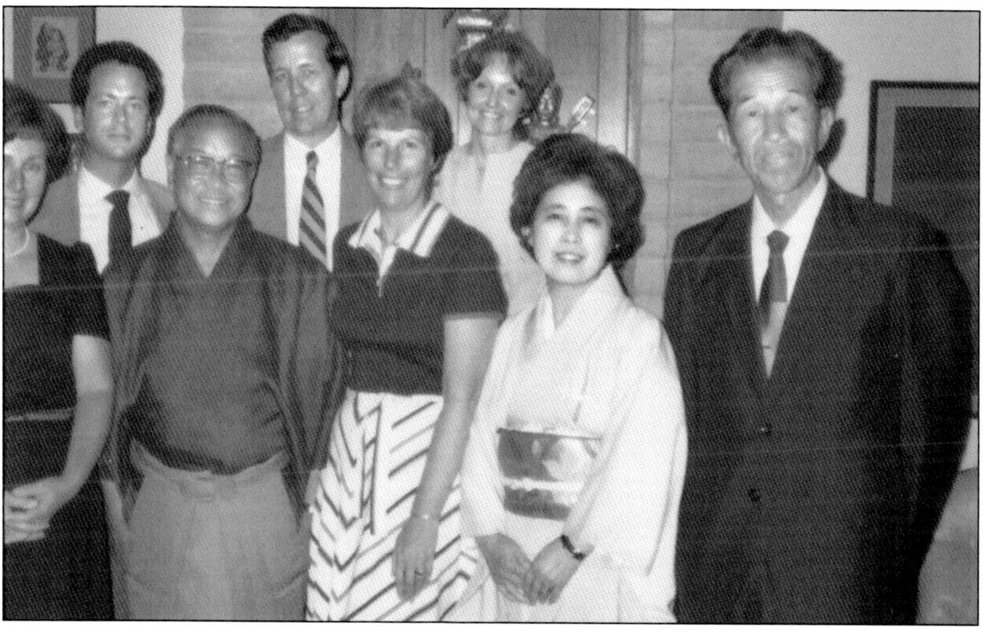

After signing the official sister city agreement, Muko representatives visited Saratoga to plan a major gift, a new Hakone bamboo garden. At the celebration party are, from left to right: Marty Clevenger and David Moyles, Saratoga City Council; Kiyoshi Yasui, Muko Sister City; Jack Mallory and Linda Callen, Saratoga City Council; Cheryl Jensen, future Saratoga City Council; and Noriko Yasui and Takashi Tamiaki, Muko Sister City members. (Courtesy of Jack Mallory.)

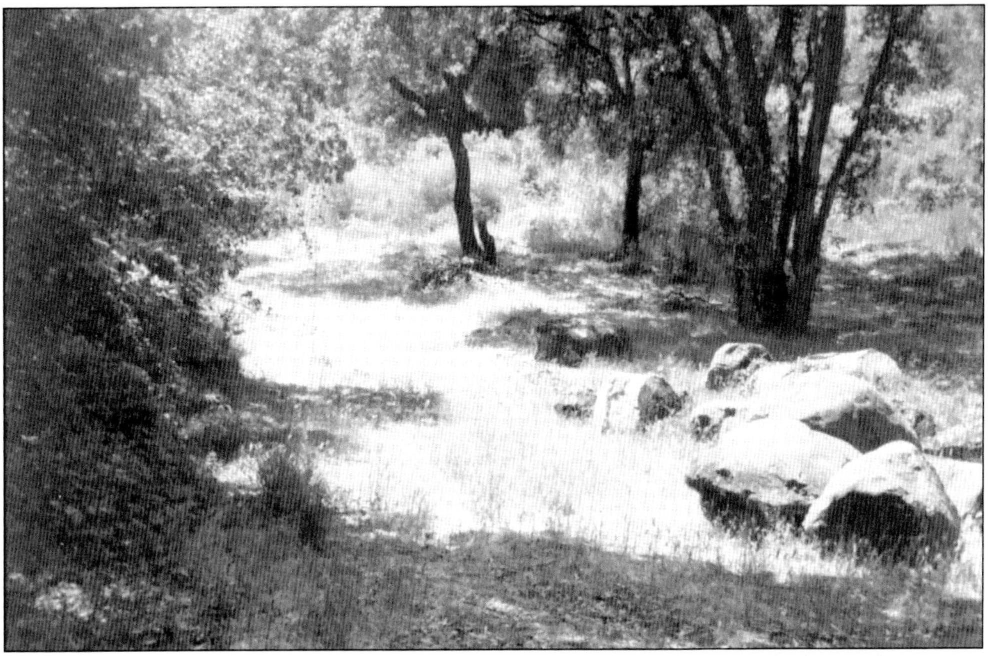

Prior to the bamboo garden, the hillside was in a natural state. The recently donated two acres were for both the bamboo garden and parking lot. Mayor Moyles and Bill Glennon secured the donation. The land developer also put in a fire hydrant next to the new emergency gate. The city then received a Caltrans grant to pave the parking lot. (Courtesy of Elaine Salter.)

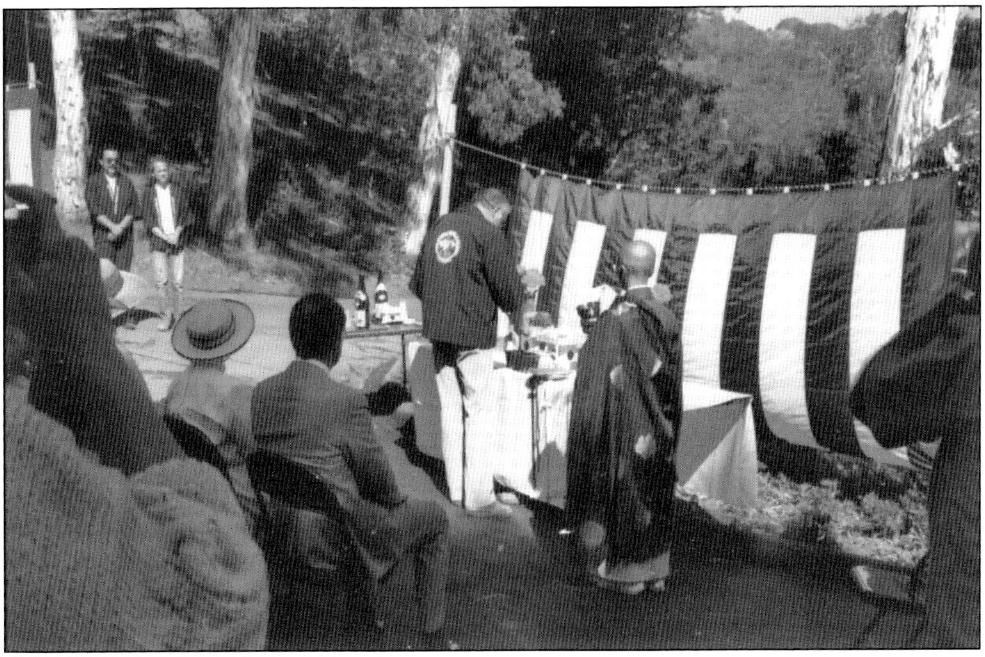

At the August 1984 dedication to begin the construction of the Kizuna-en (Friendship Bamboo Garden), volunteer leader Bruce Parker is pictured with Rev. Shozen Hosokawa, a Shinto priest at the San Francisco Soto Zen Church. Afterward, volunteers graded and designed the new garden in preparation for planting the donated bamboo. (Courtesy of David Moyles.)

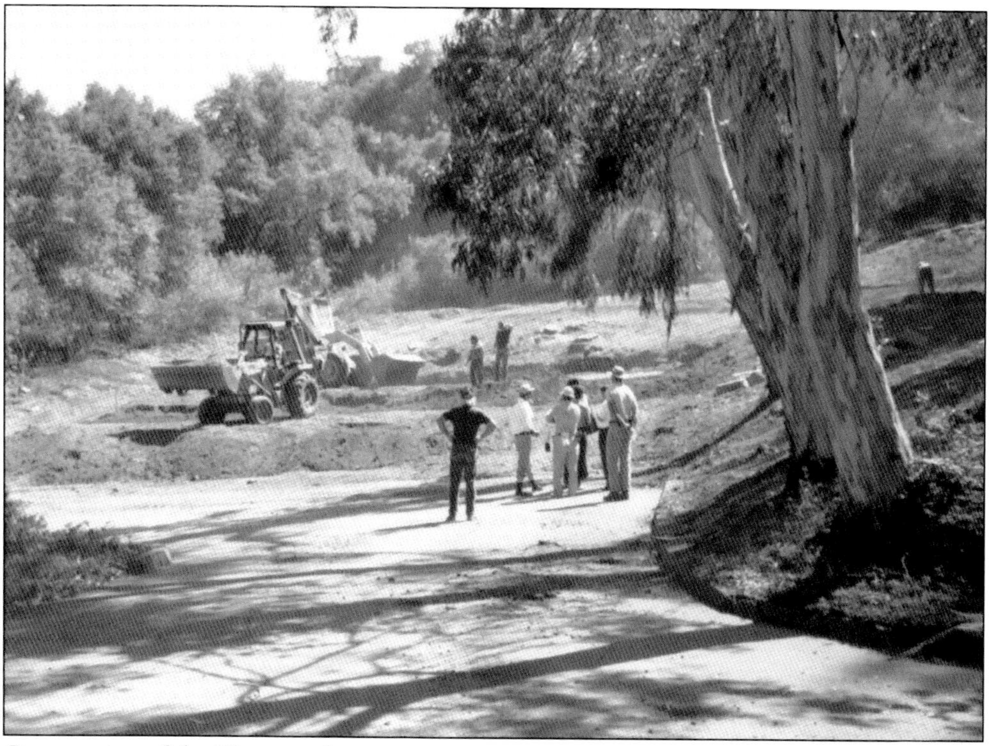

Construction of the Kizuna-en began with clearing and grading land and bringing in stones for the walls and steps. Kiyoshi Yasui, who designed the new garden, was senior director of his family architectural firm in Muko. He and his nephew Hiroshi Yasui are among those pictured here. The firm has provided architects to the imperial family for 15 generations. (Courtesy of Hakone Foundation.)

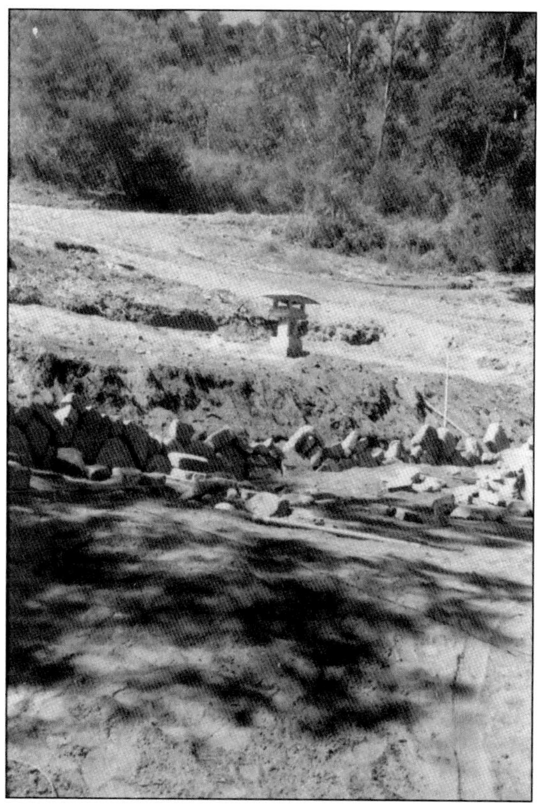

As construction of the Friendship Bamboo Garden began in August 1984, volunteers first placed the individual stones and stone lanterns. Muko Sister City donated the lantern near the new steps to "light the way" between the two cities and sister city groups. The land for the garden had been recently donated by a developer, who negotiated a housing development next to Hakone. (Courtesy of David Moyles.)

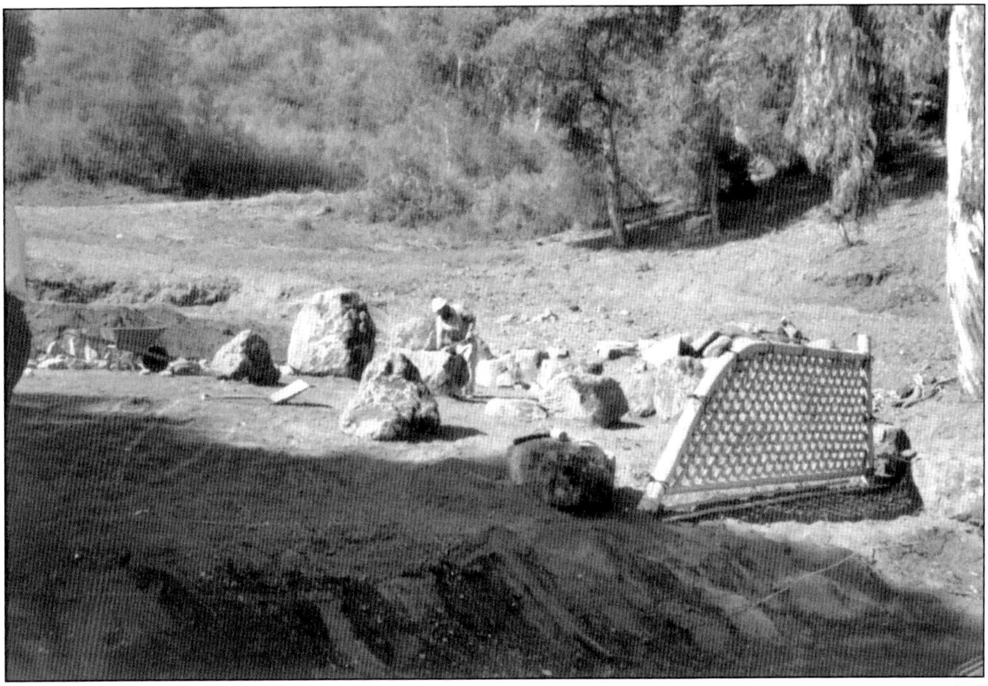

The arrangement of large irregular stones is one of the most important elements in Japanese garden design. Both the lanterns and the stones have to be placed before the planting of the moss and bamboo. The edge of the garden is then defined by bamboo fencing. (Courtesy of David Moyles.)

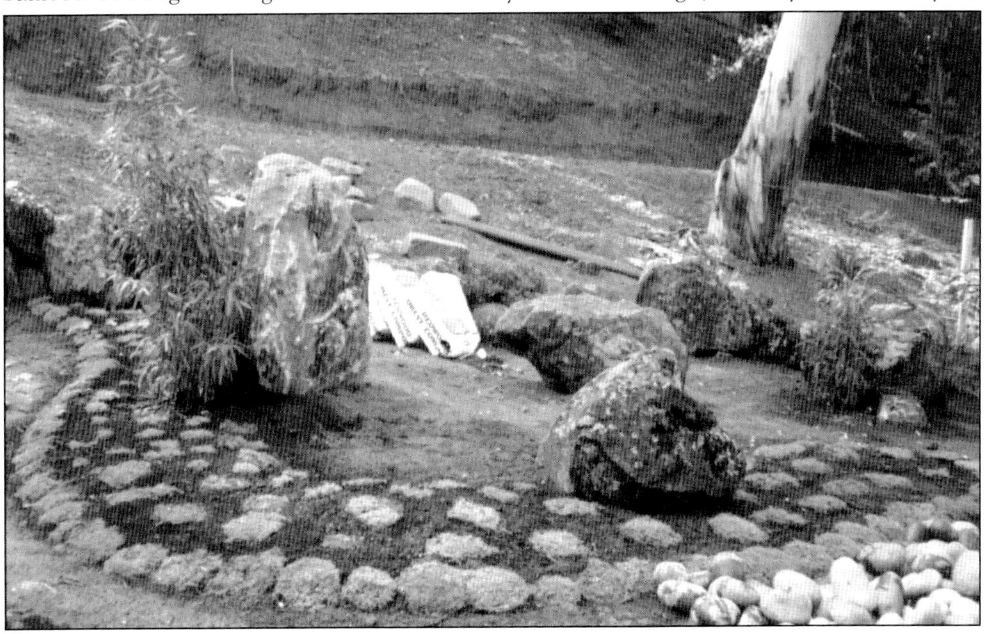

Within days, there was progress in planting moss and mondo grass among the stones. Some of the special bamboo had also been planted. The donated bamboo had arrived from Japan several years prior—the United States required two years of quarantine before planting. The plants came from the Japan Society of Bamboo Development and Protection, guided by bamboo authority Dr. Koichiro Uega, working with the Japanese government. (Courtesy of Hakone Foundation.)

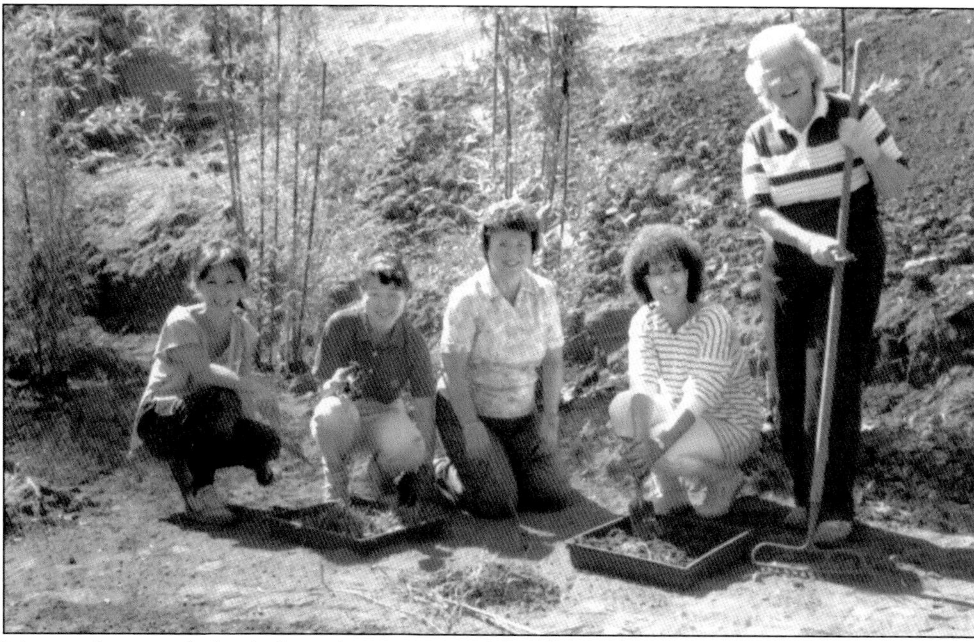

Many volunteers helped plant the grasses and bamboo. From left to right, volunteers Cathy Yoshimoto, Izumi Shibata, Jan Morgan, Elaine Salter, and Marion Card rest after planting flats of dwarf mondo grass. Izumi Shibata was one of the first students from Japan in the sister city student exchange program. She loved the experience and returned to the Bay Area for college. (Courtesy of Hakone Foundation.)

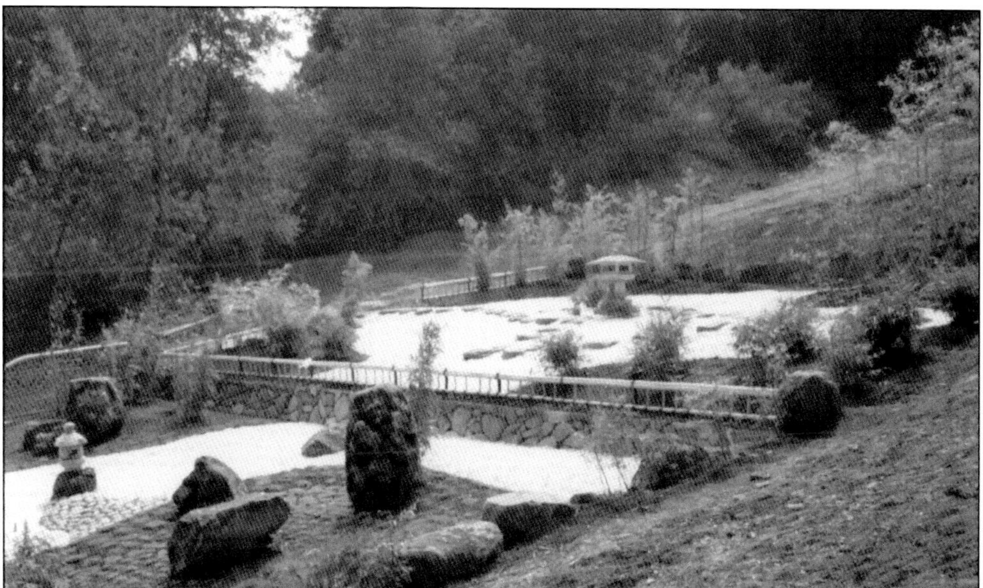

By the end of August, the major plantings were in and the white gravel spread. The white gravel represents the ocean in Japanese landscape philosophy. The larger bamboo garden that would later surround this friendship garden was still to be planted. As the watering system was yet to be established, hand watering was laboriously done through the dry California summer. (Courtesy of Hakone Foundation.)

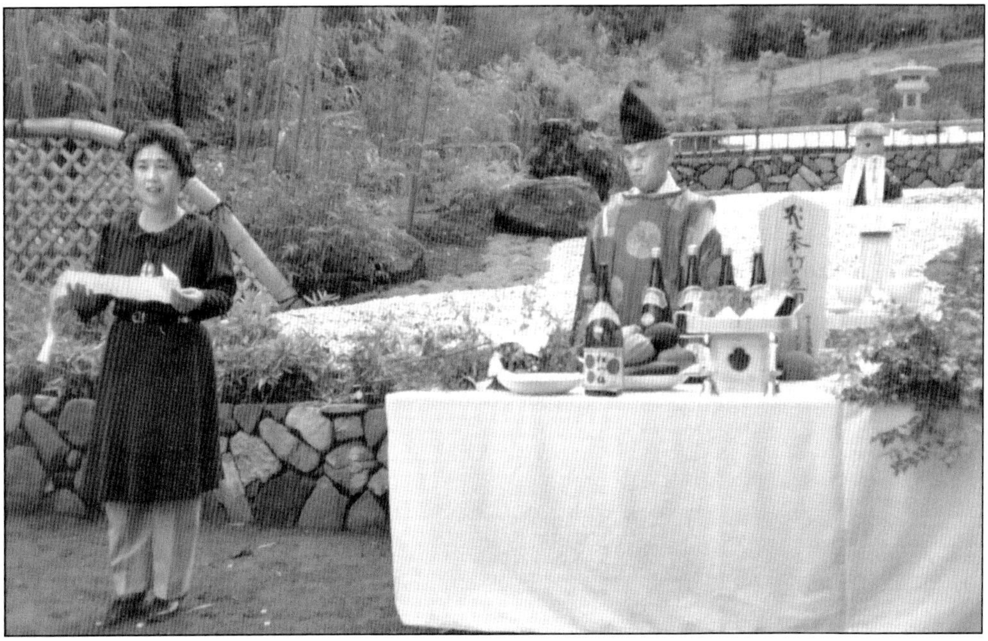

By November, the remainder of the bamboo garden was planted. The sister cities' representatives held a ribbon-cutting and a Shinto purification ceremony. Candles were lit in both lanterns, and representatives from US and Japanese consulates poured ceremonial sake over both lanterns. Noriko Yasui, wife of Kiyoshi Yasui, delivered a message along with speeches by other dignitaries. (Courtesy of Hakone Foundation.)

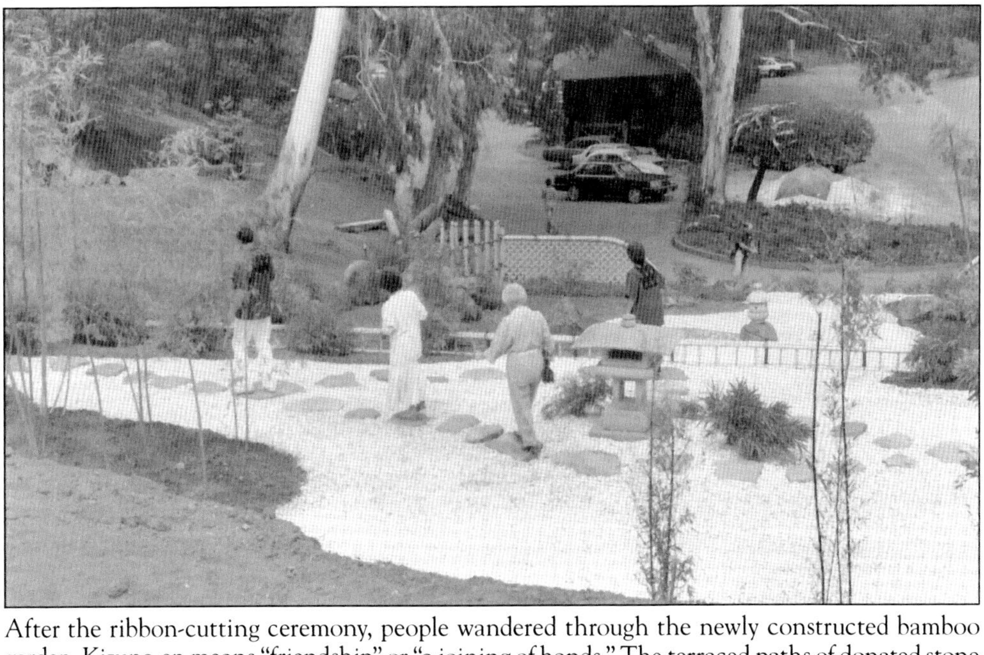

After the ribbon-cutting ceremony, people wandered through the newly constructed bamboo garden. Kizuna-en means "friendship" or "a joining of hands." The terraced paths of donated stone steps represent the number of city council members in each of the sister cities: 5 for Saratoga and 25 for Muko. The people in white outfits are Elaine Salter (left) and Gladys Armstrong, sister city members, volunteers, and docents. (Courtesy of Elaine Salter.)

In 1986, Bud and Marion Card, sister city members and major supporters of Hakone, visited with Jacqueline Stine (center), granddaughter of Hakone's founder. They sit near Hakone's Lower House. (Courtesy of Elaine Salter.)

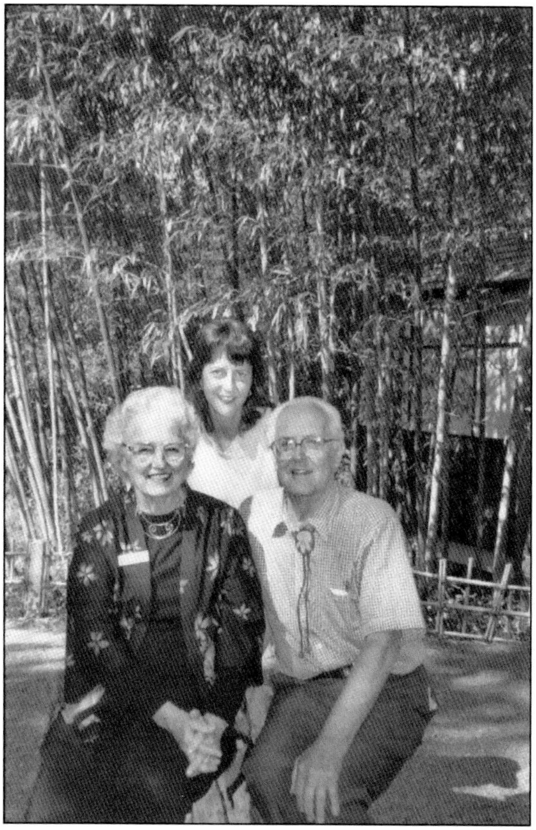

In 1986, Helen and Ralph M. Metcalf, sister city members, volunteer in the Hakone gift shop. The gift shop is in a restored two-car garage built during the Tilden ownership era. Helen was also on the first foundation board. Ralph was a retired Navy rear admiral and a highly decorated World War II submarine commander. The Metcalfs shared a deep interest in Japanese art and culture and love of Hakone. (Donated by Marshall Metcalf Seymour, courtesy of Elaine Salter.)

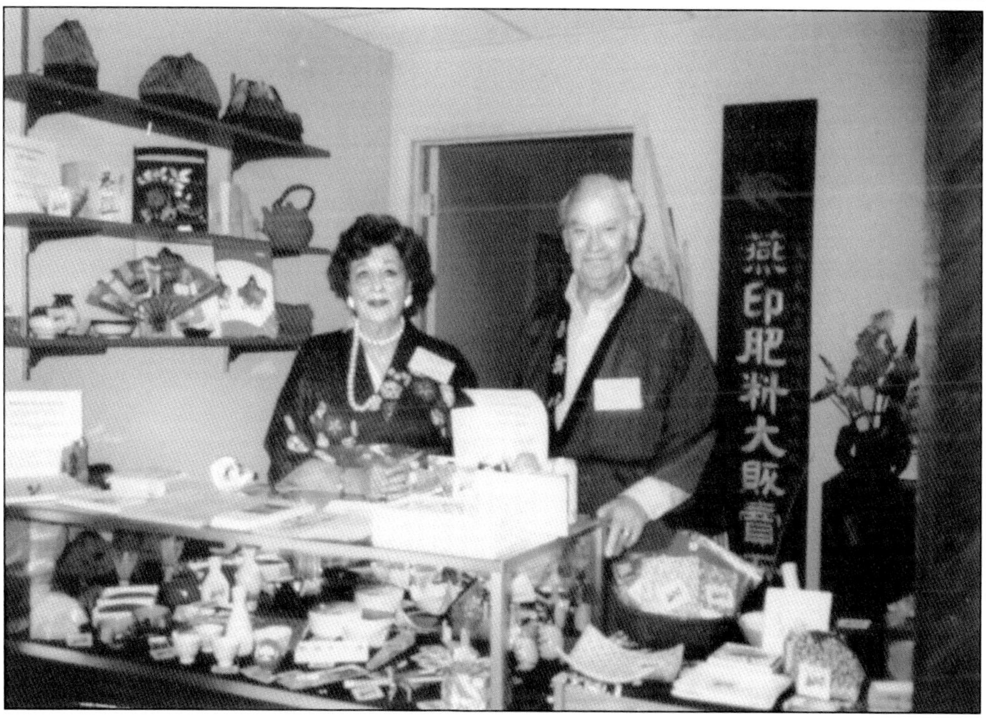

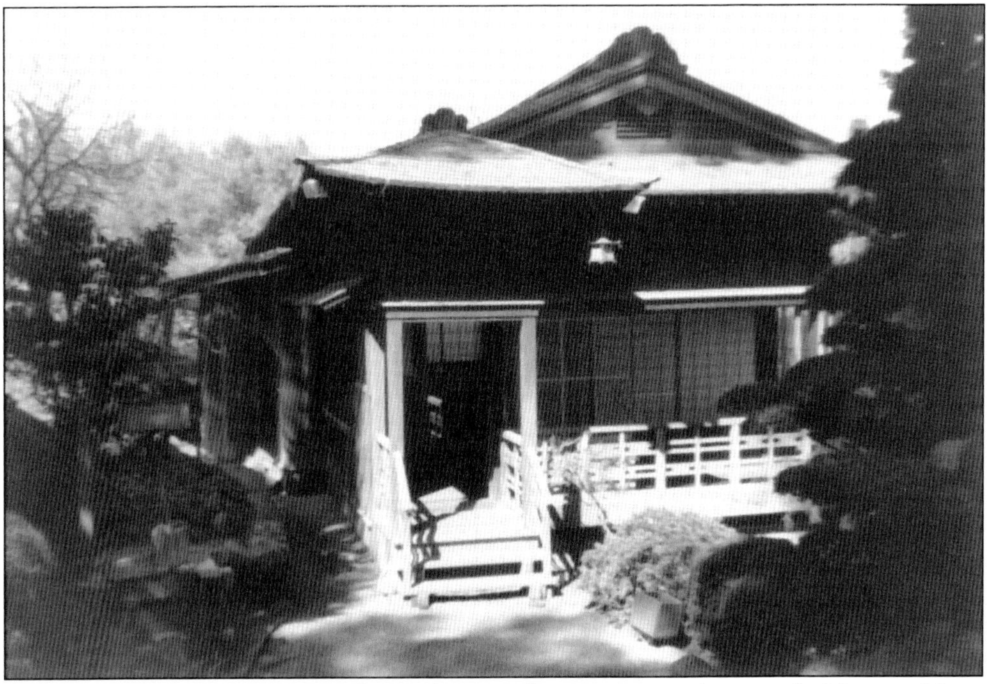

In 1986, Muko Sister City gave a gift to Hakone of a lantern that was hung on the Upper or Moon Viewing House eaves. During a visit, the mayors of Muko and Saratoga lit the lantern as a symbol of friendship between the cities. It remains in place to the present day. (Courtesy of Peter Marra.)

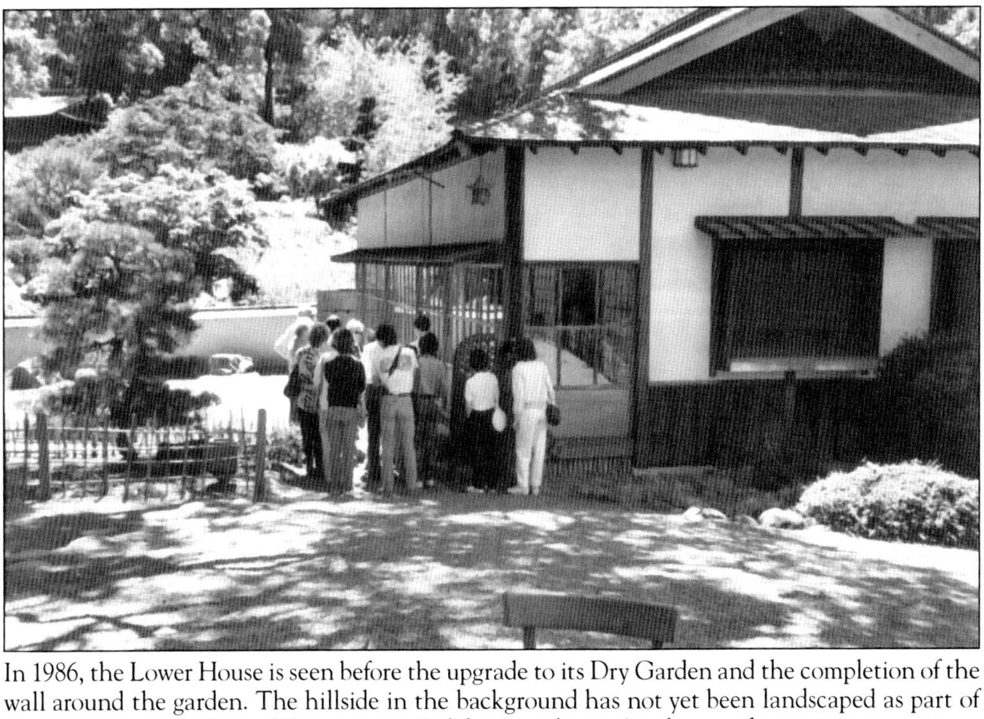

In 1986, the Lower House is seen before the upgrade to its Dry Garden and the completion of the wall around the garden. The hillside in the background has not yet been landscaped as part of the Japanese garden but still hosts native Californian plants. A volunteer docent is giving visitors a tour of the garden. (Courtesy of Peter Marra.)

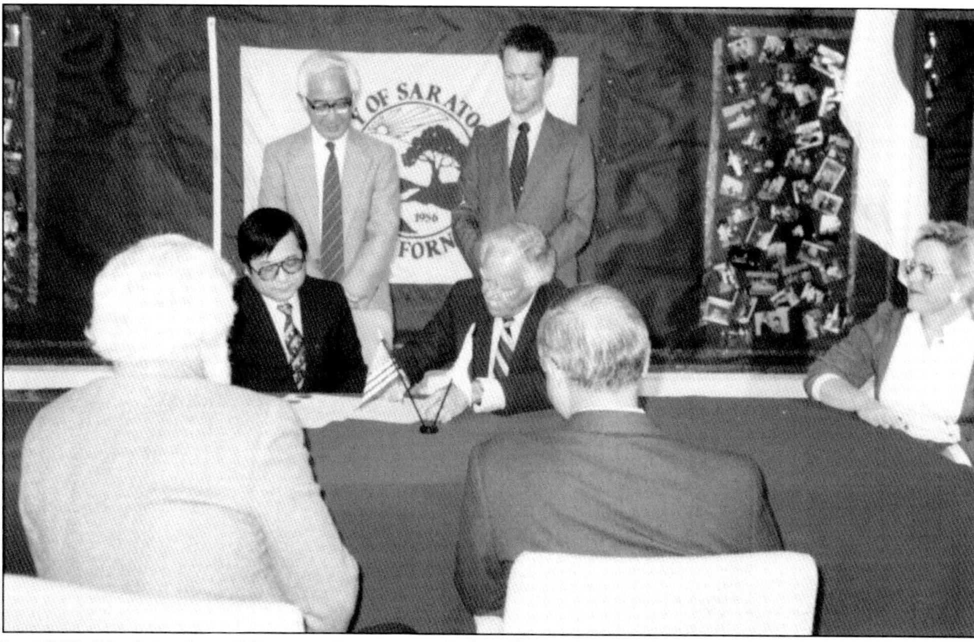

In 1987, Dr. Morihito Nagai, a Japanese philanthropist and friend of Kiyoshi Yasui, pledged $250,000 for a new cultural center at Hakone. At the signing ceremony in Saratoga City Hall are (from left to right) Don Miller, Saratoga Sister City president; Dr. Morihito Nagai; John Tauchi, Saratoga Sister City; David Moyles, Saratoga mayor; William Glennon, former mayor; Kiyoshi Yasui (back to camera); and Karen Anderson, city council. (Courtesy of Hakone Collection.)

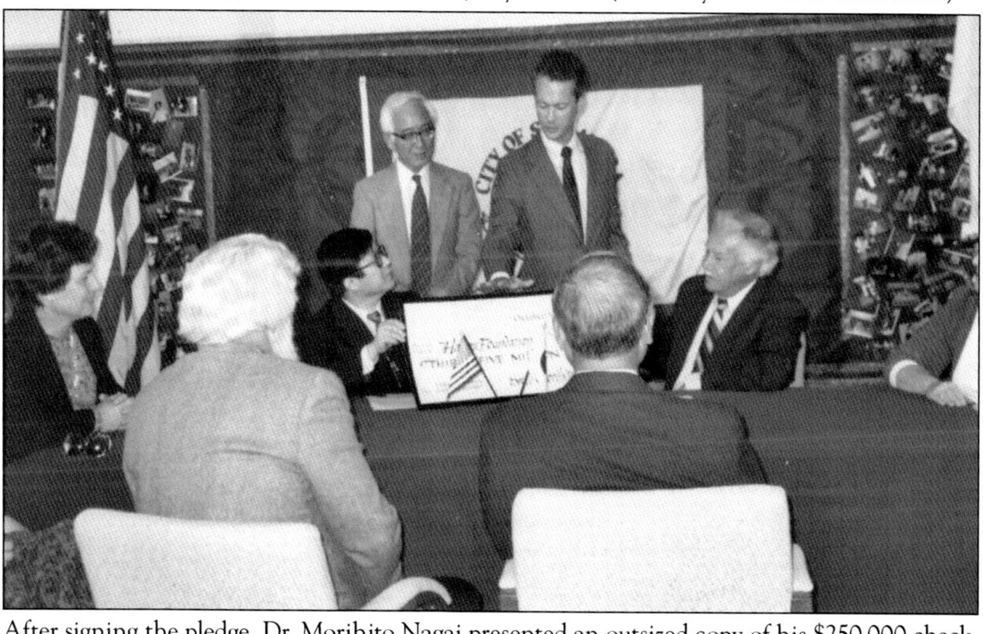

After signing the pledge, Dr. Morihito Nagai presented an outsized copy of his $250,000 check. It was a challenge grant to Hakone Foundation, the city, and the public to raise the remaining costs for the building. From left to right are Marty Clevenger, city council; Don Miller; Dr. Nagai; John Tauchi; Mayor Moyles; Kiyoshi Yasui; and former mayor Glennon. (Courtesy of Hakone Foundation.)

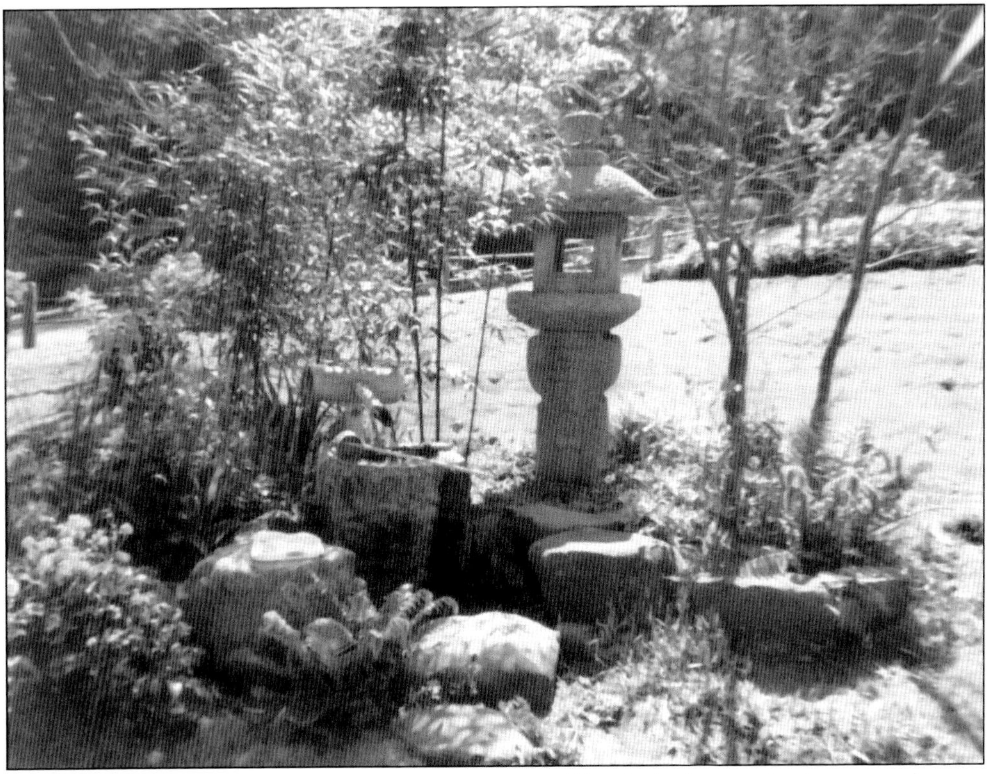

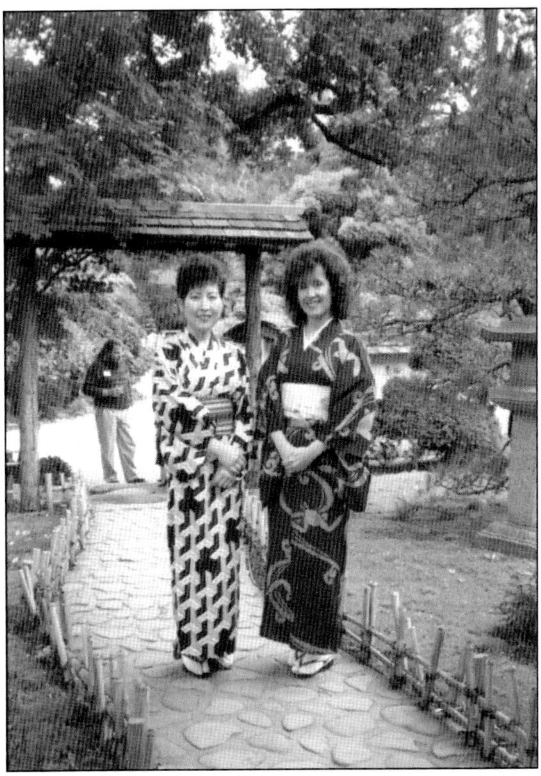

The Oribe lantern in the tea garden was a gift from Kyoto Rotarian Taneo Inoue from Muko. It was installed in April 1987. The sister city representatives indicated that it was an unusual antique lantern with a Christian cross carved in it and was originally used by a group of Japanese Christians. It remains standing in Hakone's tea garden. (Courtesy of Peter Marra.)

One of the favorite things to do at Hakone, both past and present, is to participate in a Japanese tea service. Hakone volunteers provide tea-serving events and teach the art of the tea ceremony. In 1988, Elaine Salter (right) and Mako take a moment out from assisting Minako Tsuji, who served the tea. (Courtesy of Peter Marra.)

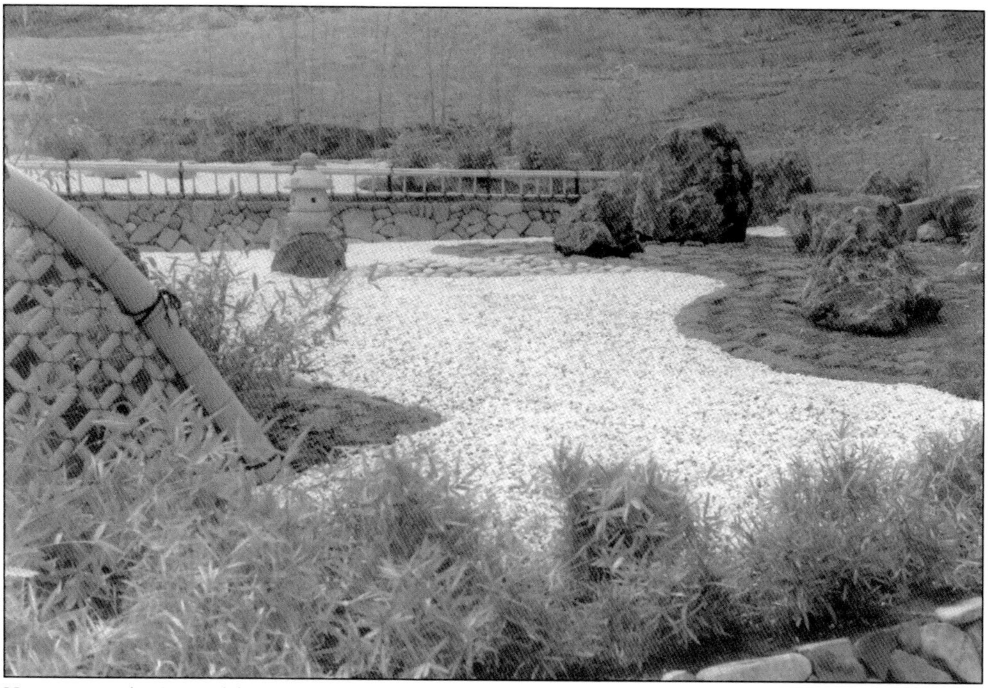

Kizuna-en, the Friendship Bamboo Garden, is shown at two years old in 1987. The bamboo is quickly growing, and the ground cover of bamboo grass is filling in between the stone paths. Visitors are enjoying the variety of bamboo that has been planted. (Courtesy of Elaine Salter.)

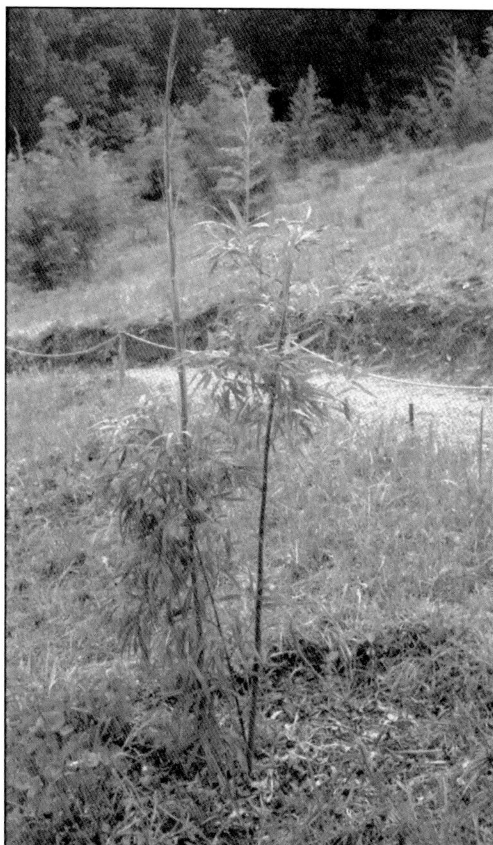

Hakone gratefully accepted donations of unusual bamboo from Japanese donors and from American enthusiasts to establish a remarkable bamboo garden. One such plant was the tortoise-shell bamboo, newly planted in 1989. The young shoots are straight, but as it matures, its trunk twists to resemble a turtle shell. (Courtesy of Peter Marra.)

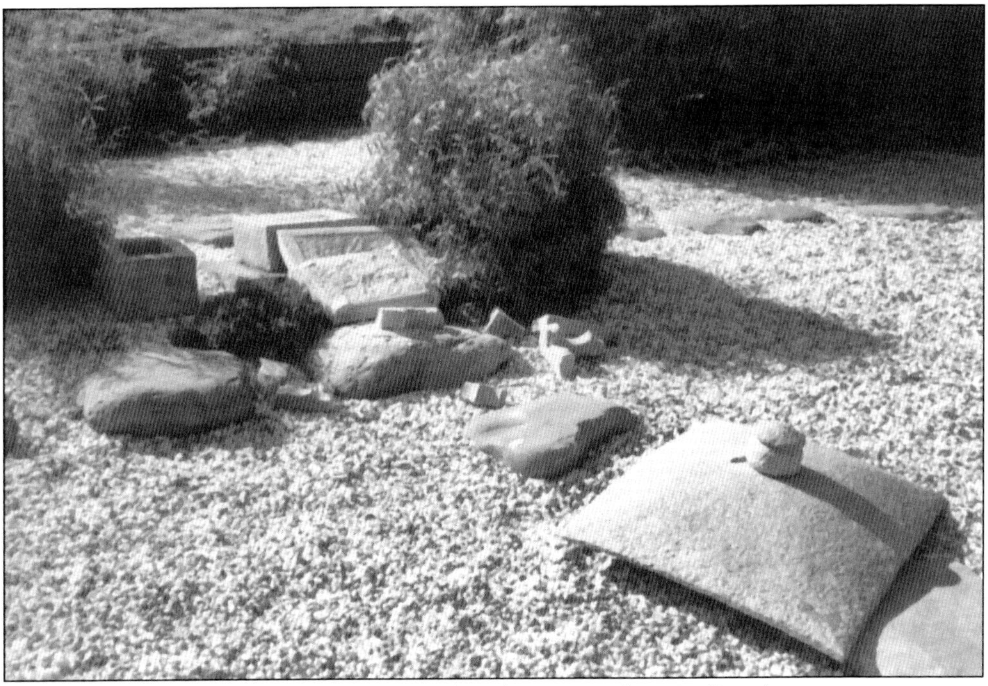

In 1989, the devastating Loma Prieta earthquake occurred in the Bay Area, registering at a magnitude of 6.9. It damaged the San Francisco Bay Bridge, businesses, and homes in many parts of the region. However, at Hakone, there was only minor damage to the old Japanese structures. One of the new Friendship Bamboo Garden lanterns was tipped over, but as it was not damaged, it could be set upright again. (Courtesy of Elaine Salter.)

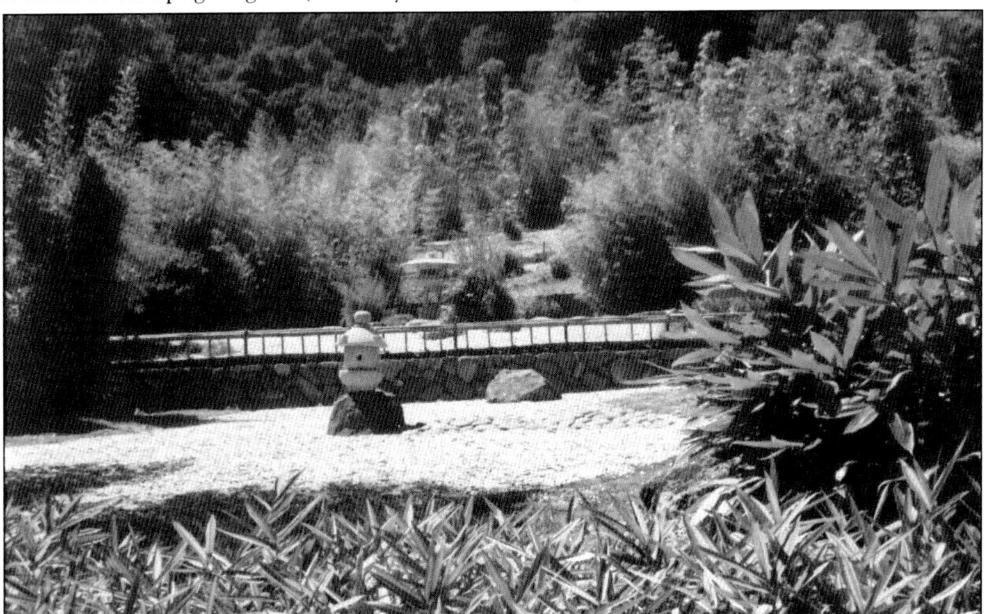

In 1989, Kizuna-en is now four years old. Note the lush, rapid growth of the bamboo. Plants grow fast in the temperate climate of Saratoga. The lantern is back in its place after the earthquake. (Courtesy of Peter Marra.)

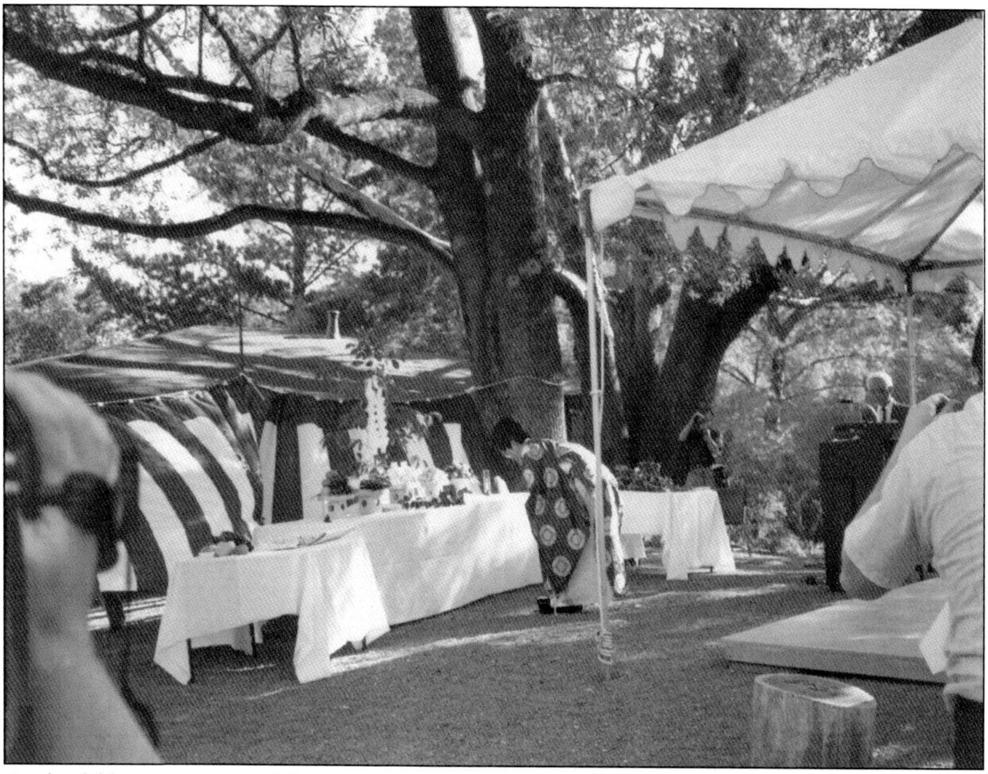

At the fifth anniversary of the sister cities organization, November 4, 1989, Muko representatives visited Hakone. Yoshitsuga Mutobe, a Shinto priest from the Muko City Shrine, is blessing Hakone and its new bamboo garden. (Courtesy of Peter Marra.)

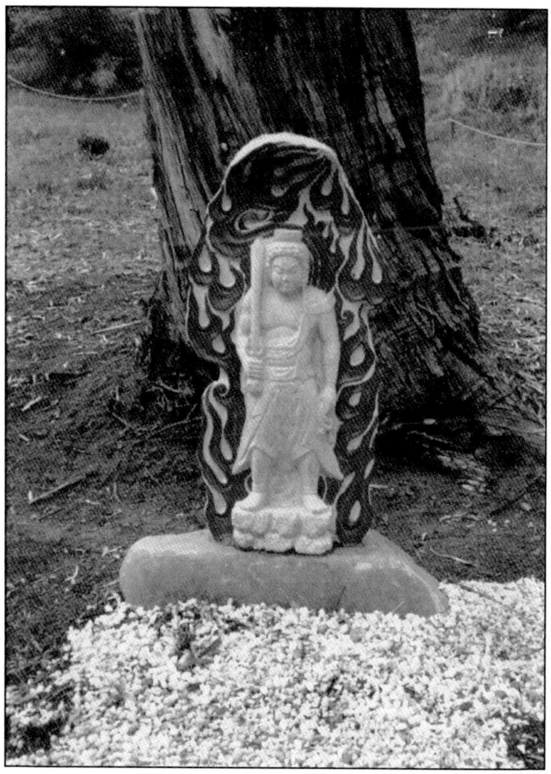

At the fifth-anniversary gathering, Muko Sister City presented a granite statue for the bamboo garden representing the Shinto fire god Fudo. On the back of the statue is an invocation in Japanese. It states that Fudo protects both Hakone Gardens and Saratogans from natural disasters. (Courtesy of Peter Marra.)

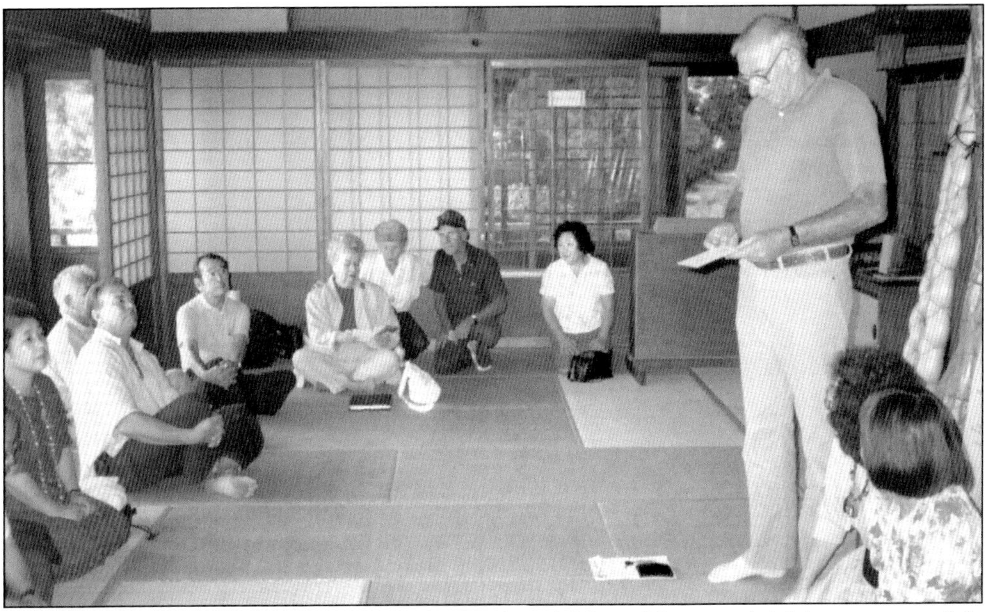

Saratoga Bamboo Society volunteers meet in Hakone's Upper House with Muko visitors in July 1989. The society was formed by Kiyoshi Yasui, Tanso Ishihara (Hakone's head gardener), Jack Tomlinson (assistant gardener), Bruce Parkinson, Stewart Lenox, Syd Dunton, and Jim Marshall to promote a bamboo garden section within Hakone. From left to right are Syd Dunton, Bob Hall, unidentified, Gladys Armstrong, Dodi Walker, Jim Marshall, Teru Ishihara, and Bruce Parkinson. (Courtesy of Peter Marra.)

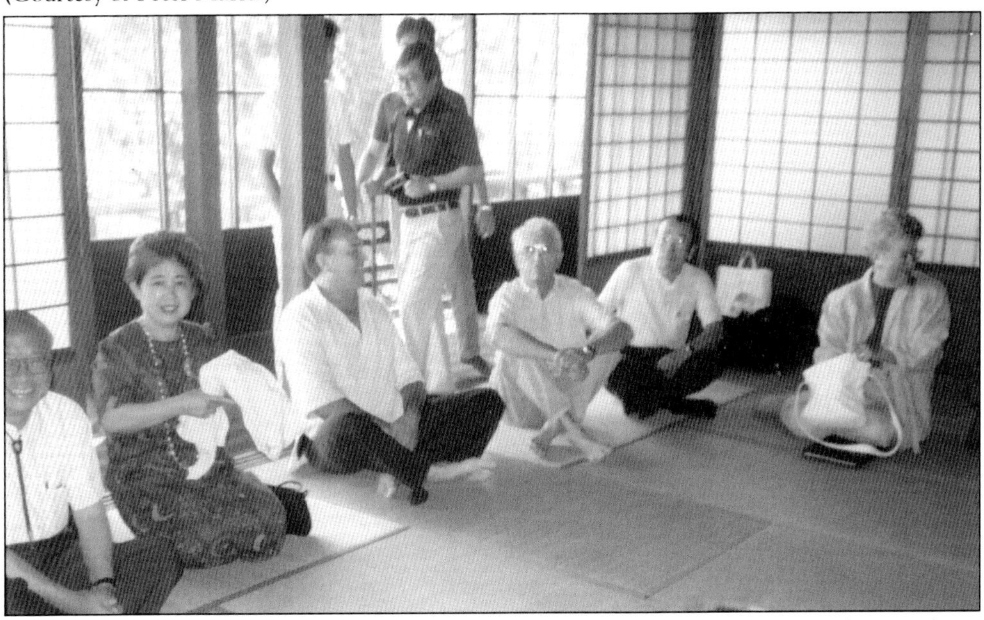

Participants at this congenial meeting were dedicated to the society's mission "to share, inform, and encourage others of the enjoyment, uses, beauty, and care of the varieties of bamboo, plus an appreciation of the Japanese culture in the development of a strolling bamboo garden." From left to right are Kiyoshi Yasui, Noriko Yasui, Bob Hall, Dr. Morihito Nagai (standing), Andy Hardin, unidentified, and Gladys Armstrong. (Courtesy of Peter Marra.)

Head gardener Jack Tomlinson (left) participates in the same Saratoga Bamboo Society meeting in Hakone's Upper House. After the untimely death of head gardener Tanso Ishihara in 1980, Tomlinson became the head gardener, remaining dedicated to Hakone for 30 years. Standing behind Tomlinson is Dr. Morihito Nagai, a Japanese philanthropist who donated a pledge grant for a new cultural building for Hakone. (Courtesy of Peter Marra.)

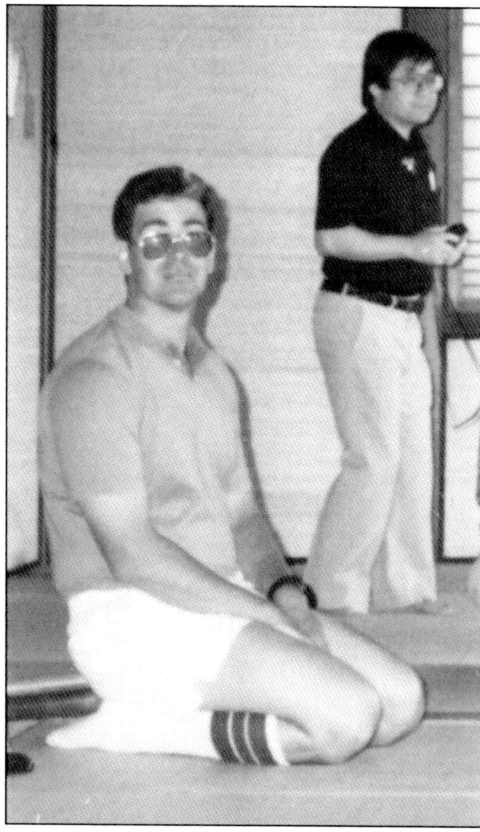

In 1989, Kioshi Yasui, from Muko Sister City, visited Hakone and led an information session on the differences between the growth habits of bamboo in California and Japan. In the background wearing a white cap is Don Miller, and on the right with his back to the camera is Syd Dunton, both longtime volunteers. (Courtesy of Peter Marra.)

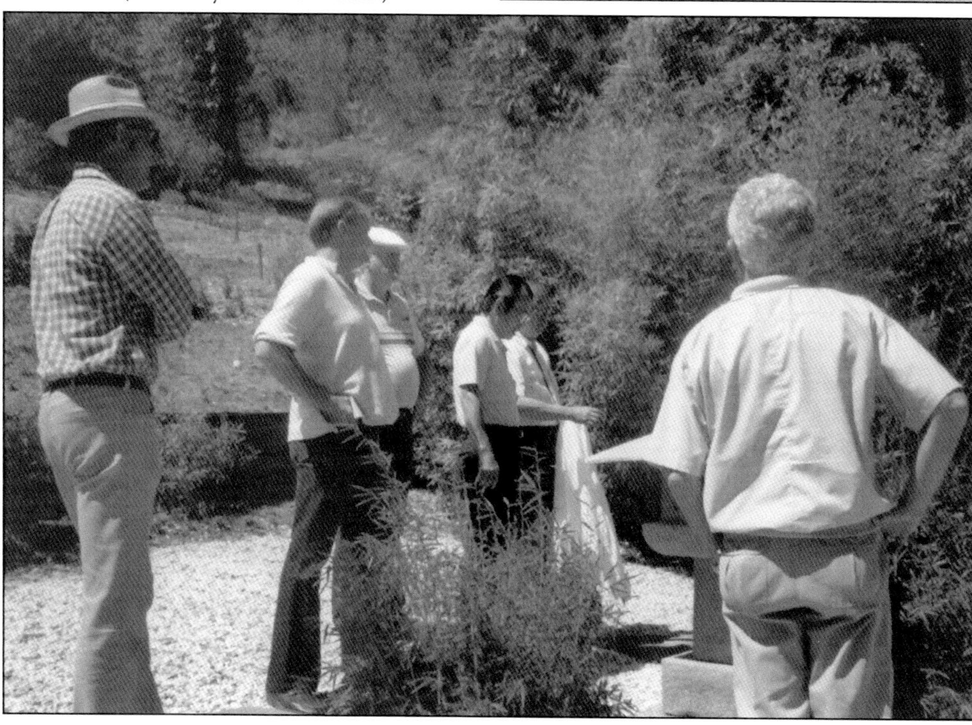

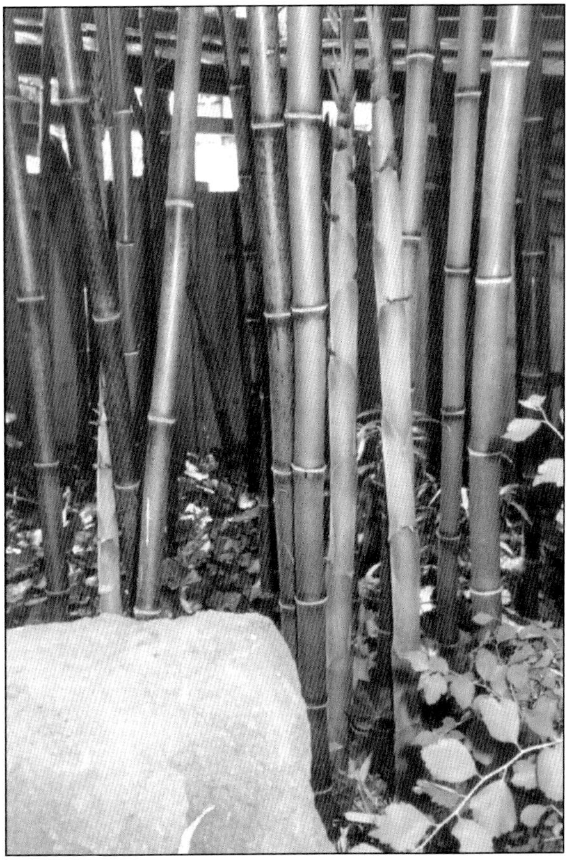

By 1989, the unusual variety of black bamboo had grown up in the bamboo garden of Hakone. Now it is a thick grove of beautiful, rare bamboo. (Courtesy of Peter Marra.)

In 1990, this tea-serving cart was built and donated by Syd Dunton from the Saratoga Bamboo Society; it is still in use today, albeit as a wine bar. On the right is Bruce Parkinson, also a Saratoga Bamboo Society member. The cart has wheels for easy movement. In the background is the Lower House Dry Garden before being enclosed by a Japanese-style stucco wall. (Courtesy of Peter Marra.)

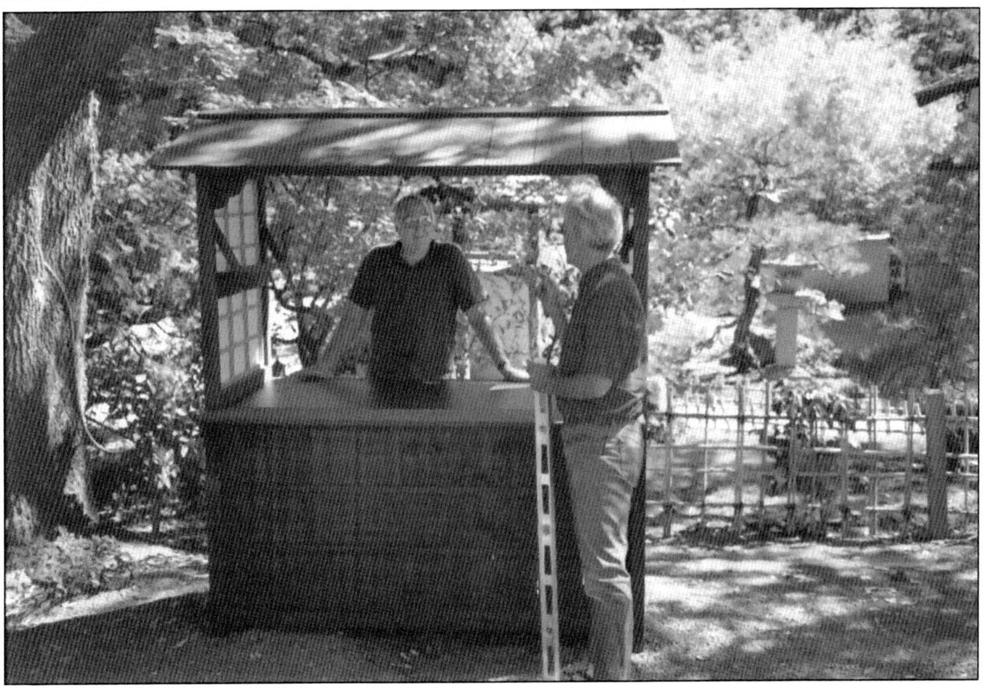

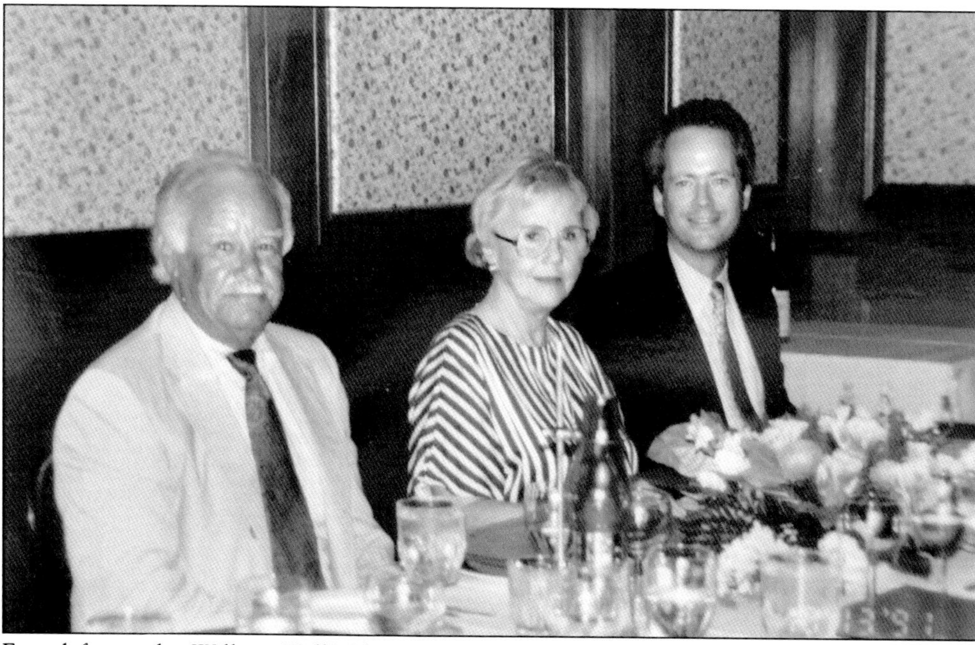

From left to right, William "Bill" Glennon, his wife, Susie Glennon, and David Moyles attend a 1991 sister city event. Continuing to support Hakone Gardens, the Glennons were sensitive to local racism because of their own Latino background. They started a foundation to help immigrant children. Born to immigrant parents, Bill understood the stress that these children can face. David Moyles, an attorney, assisted the Glennons with their foundation. (Courtesy of Glennon family.)

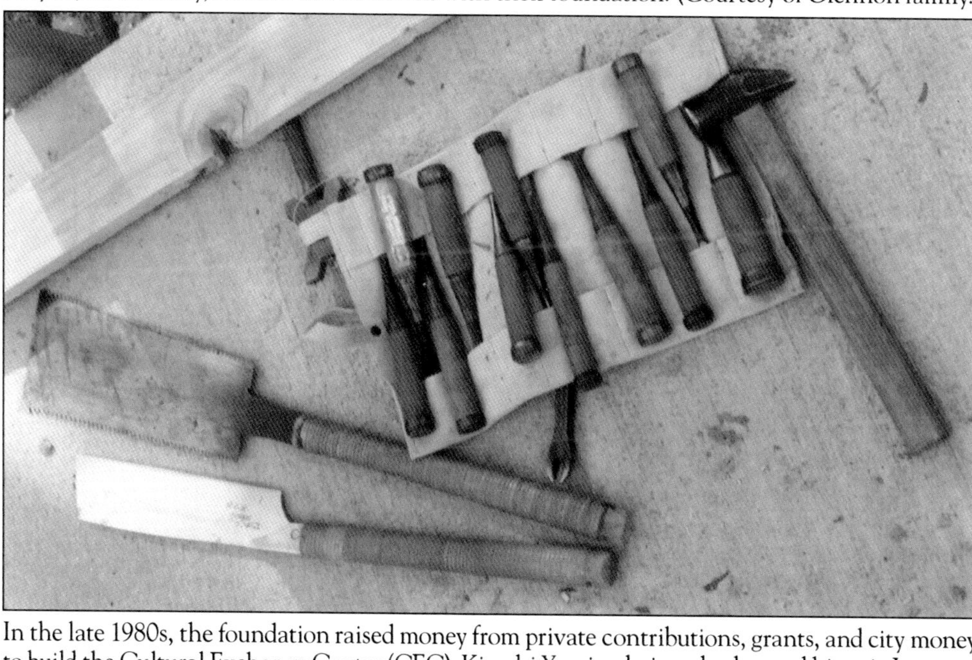

In the late 1980s, the foundation raised money from private contributions, grants, and city money to build the Cultural Exchange Center (CEC). Kiyoshi Yasui redesigned a donated historic Japanese building. It was deconstructed and the pieces were sent to Saratoga, where it was reassembled by a team of Japanese builders. They used traditional Japanese tools and the mortise-and-tenon method of construction without nails. (Courtesy of Elaine Salter.)

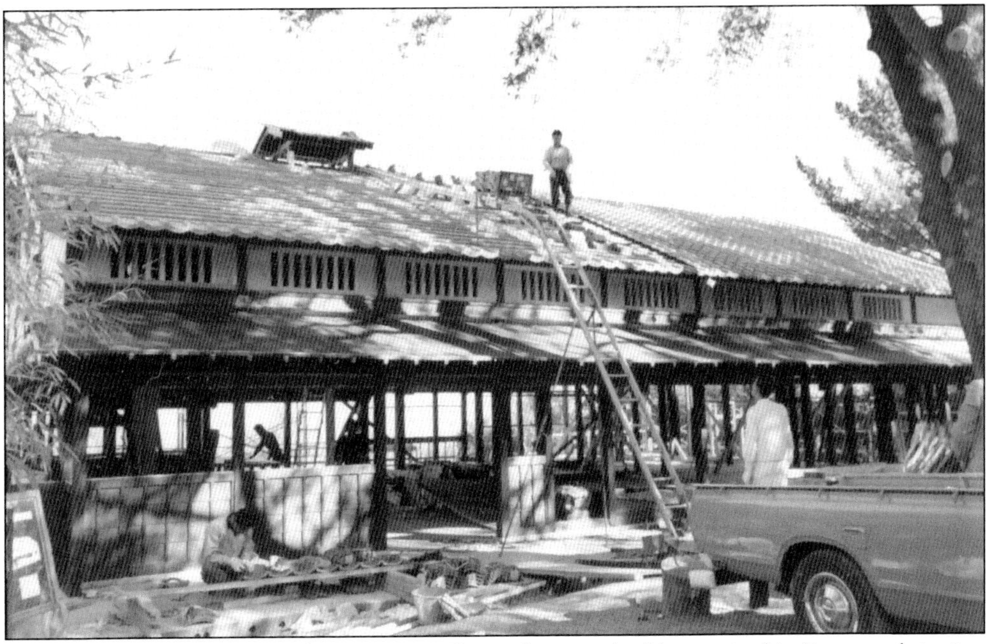

The construction of the CEC began in 1991. Seven Japanese builders arrived in Saratoga, bringing the parts of the Japanese building. Mayor David Moyles graciously loaned the Japanese builders his condo in the village. The builders could then walk to Hakone each day during the months of construction. (Courtesy of Elaine Salter.)

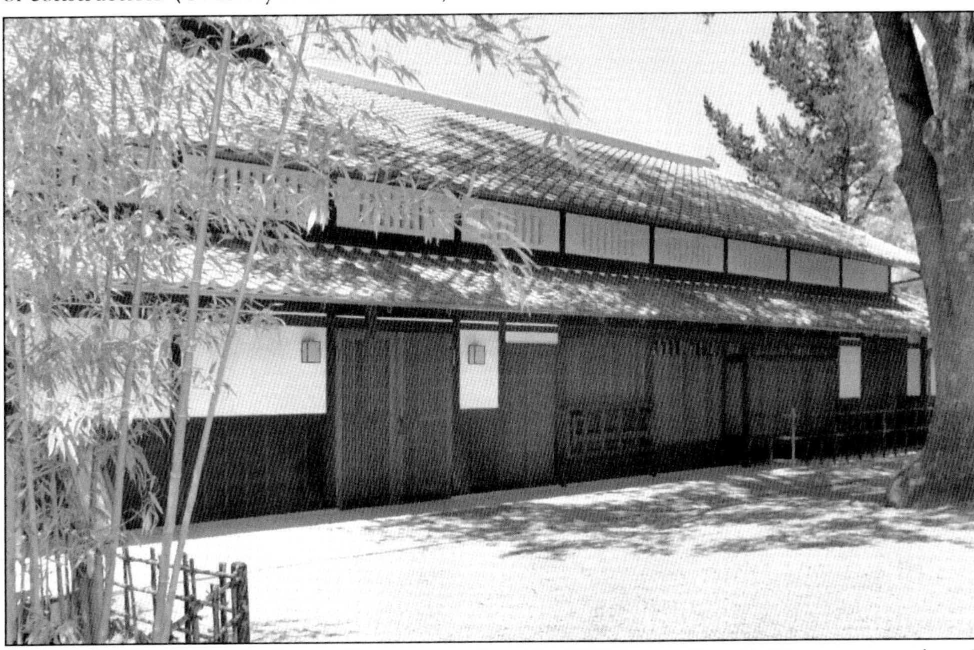

The beautiful Cultural Exchange Center, completed in 1992, is a replica of a Kyoto tea merchant's home. The interior was configured so that art exhibits and cultural programs can be held. Both the interior and exterior were redesigned to meet California safety and ADA standards. The CEC is a major attraction and is available for rentals, private events, and meetings. (Courtesy of Hakone Foundation.)

US congressman Norman Mineta delivered the keynote speech at the CEC dedication. Born in San Jose, he and his parents were incarcerated at Heart Mountain, Wyoming, during World War II. Mineta was San Jose's 59th mayor, US secretary of commerce, and secretary of transportation during September 11, 2001. Norman Y. Mineta International Airport in San Jose is named after him. In 2006, he was awarded the Presidential Medal of Freedom. (Courtesy of Hakone Foundation.)

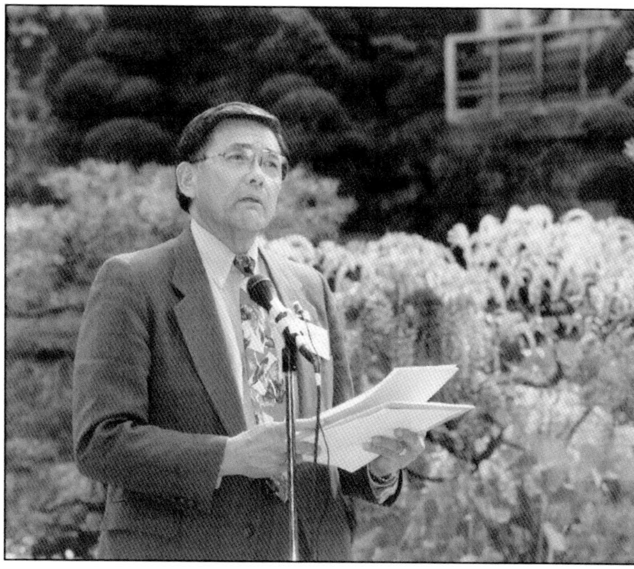

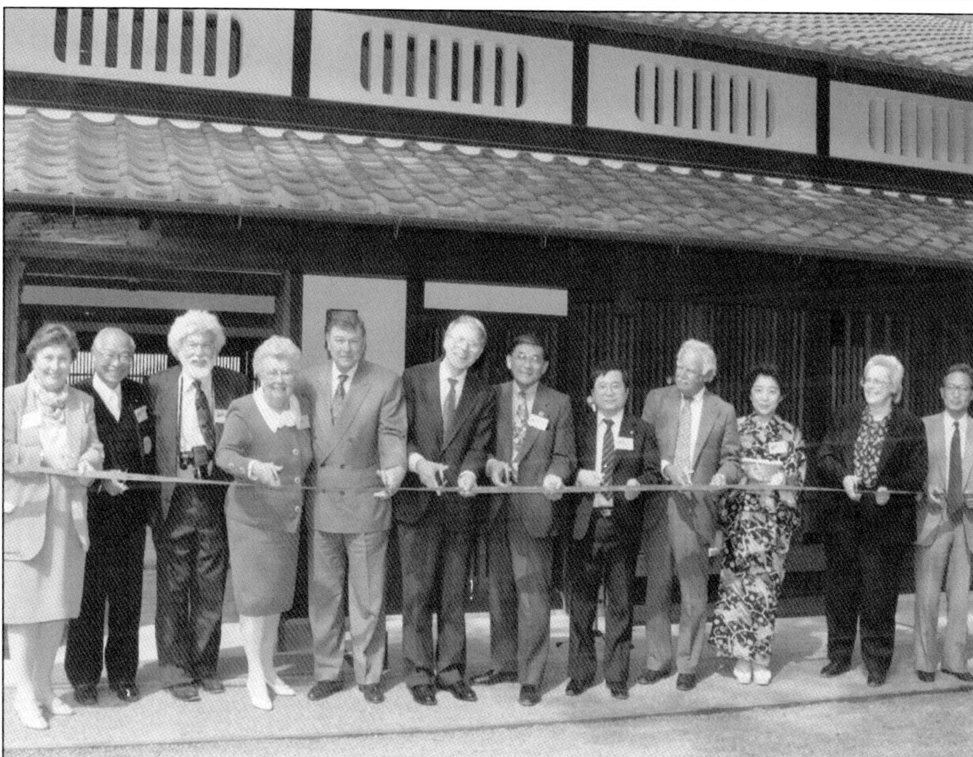

Pictured at the dedication of the CEC are, from left to right, Martha Clevenger, Saratoga City Council and past mayor; Kiyoshi Yasui, architect; Donald B. Miller, president, Hakone Foundation; Gladys Armstrong, vice president, Hakone Foundation; Harry Peacock, Saratoga city manager; Willem Kohler, mayor; Norman Y. Mineta, US congressman; Dr. Morihito Nagai, major donor; William Glennon, former mayor and former chairperson, Hakone Foundation; Midori Hirano, architect Yasui's daughter; Karen Anderson, Saratoga City Council and past mayor; and Atsushi Tokinoya, Japanese consul general, San Francisco. (Courtesy of Hakone Foundation.)

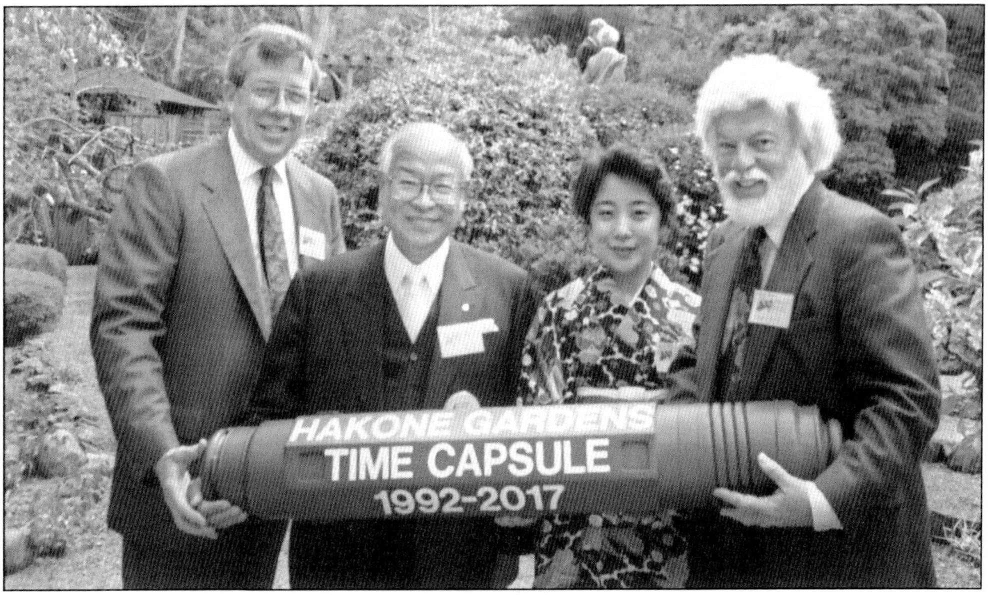

At the dedication of the CEC, a time capsule filled with memorabilia was buried in the basement. Jack Mallory oversaw the project. From left to right are Mallory, Saratoga Sister City member; Morihito Nagai and Midori Yasui, sister city members; and Don Miller, president, Saratoga Sister City. Twenty-five years later, during a celebration in 2017, the capsule was opened to an enthusiastic audience. (Courtesy of Mallory family.)

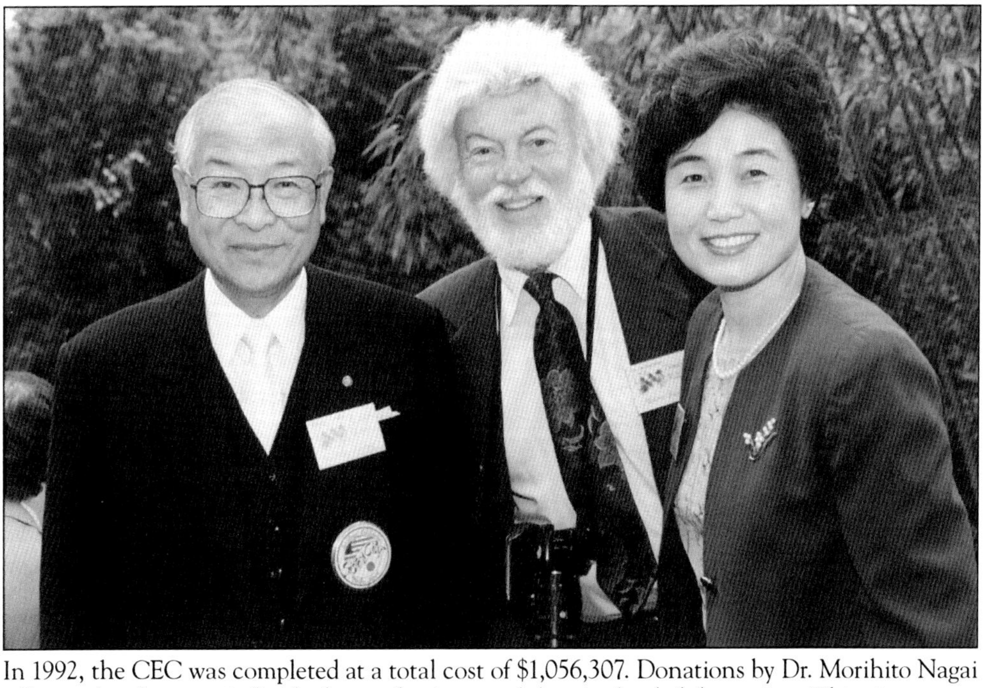
In 1992, the CEC was completed at a total cost of $1,056,307. Donations by Dr. Morihito Nagai of Japan, local grants, individual contributions, and the city funded the project. This picture was taken at the opening celebration on April 11, 1992. From left to right are Dr. Morihito Nagai; Don Miller, president of Saratoga Sister City; and Aiko Tauchi, sister city member and translator. (Courtesy of Tauchi family.)

Five

Celebrating Hakone

A Historic Site of Culture and Ideals

The City of Saratoga was financially struggling in 2000, and with the burden of maintaining Hakone, the council rewrote the agreement of the foundation, realizing a nonprofit foundation would be most effective in securing funding for the park. With seed funding from the David and Lucille Packard Foundation, the new Hakone Foundation began to draw on support of members, private donations, visitor admission fees, and private rentals. With the influx of new residents of Asian ancestry and the popularity of Indian, Korean, Vietnamese, and Thai, as well as Chinese and Japanese restaurants opening in the village and shopping centers, Saratoga was becoming multicultural and international. The Hakone Foundation rose to meet the changing demographics and the opportunity for potential supporters. It would be living up to its mission statement: "To conserve and enhance Hakone Estate and Gardens for the enjoyment and benefit of the public, to preserve its Japanese authenticity for future generations, to promote a deeper understanding of Asian cultures, and to serve as a global forum for art, music, culture, and ideas."

The foundation observed Hakone's centennial over the span of three years, 2015–2017, featuring exhibits, a themed gala each year, and a documentary video. There was much to celebrate with a rise in Hakone's popularity and achieving national recognition as one of the oldest Japanese gardens in the Western Hemisphere. The centennial gave the foundation an opportunity to appeal for financial support in maintaining Hakone's aging historic buildings and koi pond.

Hakone, now known as Hakone Estate and Gardens, was becoming nationally recognized. It received the prestigious National Trust for Historic Preservation "Save America's Treasures" designation and is listed in the National Register of Historic Places. It continues to be a timeless oasis for strolling the "hill and pond" garden, ascending the Moon Bridge, sipping tea overlooking the dry landscape garden, or enjoying quiet reflection in the bamboo garden. The resurgence of nativism and racism in America since 2016, so deeply offensive to this diverse community, has motivated its citizens toward activism and political involvement. Hakone Gardens has become the site for events of diverse cultures and is ever invigorated by new members, volunteers, and a dedicated staff. The mission of the Hakone Foundation reaches beyond Silicon Valley, welcoming people from everywhere to be enriched by the legacy of the historic garden. Saratoga is proud that its public park, Hakone, stands for something: the true American ideals of inclusion, social justice, and international peace through understanding.

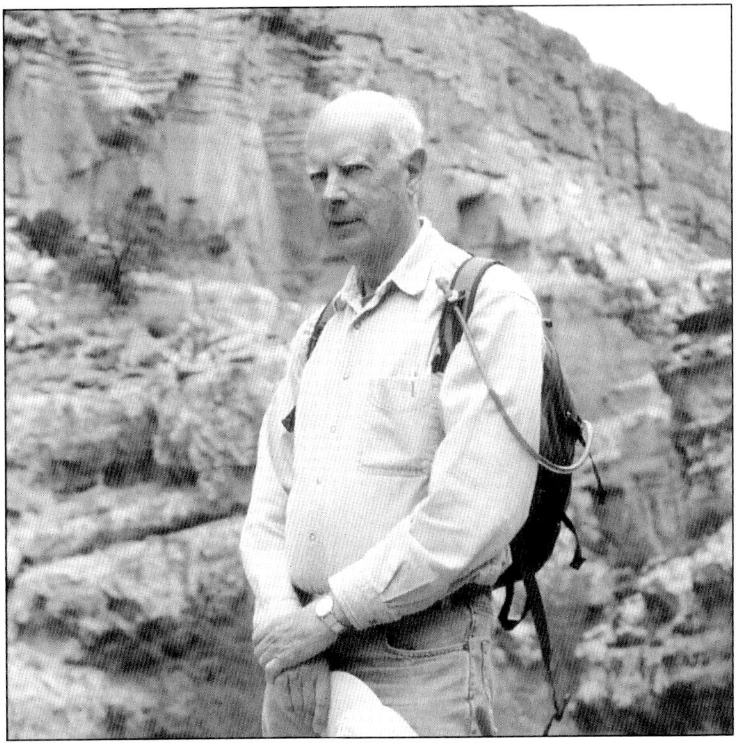

Cole Wilbur, former president of the David and Lucille Packard Foundation, was instrumental in developing the second foundation of Hakone Gardens in 2000. He facilitated the awarding of the $150,000 seed grant so that the second Hakone Foundation could begin. With the grant, the new foundation could hire professional staff and promote outreach and advertising to the wider public. (Courtesy of Cole Wilbur.)

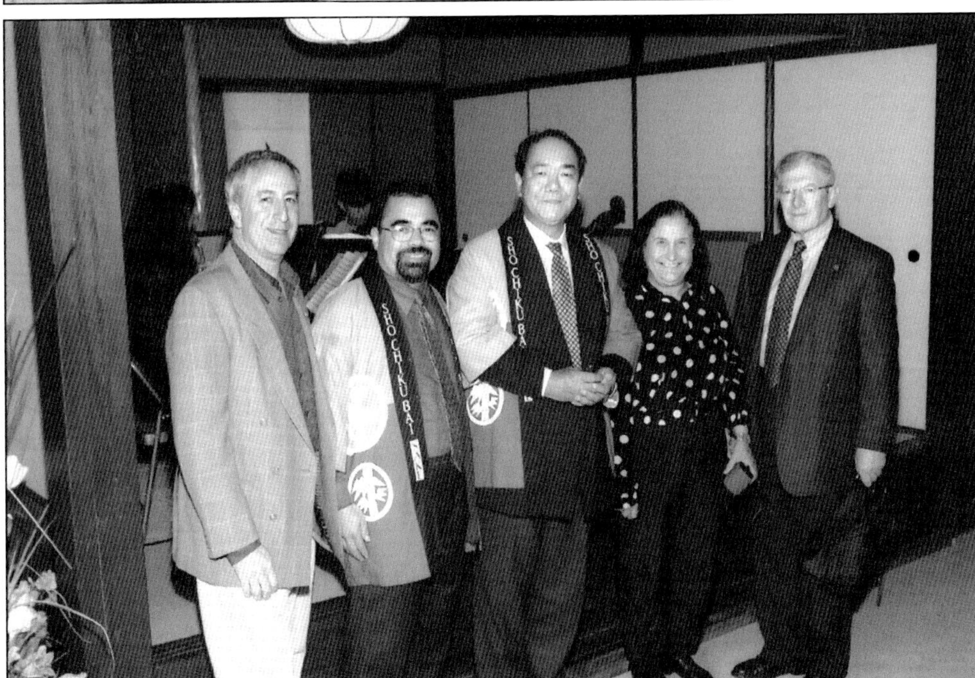

The new Hakone Foundation began fundraising and focusing on grant outreach priorities. In May 2003, the foundation celebrated its progress at an event. From left to right are Ron Cohn, foundation trustee; Lon Saavedra, foundation CEO; Consul General Shigeru Nakamura of Japan; unidentified; and Don Korn, foundation trustee. (Courtesy of Don Korn.)

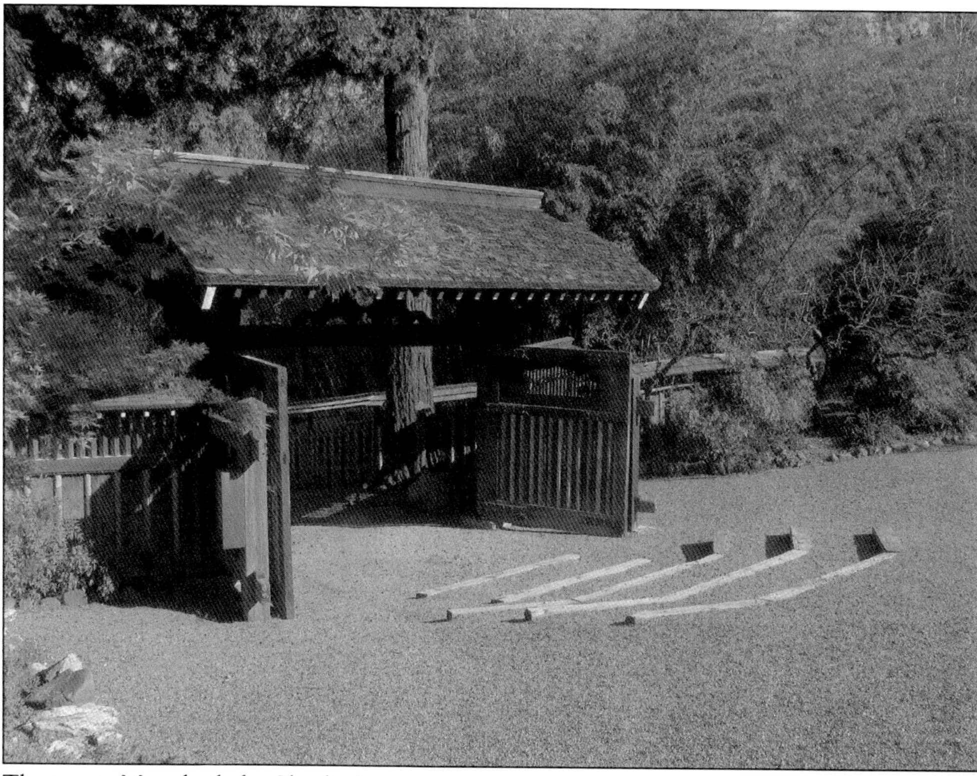

The iconic Mon, built for Charles Lee Tilden by the Nishiura brothers of San Jose, was constructed downhill from the pond. In 2006, the foundation, seeing the need for more level space in the garden, had the Mon raised onto a six-foot-high foundation with leveling fill behind it. Steps were then built on the eastern side, and the result was an even more dramatic entrance. (Courtesy of Mike Story.)

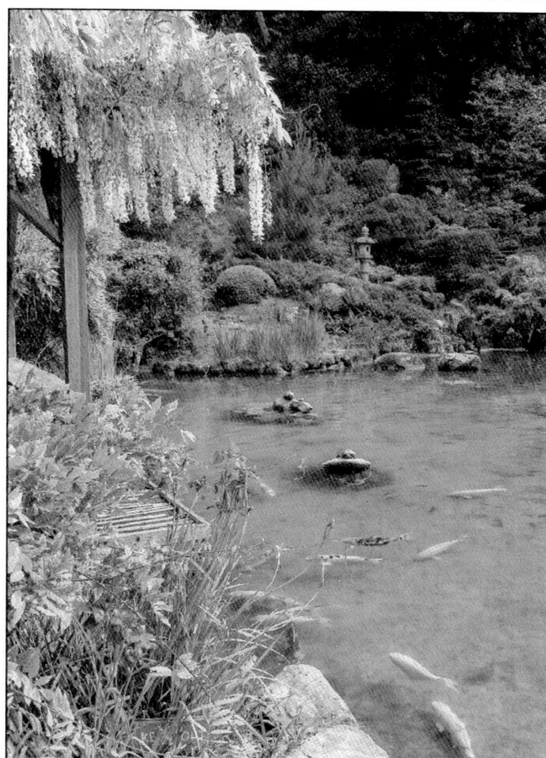

The irregular-shaped pond, with its spectacular, multihued koi, is the liveliest attraction of the garden. In Hakone's early days, it served as a pool for the Stine children and their friends to wade and paddle canoes in the summer. The Lower Wisteria Pavilion, on the left, is where visitors may view the koi gliding in the water and enjoy the lush surrounding landscape. Directly ahead is the waterfall area. (Courtesy of Mike Story.)

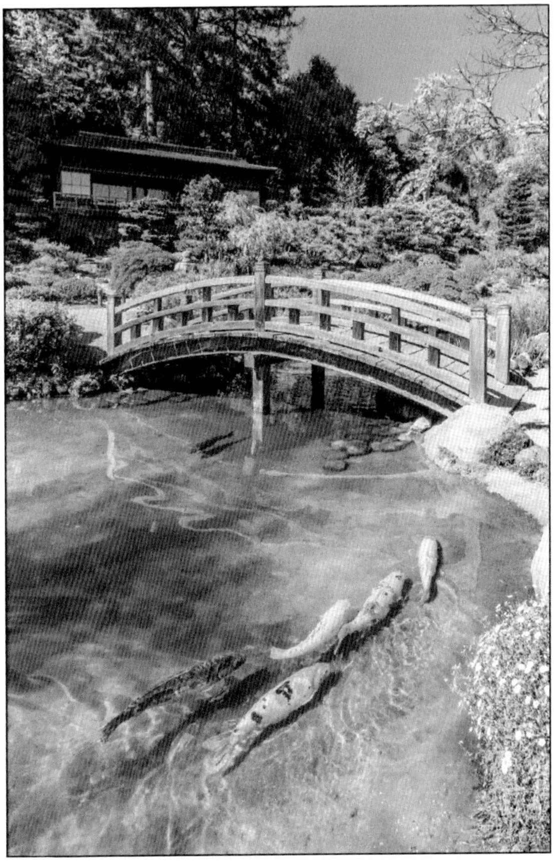

The arched wooden-trestle Moon Bridge is the central feature of the pond. It was designed and built by Naoharu Aihara for Isabel Stine and was rebuilt for Maj. Charles Tilden by Gentaro Nishiura in 1939. In the public era of Hakone, it is the most picturesque place for visitors. Note that behind the Upper House, large California redwoods and oak trees now fill in the landscape. (Courtesy of Mike Story.)

The tame koi fish are always an attraction for visitors to watch and feed. The graceful, gentle koi gliding among water plants and reeds in Hakone's pond are a variety of carp deeply loved by Japanese. The Japanese word *koi* means "good fortune or luck." The koi are also associated with perseverance in adversity and strength of purpose. (Courtesy of Mike Story.)

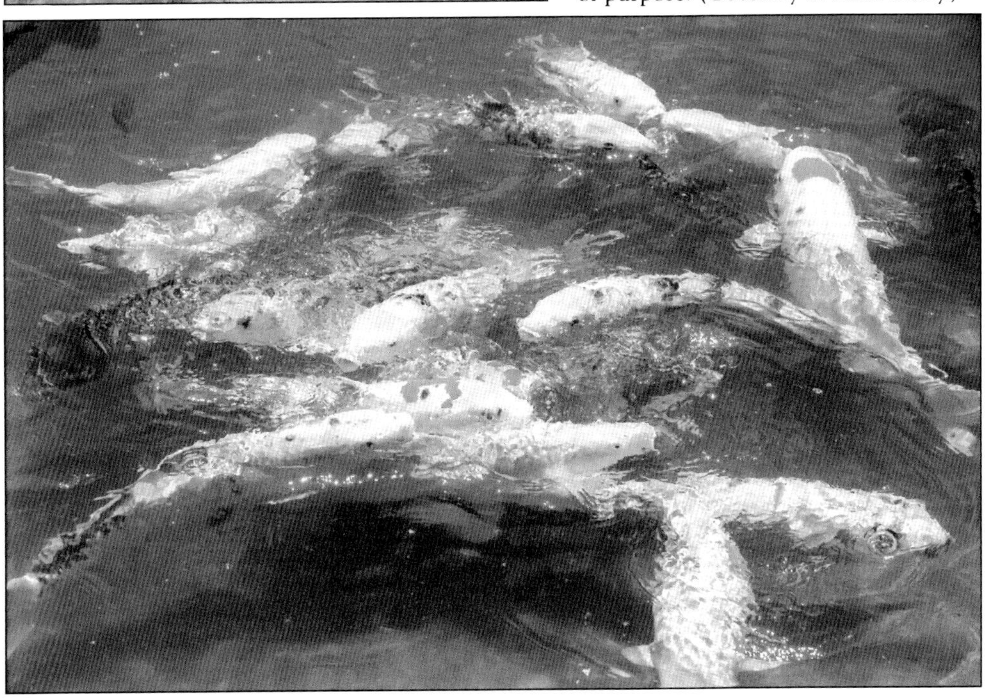

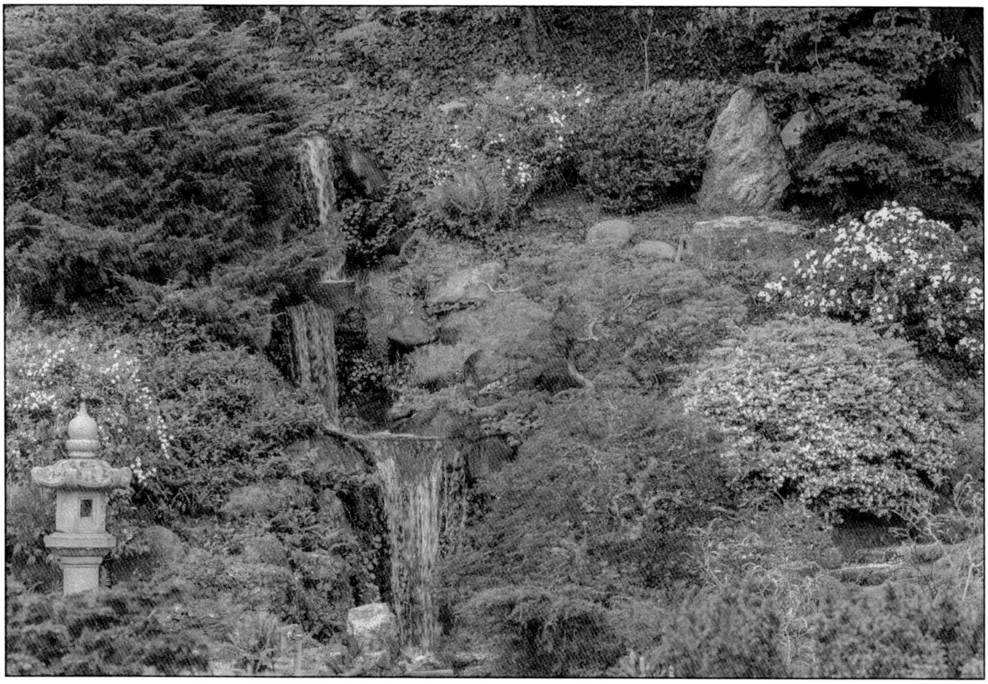

Comparing the pond's waterfall and landscaping to the original 1918 landscaping, no remnants of the bare logged hillside remain. With watering and tender care, the hillside is lush with an azalea grove, a camellia grove, and tea plants. The camellias were donated by the Richard Roggia family in the 1970s. The Master Stone, central to Japanese landscape principles, is visible at upper right. (Courtesy of Mike Story.)

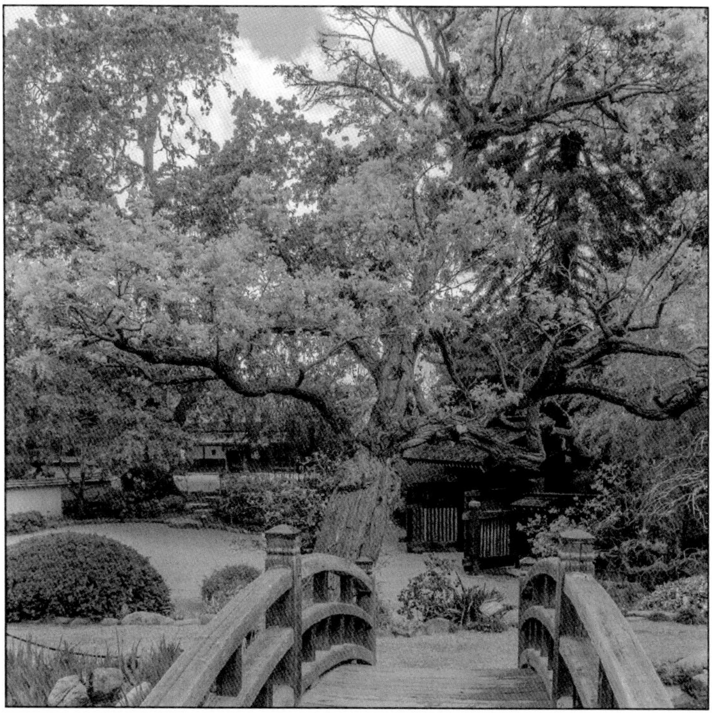

From the top of the Moon Bridge is a panoramic view of the Lower House, its walled Dry Garden, the CEC directly in front, and the Mon to the right. After 100 years, the garden landscape is mature, and the surrounding redwood and oak trees enclose the garden space in a green embrace. (Courtesy of Mike Story.)

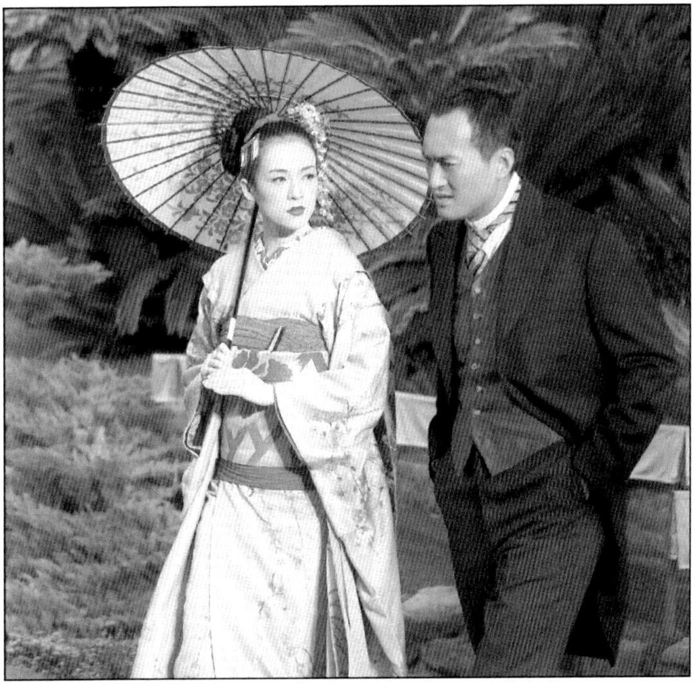

Hakone was a dramatic location for *Memoirs of a Geisha*, the acclaimed 2005 motion picture starring Ziyi Zhang and Ken Watanabe. Hakone provided a spectacular set for portraying garden scenes of Japan. Based on Arthur Golden's novel, the movie won three Academy Awards: Best Cinematography, Best Art Direction, and Best Costume Design. (Courtesy of Columbia Pictures, ©2005 Columbia Pictures Industries, Inc., DreamWorks, LLC, and Spyglass Entertainment Group, LLC, all rights reserved.)

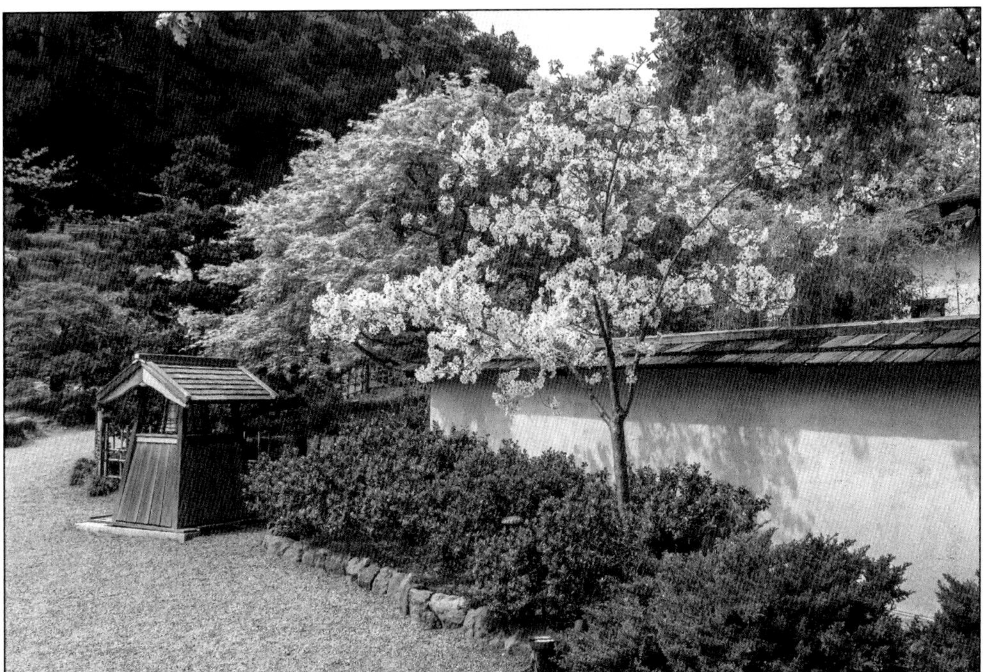

In 2003, Saratoga Sister City and the Hakone Foundation commemorated the 150th anniversary of the Japanese-American friendship treaty. The ceremony included planting a Japanese cherry tree. Certificates were presented to Consul General Shigeru Nakamura, Kiyoshi Yasui, and Dr. Morihito Nagai. Commodore Matthew Perry's great-granddaughter attended the ceremony. Perry led the opening of Japan to the West with the Convention of Kanagawa in 1854. The tree continues to blossom annually. (Courtesy of Mike Story.)

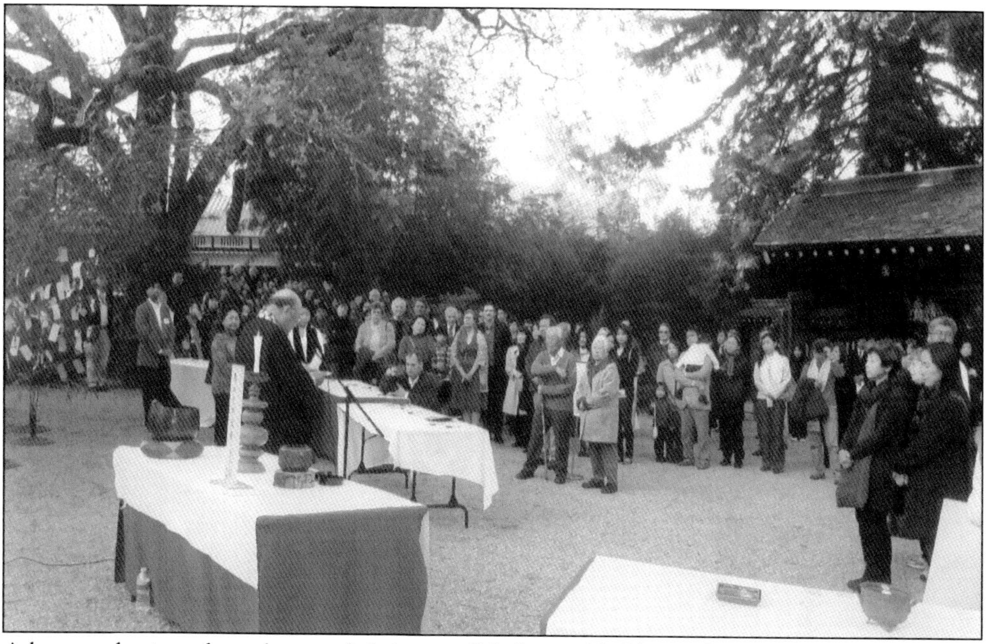

A large gathering of people attended the candlelight vigil held at Hakone Gardens for the more than 20,000 victims of the Great Sendai Earthquake, a devastating disaster followed by a tsunami that occurred in northeastern Japan on March 11, 2011. The somber vigil took place in the large area in front of the Mon. (Courtesy of Hakone Foundation.)

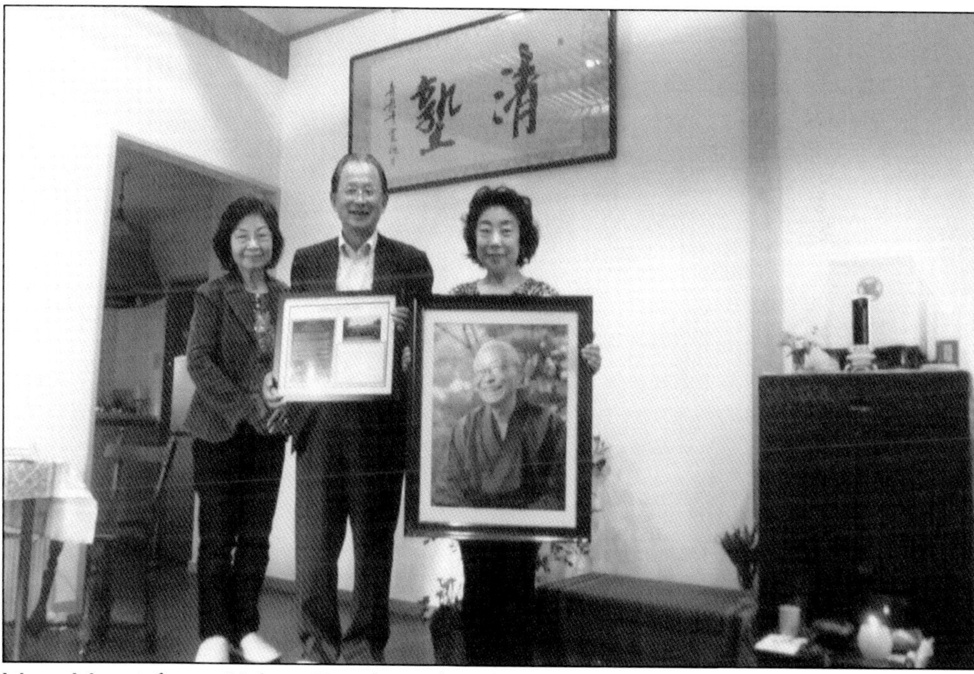

Marty Matsui, former Hakone Foundation board president, and his wife, Tazu, pose with Midori Yasui, daughter of Kioshi Yasui; Midori is holding her father's portrait. They visited the late Kioshi Yasui's daughter to express the foundation board's appreciation for his service to Hakone Gardens and Saratoga Sister City on May 21, 2011. (Courtesy of Hakone Foundation.)

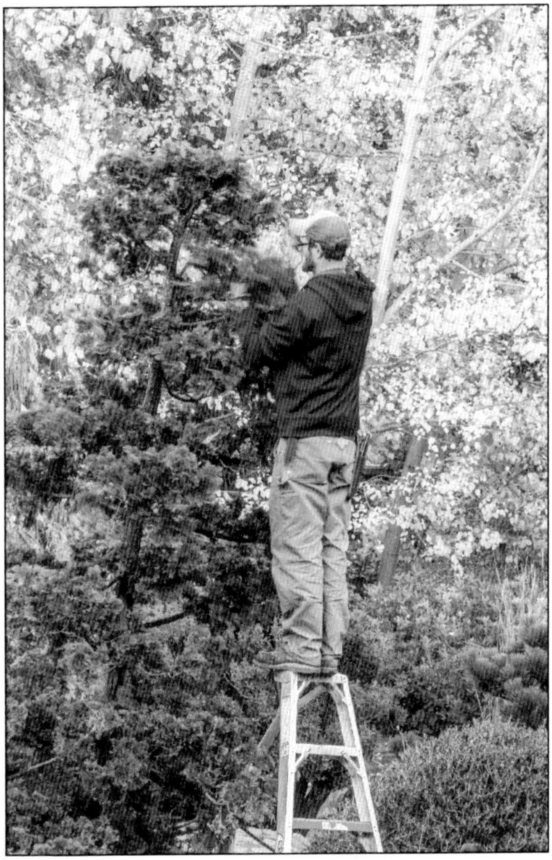

Jacob Kellner, head gardener, trims the trees of Hakone. Since 2008, he has cared for Hakone's treasured grounds and oversees a small trained staff of gardeners who manage the many beautiful Japanese landscaped areas of the garden. (Courtesy of Mike Story.)

Saratoga's *taiko* drummer group, formed in 1992, represents the sister city group, connected to Hakone, and provides entertainment as well as intercultural understanding by performing at schools and organizations, such as senior centers and civic organizations. Their first drums were originally made by supporters John Tauchi, Syd Dunton, and Art Okuno using old whiskey barrels with cowhide drumheads. The group's enthusiasm is infectious. (Courtesy of Peter Marra.)

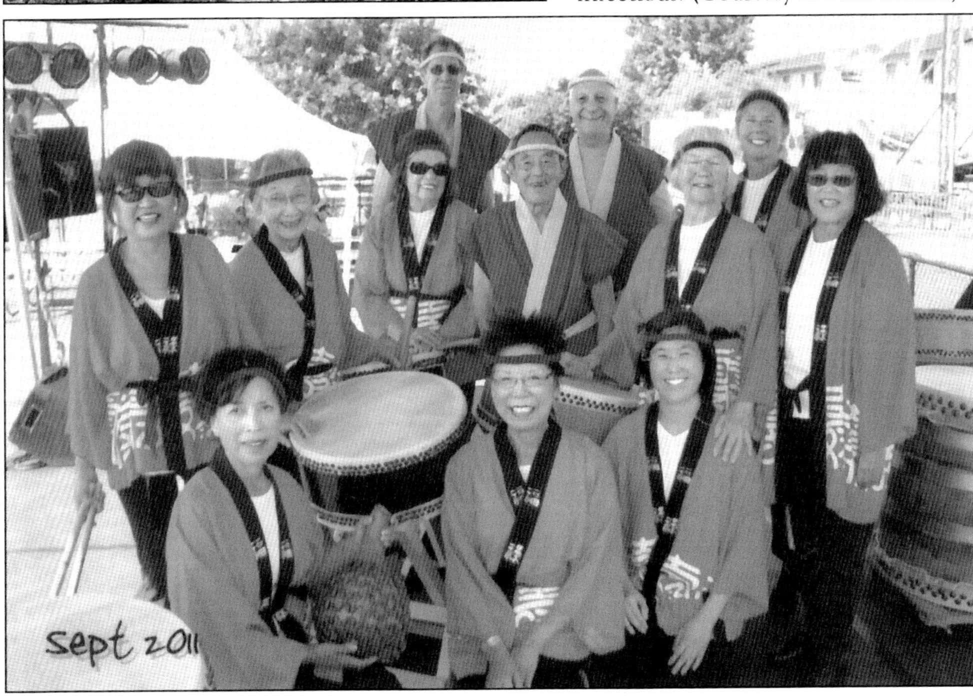

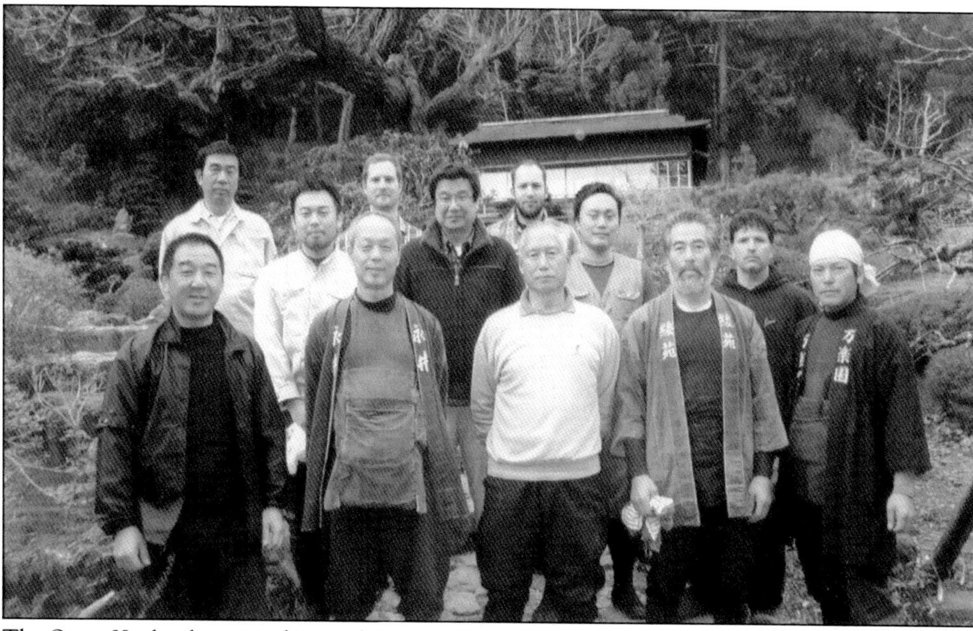

The Ogata Kai landscape architects from Japan, on their second visit to Hakone in 2011, volunteered to work on an area in the garden. The Ogata Kai are professional garden architects, or *niwashi* in Japanese. Dr. Takao Donuma (in black) is in the center of the group, with head gardener Jacob Kellner behind him. (Courtesy of Shozo Kagoshima.)

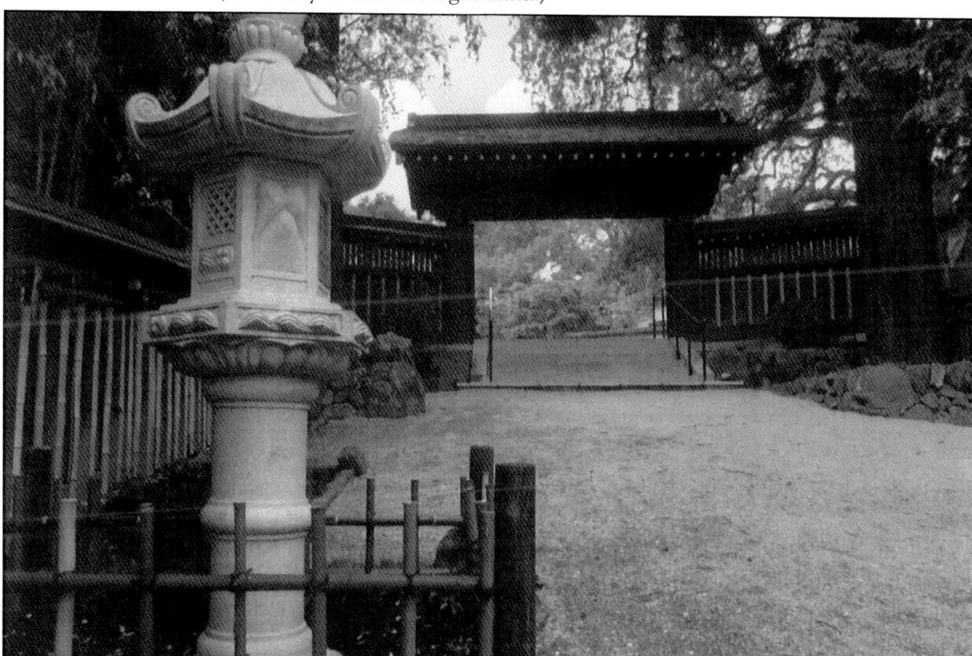

This shows the completed placement of lanterns and the new landscaping around the lanterns done by the Ogata Kai visiting volunteer gardeners from Japan in 2011. In addition, note that the Mon is in its present position on a six-foot-high foundation with steps up to the garden. It is now a very dramatic entrance for the century-old garden. (Courtesy of Shozo Kagoshima.)

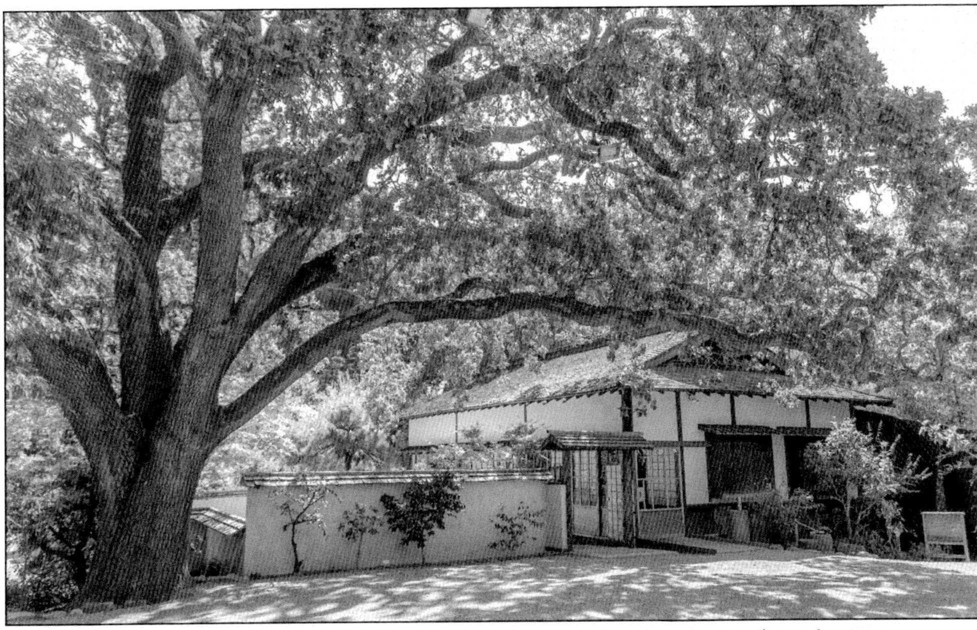

Isabel Stine's dream garden design has been augmented and enhanced in the 21st century. Originally there was open landscaping in front of the Lower House, and now a high stucco wall encloses the Dry Garden, or Karensansui, which has expanded into the wider area. The lovely building is an ideal place for tea ceremonies and is in popular demand for meetings and social events. (Courtesy of Mike Story.)

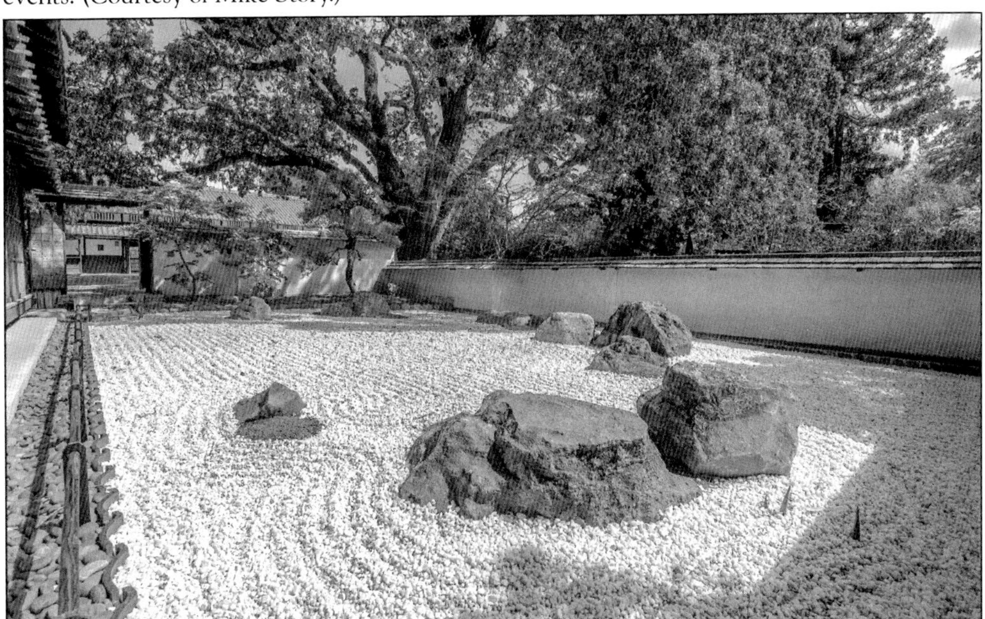

The Japanese dry garden creates a miniature stylized landscape through careful arrangements of rocks, water features, moss, pruned trees, and bushes, and uses raked gravel or sand to represent ripples in water. Hakone's Dry Garden was renovated and expanded in 2014 by the Ogata Kai, Japanese landscape architects. This was their third official volunteer visit to Hakone. (Courtesy of Mike Story.)

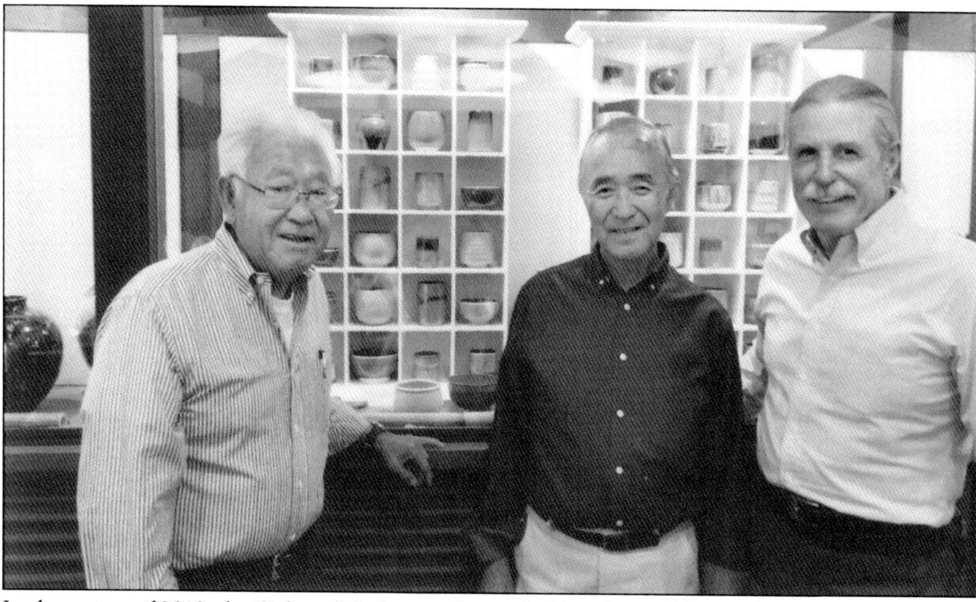

In the spring of 2013, the Cultural Exchange Center held its first public art show, Japanese-Inspired American Ceramics, curated by Paul Sakamoto, a longtime supporter of Hakone. Sakamoto, on the left, stands in front of his collection of pottery with the featured ceramicists, Ben Horichi (center) and Bill Geisinger, who personally installed their work. Both artists have led groups of students to visit potters in Japan. (Courtesy of Hakone Foundation.)

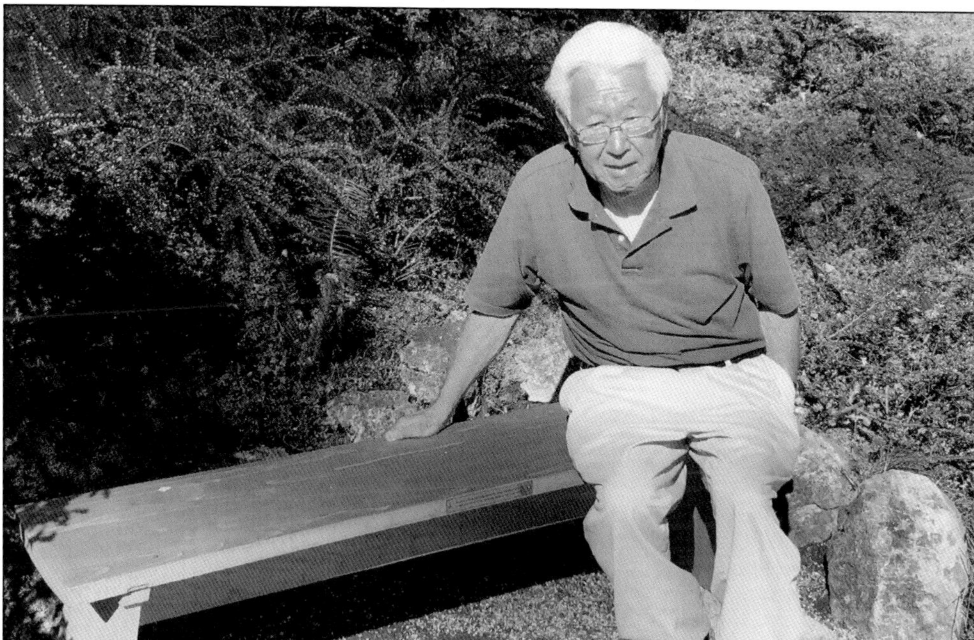

Paul Sakamoto, educator, horticulturist, and artist, was honored at the 2015 centennial gala for his generous support of Hakone. He has donated many plants, cherry trees, and artwork and inspired the foundation to delve deeply into Hakone's fascinating history. He was a founding board member of Asian Americans for Community Involvement. He is pictured sitting on the wooden bench dedicated in his honor. (Courtesy of Shozo Kagoshima.)

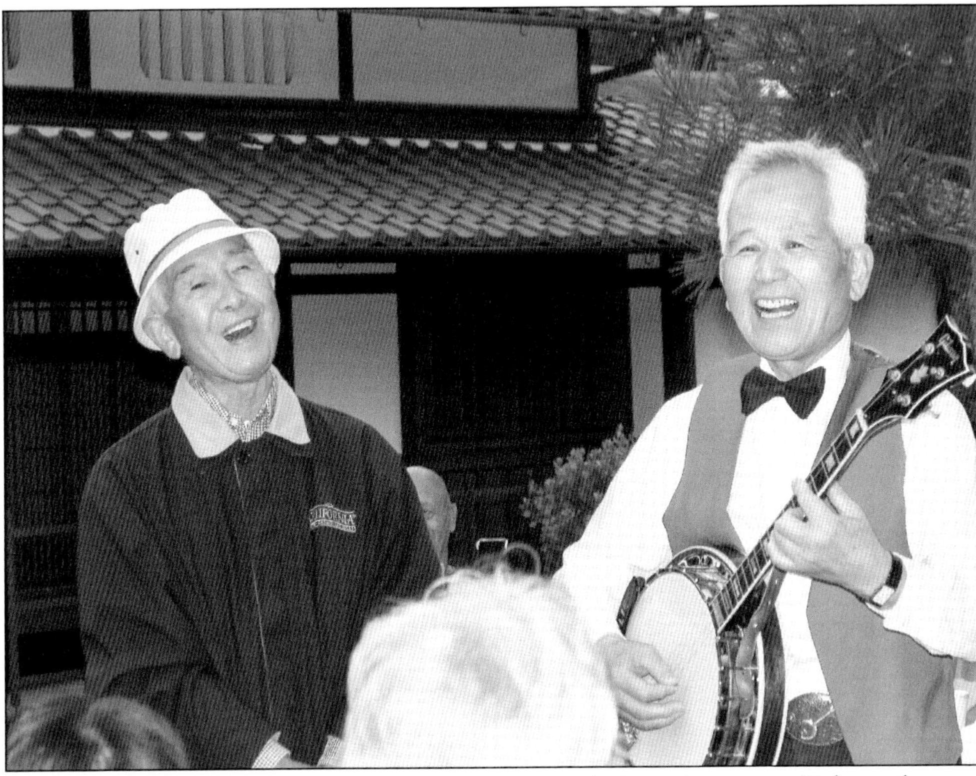

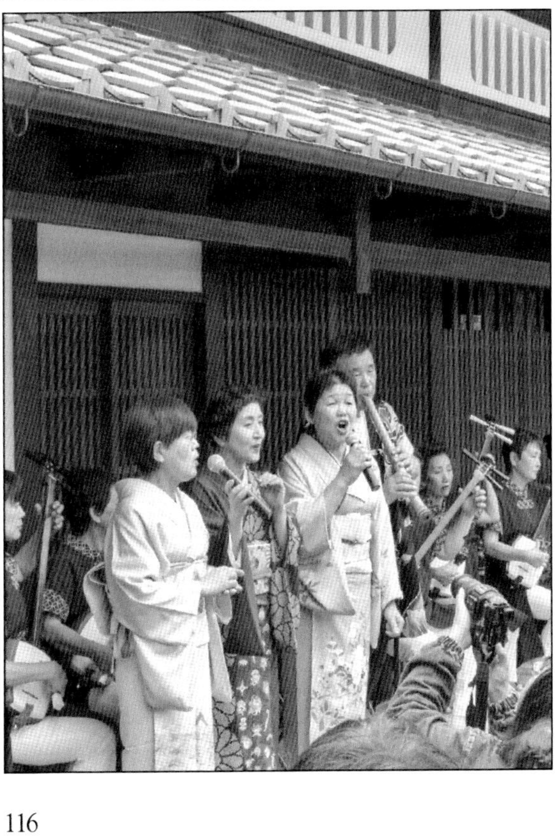

A sister city event at Hakone always includes bento box dinners or potluck and entertainment. Longtime sister city leader John Tauchi (left) enjoys a banjo singalong led by Charlie Tagawa. The banjo is reminiscent of traditional Japanese instruments such as the shamisen. John Tauchi and his wife, Aiko, planned the sister city visitor exchange trips for 35 years. (Courtesy of Mike Story.)

Events at Hakone can be a mixture of old and modern entertainment for the enjoyment and education of attendees. Note the traditional shamisens and flute and kimono-clad singers performing traditional Japanese songs and American folk songs. This event took place in the open area in front of the CEC. (Courtesy of Mike Story.)

Hakone provides weekly tea ceremonies for public enjoyment as well as classes in the tea ceremony. Kimono-clad experts, along with helpers, present the elements of the ceremony and end with all participants enjoying a bowl of tea. Three public tea-serving areas and a yearly tea masters gathering make Hakone a mecca for Japanese tea ceremony lovers. (Courtesy of Mike Story.)

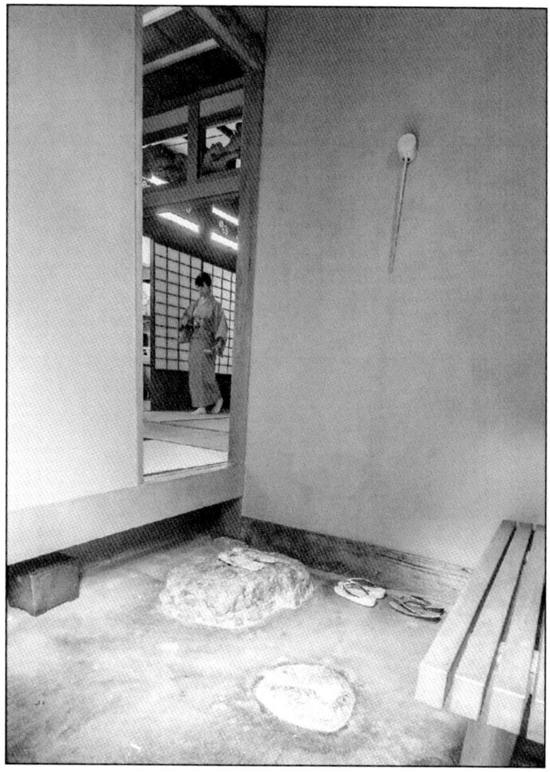

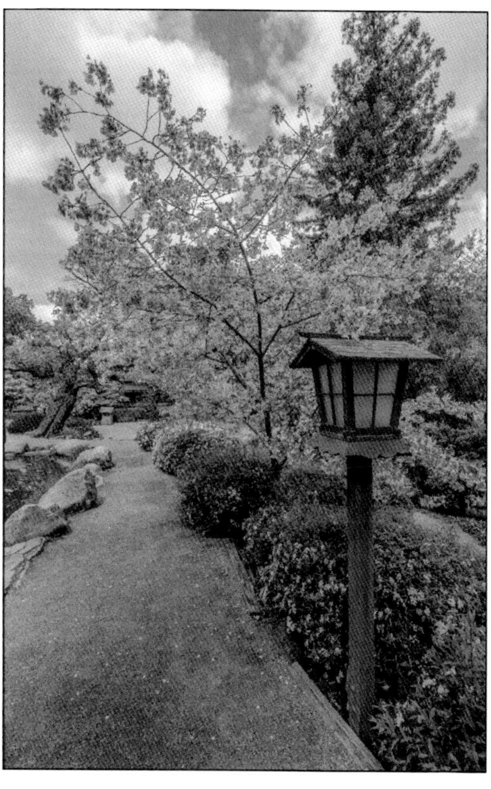

This is one of the 60 Japanese cherry trees donated by Paul Sakamoto that blossom each spring inside the garden and along Hakone's entrance driveway. The cherry trees are a major attraction in springtime and are especially memorable when Hakone hosts an exquisite event called Hanami, the viewing of cherry blossoms in the moonlight. (Courtesy of Mike Story.)

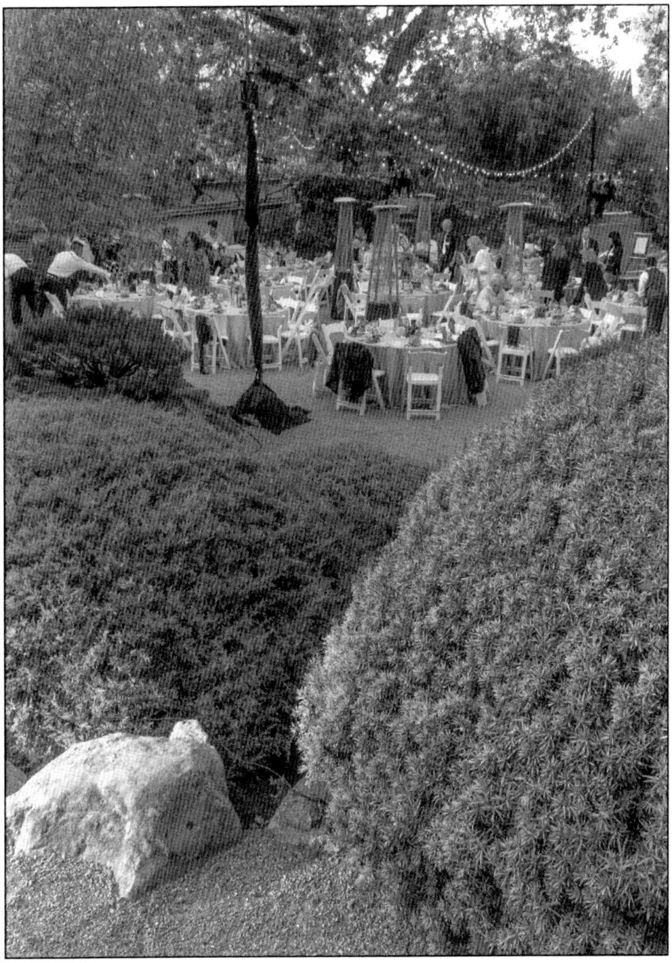

Guests are gathering for a dinner in the garden at the 2016 centennial gala celebrating the Tilden era of Hakone. During the program, a fine wooden bench was dedicated in memory of Charles Lee Tilden and another in memory of James Sasaki, his gardener. (Courtesy of Mike Story.)

Bunkichi Ito, from the Northern Culture Museum (NCM) in Japan, visited Hakone and was a guest of honor at the 2016 gala. From left to right are Mikiko Shimabe, Hakone trustee; Bunkichi Ito; Robert Handa of NBC Bay Area News and master of ceremonies; Aiko Tauchi, Saratoga Sister City; and Kitaro, Bunkichi Ito's friend. Kitaro is an award-winning Japanese recording artist and composer noted for his electronic-instrumental music. (Courtesy of Brian Satoh.)

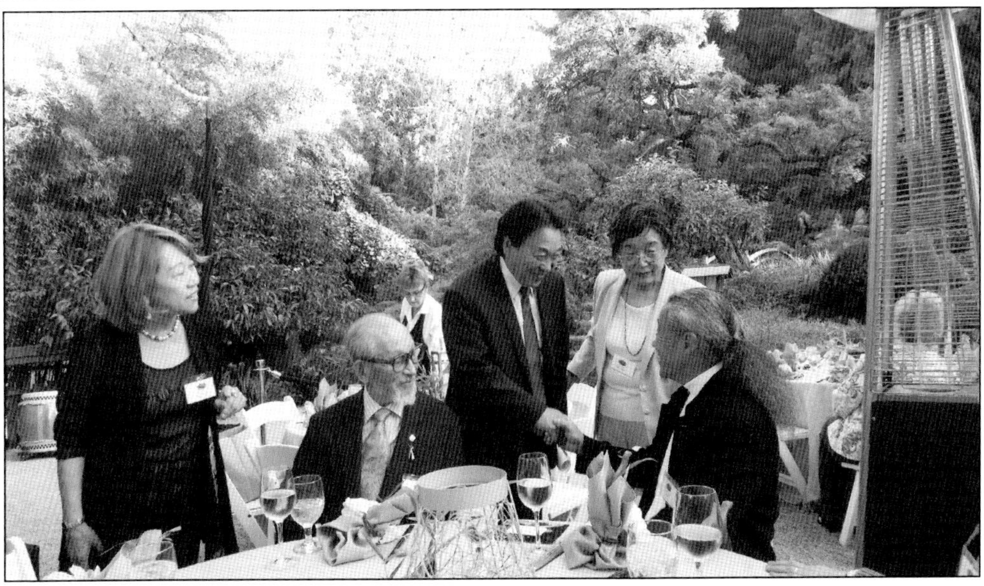

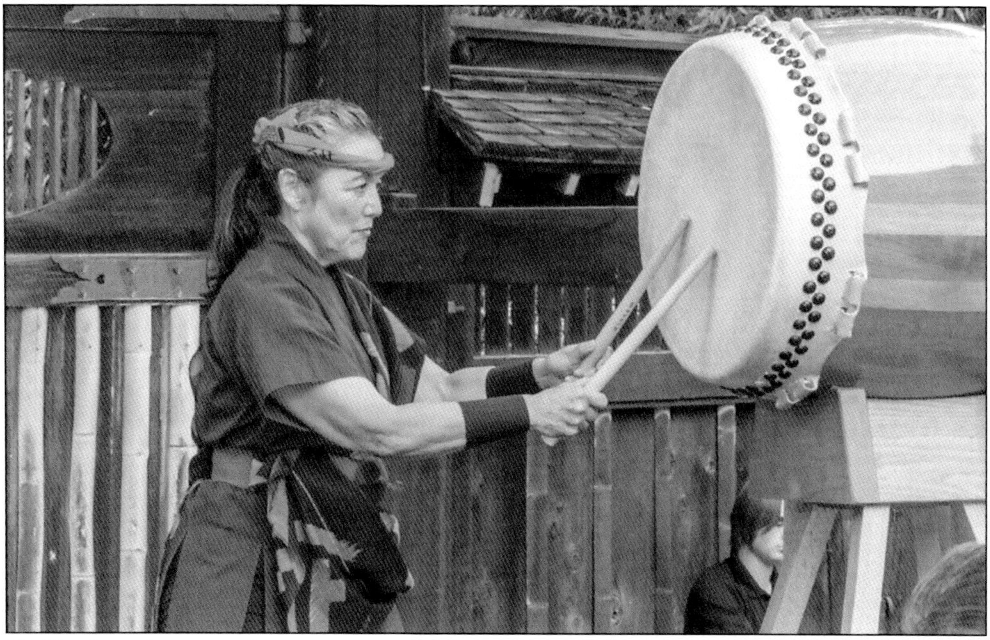

P.J. Hirabayashi gave a heart-stopping taiko performance at the 2016 centennial gala with her husband, Roy. P.J. has been long involved in the arts and culture of San Jose's Japantown, and Roy was the cofounder of San Jose Taiko, the acclaimed world-class drumming group. Taiko drumming comes from a long sacred tradition and now represents a Japanese cultural experience. (Courtesy of Mike Story.)

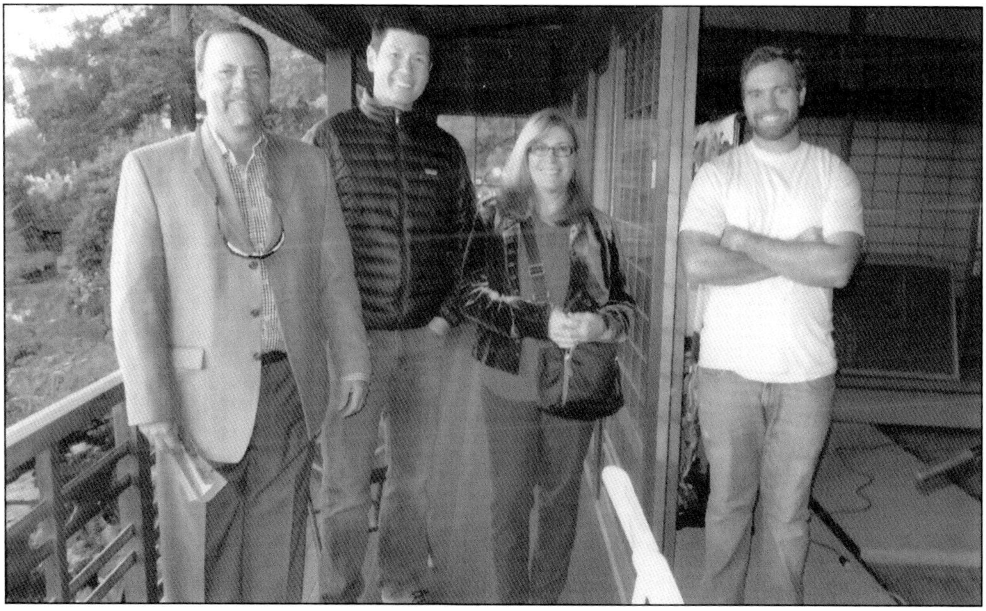

A documentary video, *Hakone: A Century of Beauty and Endurance*, was produced for the centennial by Barre Fong and Connie Young Yu. It features historic photographs, interviews, and scenes of Hakone's remarkable beauty through the ages. Standing at the Lower House after a shoot are, from left to right, Peter Stine, grandson of Isabel and Oliver Stine; filmmaker Barre Fong; Peter's wife, Ann Chrisney Stine; and Jeff Hallenbeck, Hakone staff. (Courtesy of Yu family.)

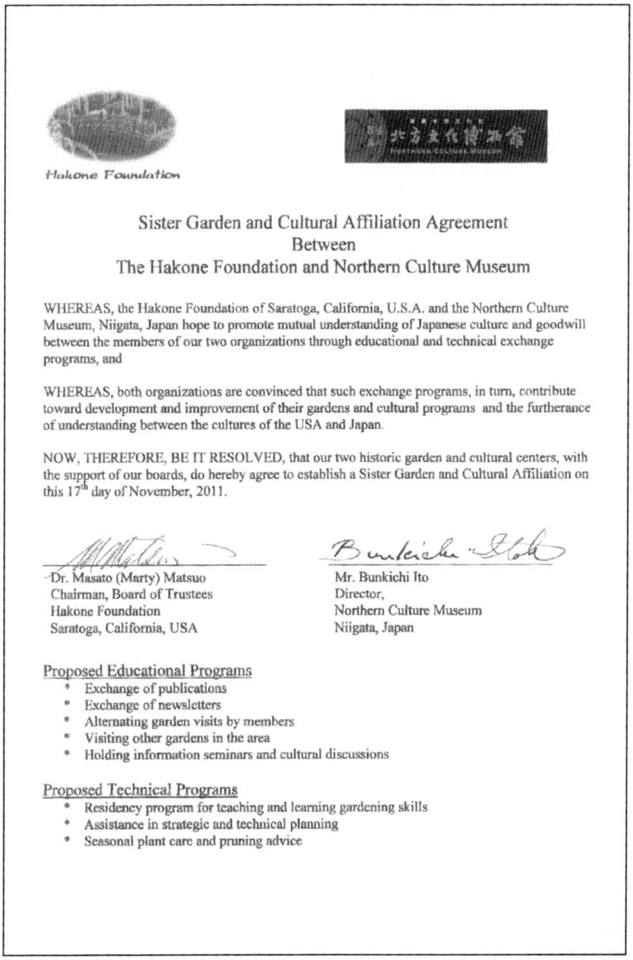

Hakone Foundation

北方文化博物館
NORTHERN CULTURE MUSEUM

Sister Garden and Cultural Affiliation Agreement
Between
The Hakone Foundation and Northern Culture Museum

WHEREAS, the Hakone Foundation of Saratoga, California, U.S.A. and the Northern Culture Museum, Niigata, Japan hope to promote mutual understanding of Japanese culture and goodwill between the members of our two organizations through educational and technical exchange programs, and

WHEREAS, both organizations are convinced that such exchange programs, in turn, contribute toward development and improvement of their gardens and cultural programs and the furtherance of understanding between the cultures of the USA and Japan.

NOW, THEREFORE, BE IT RESOLVED, that our two historic garden and cultural centers, with the support of our boards, do hereby agree to establish a Sister Garden and Cultural Affiliation on this 17th day of November, 2011.

Dr. Masato (Marty) Matsuo
Chairman, Board of Trustees
Hakone Foundation
Saratoga, California, USA

Mr. Bunkichi Ito
Director,
Northern Culture Museum
Niigata, Japan

Proposed Educational Programs
* Exchange of publications
* Exchange of newsletters
* Alternating garden visits by members
* Visiting other gardens in the area
* Holding information seminars and cultural discussions

Proposed Technical Programs
* Residency program for teaching and learning gardening skills
* Assistance in strategic and technical planning
* Seasonal plant care and pruning advice

In 2011, Hakone Estate and Gardens and the Northern Culture Museum in Niigata, Japan, signed a sister garden cultural affiliation agreement. Bunkichi Ito is the eighth generation in the family ownership of the NCM. It was a unique agreement of support between gardens. At that time, no other sister garden agreements existed between Japan and the United States. The Northern Culture Museum and Hakone promote friendship and cultural exchange with one another. (Courtesy of Hakone Foundation.)

Bunkichi Ito, from the NCM, toured Hakone in 2016 and is pictured on the Madrone Mound, between the Lower House and the CEC. From left to right are Takao Shimabe; Mikiko Shimabe; Kyoko Ito; Bunkichi Ito; Brian Satoh, executive director of the NCM, and Shozo Kagoshima, executive director of Hakone Foundation. (Courtesy of Brian Satoh.)

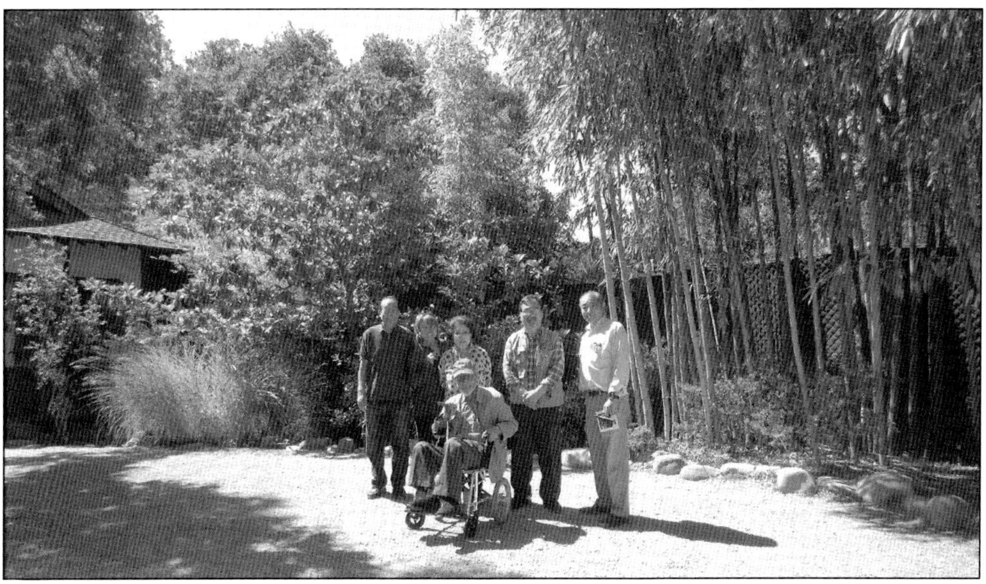

In 2016, the city and the Hakone Foundation developed a master plan with a vision for the garden's future. With increasing numbers of visitors and heavy use of the buildings for revenue-producing events, the structured plan outlined solutions for renewing the garden's aging infrastructure, the historic buildings, and the leaky koi pond. It also underscores the need for a major fundraising campaign. (Courtesy of Hakone Foundation.)

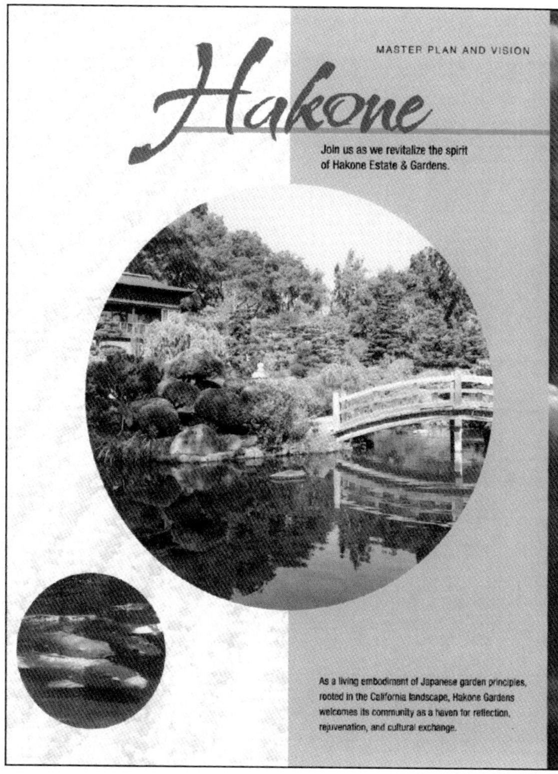

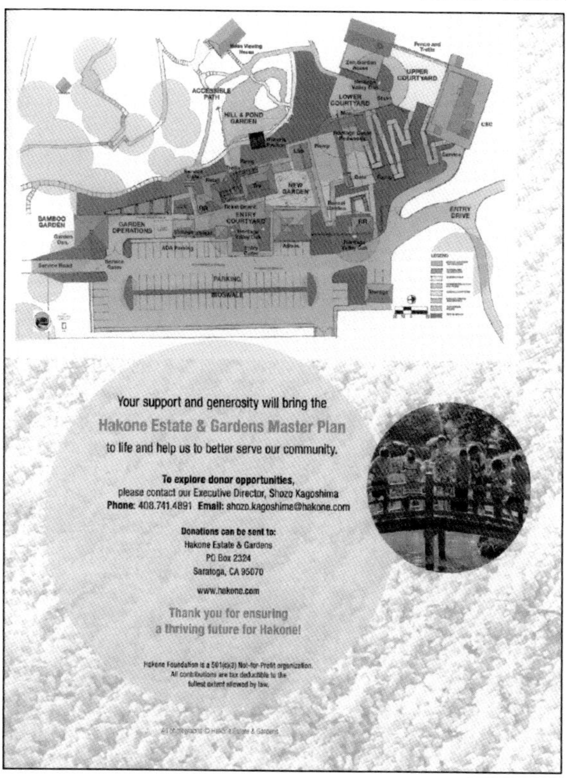

The back page of the master plan's brochure shows the layout of the garden and its historic buildings. It announces donor opportunities and a request for contributions to insure a thriving future for Hakone. Among the pressing needs outlined in the plan are a new entrance, a new gift shop, the remodeling of the heavily used Cultural Exchange Center, and additional restrooms to accommodate the increasing number of visitors. (Courtesy of Hakone Foundation.)

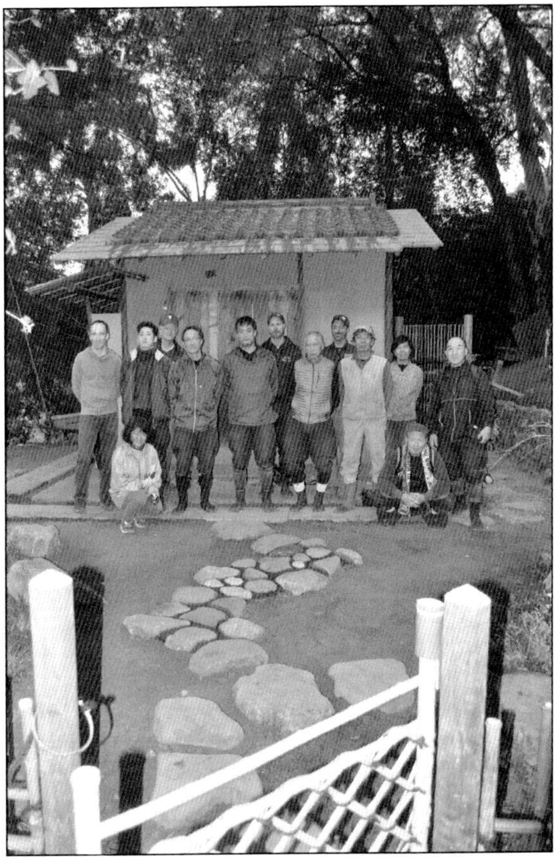

In 2018, the fourth Ogata Kai group visited. They worked on Hakone's Shogetsu-an, the historic small teahouse, its landscape area, retaining wall, and stairs in the upper garden area. The Ogata Kai, Hakone's head gardener Jacob Kellner, and local volunteers pose for a photograph in front of the Shogetsu-an before the work is completed. (Courtesy of Shozo Kagoshima.)

During the 2018 visit, the Ogata Kai group worked on the retaining wall and its stairs in the upper garden area. In this photograph, the Ogata Kai, Hakone staff and local volunteers are working on the new Japanese landscape. (Courtesy of Shozo Kagoshima.)

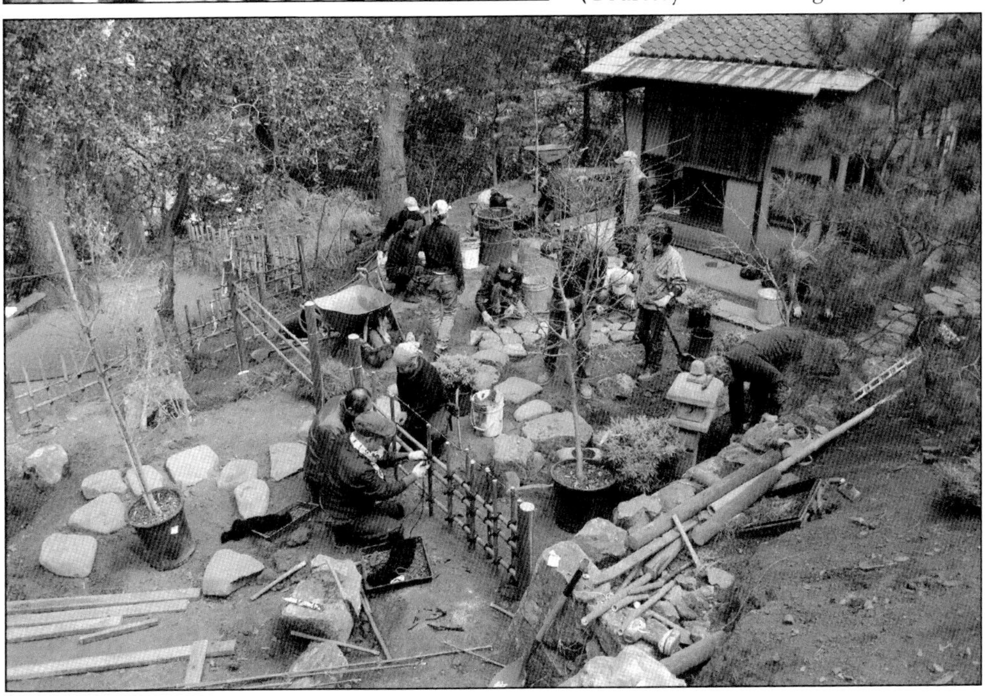

For 20 years, the annual Hakone Matsuri, or Japanese festival, has been presented in May. Japanese entertainment, food, and children's events draw large crowds. The yearly festival was organized by board member Mikiko Shimabe and her husband, Takao Shimabe, Hakone staff and volunteers. Baisho Matsumoto, a shamisen artist from Japan, was one of the regular entertainers at many festivals, seen here in 2016. (Courtesy of Mike Story.)

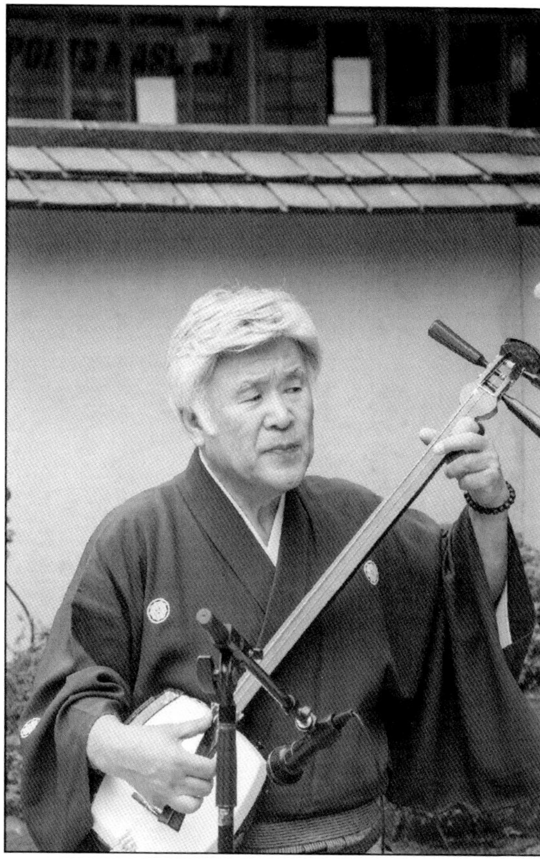

Hakone offers classes and demonstrations in traditional Japanese arts, crafts, and designs. In October 2016, the Kezurou-kai organization demonstrated how to mill and prepare beams for the vine trellis just outside of Hakone's gift shop. The Kezurou-kai members donate their expertise and time. They are a group of designers, builders, and craftsmen who are expert in Japanese woodworking, architecture, and construction. (Courtesy of Mike Story.)

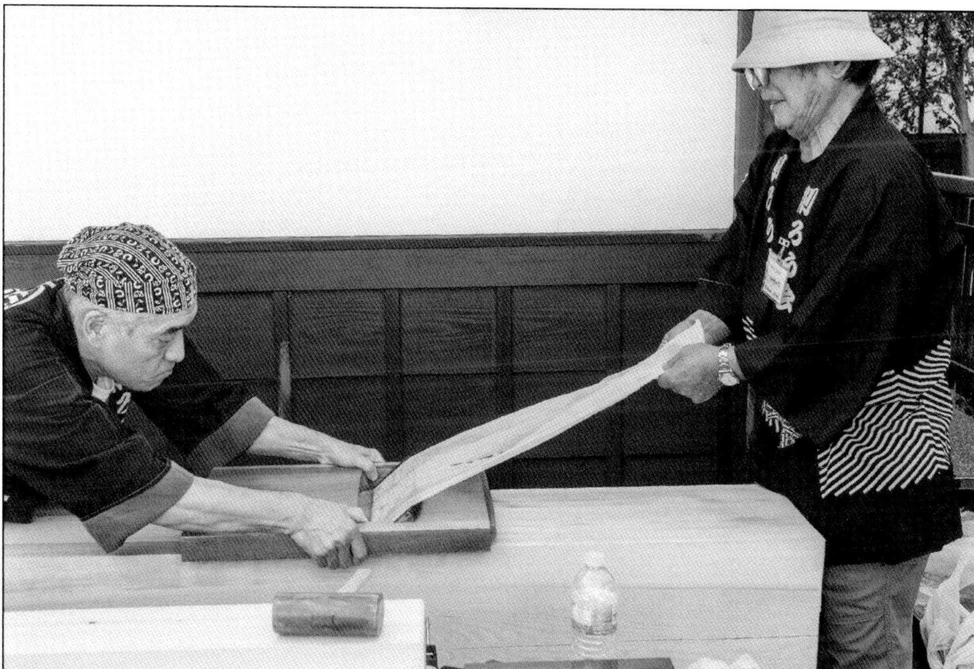

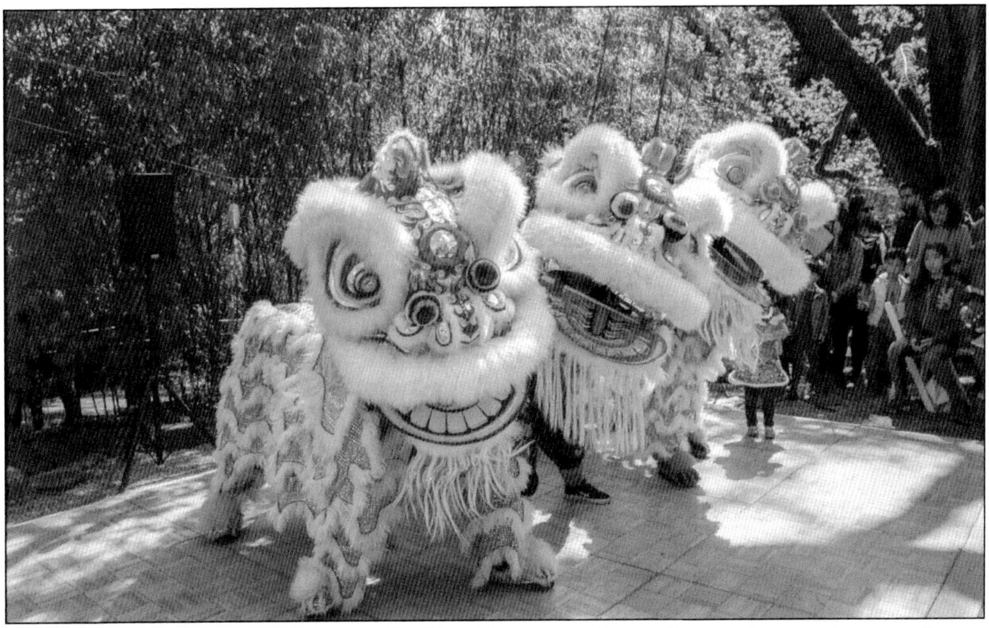

The performing lions of the famous Far East Dragon and Lion Dance Association pose for an admiring audience at Hakone's annual Lunar New Year Festival. Hakone has held this festival since 2009. The 2020 Year of the Rat festival featured a triple lion dance, a children's costume parade, arts and crafts, a Chinese trinket booth, dim sum lunch, and an entertaining program of music, magic, and martial arts. (Photograph by Frank Jang, courtesy of Emily Lo.)

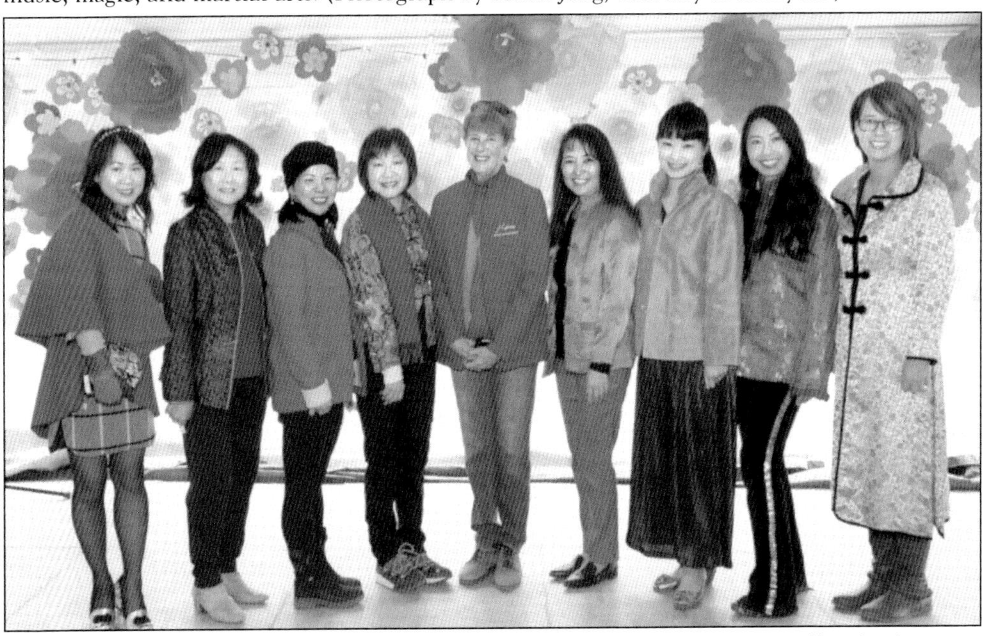

The annual Lunar New Year Festival is presented by a large, enthusiastic group of local volunteers, both adults and teens. The organizing committee, pictured here, are (from left to right) Isabelle Ip, Connie Young Yu, Wendy Chang, Emily Lo, Ann Waltonsmith (board chair but not on the committee), Beverly Harada, Wenlan Lu, Jessica Liu, and Phyllis Tung. Connie, Emily, Beverly, and Phyllis are also on the foundation board. (Courtesy of Emily Lo.)

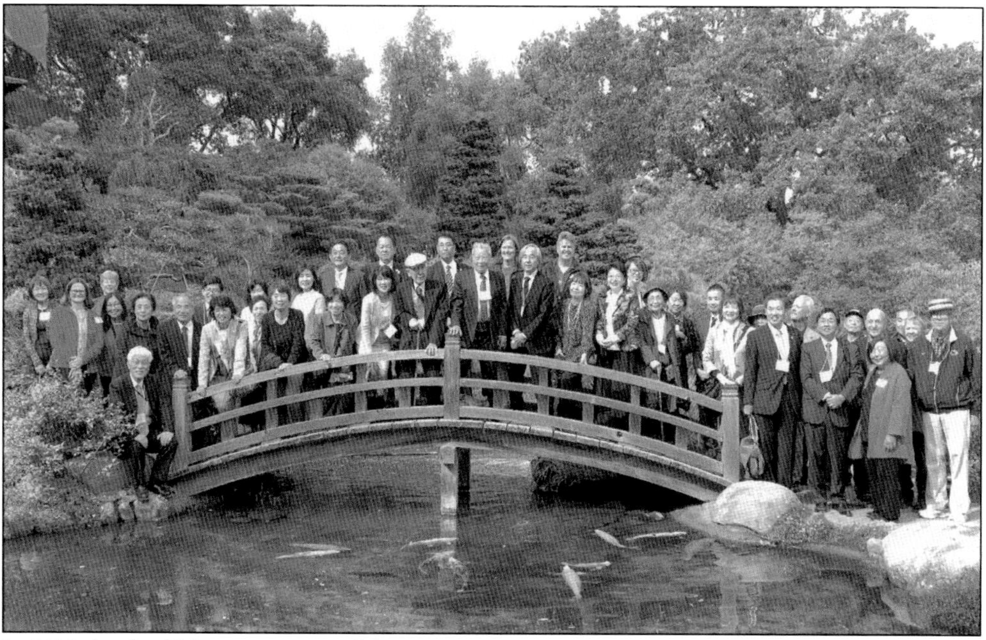

In 2019, for the 35th anniversary of the Saratoga-Muko sister city relationship, a large delegation from Muko visited Saratoga and Hakone. Here, members from both groups pose with members of the Saratoga City Council and Hakone Foundation trustees on the Moon Bridge for a photograph capturing an important moment in the century-old garden. (Courtesy of Mike Story.)

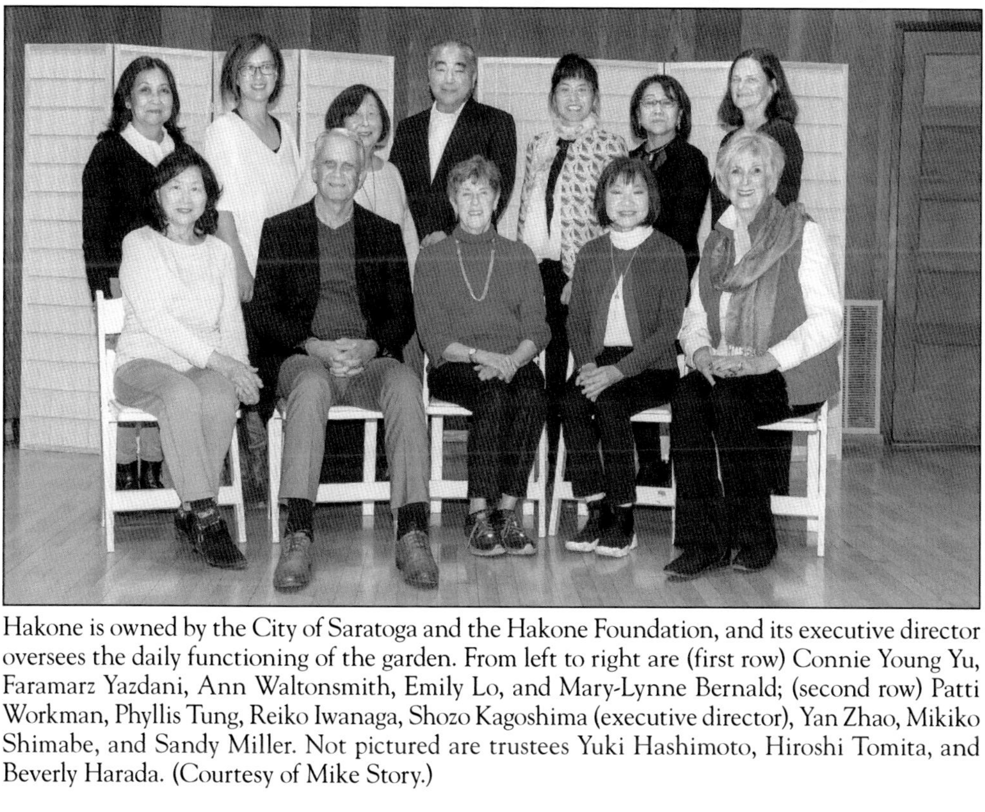

Hakone is owned by the City of Saratoga and the Hakone Foundation, and its executive director oversees the daily functioning of the garden. From left to right are (first row) Connie Young Yu, Faramarz Yazdani, Ann Waltonsmith, Emily Lo, and Mary-Lynne Bernald; (second row) Patti Workman, Phyllis Tung, Reiko Iwanaga, Shozo Kagoshima (executive director), Yan Zhao, Mikiko Shimabe, and Sandy Miller. Not pictured are trustees Yuki Hashimoto, Hiroshi Tomita, and Beverly Harada. (Courtesy of Mike Story.)

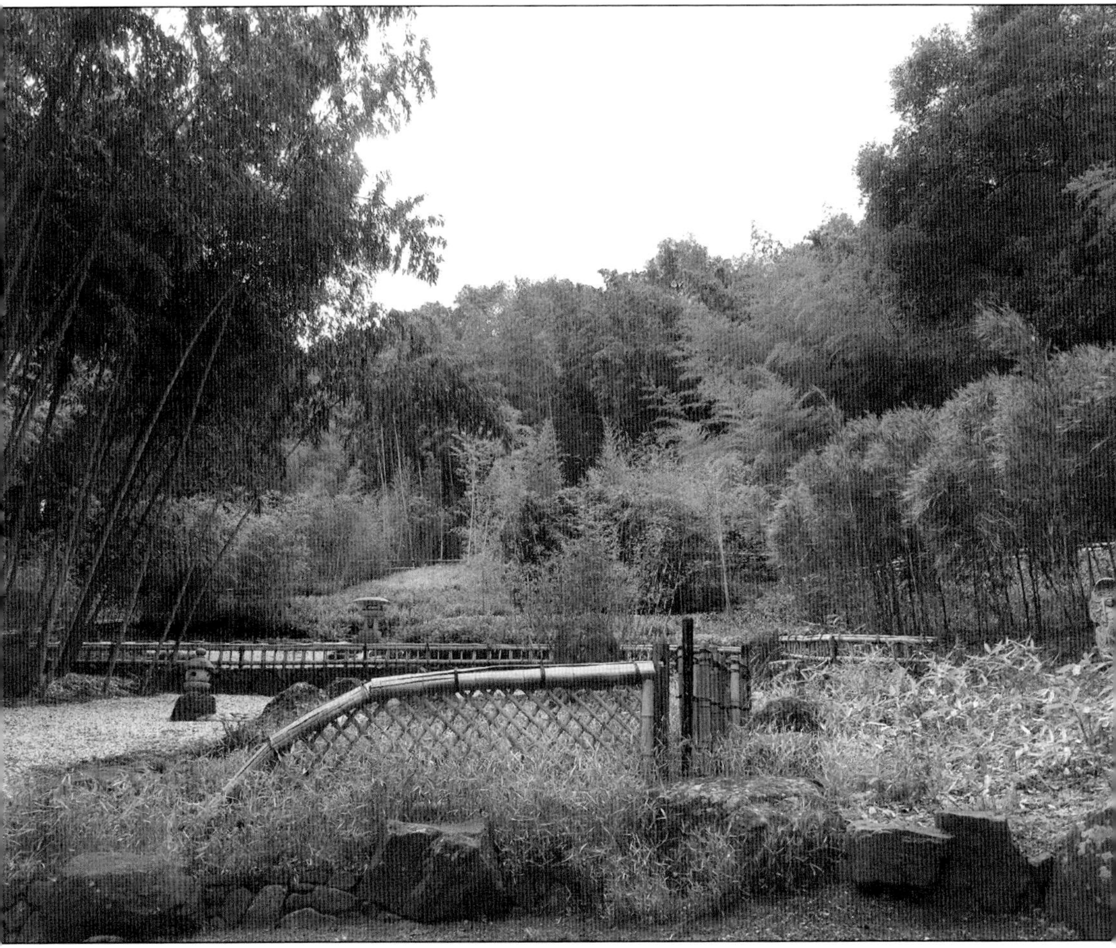

The mature bamboo garden, and within it the Kizuna-en (Friendship Bamboo Garden), draws visitors for a cool, quiet stroll, as envisioned by the Saratoga and Muko sister city donors. Fudo, the fire god statue, still sits in the garden (right) protecting Hakone and the City of Saratoga from natural disasters. This lovely specialty garden is an addition to the core of the Japanese garden estate originally designed by Isabel Stine and her master landscape architects. (Courtesy of Mike Story.)

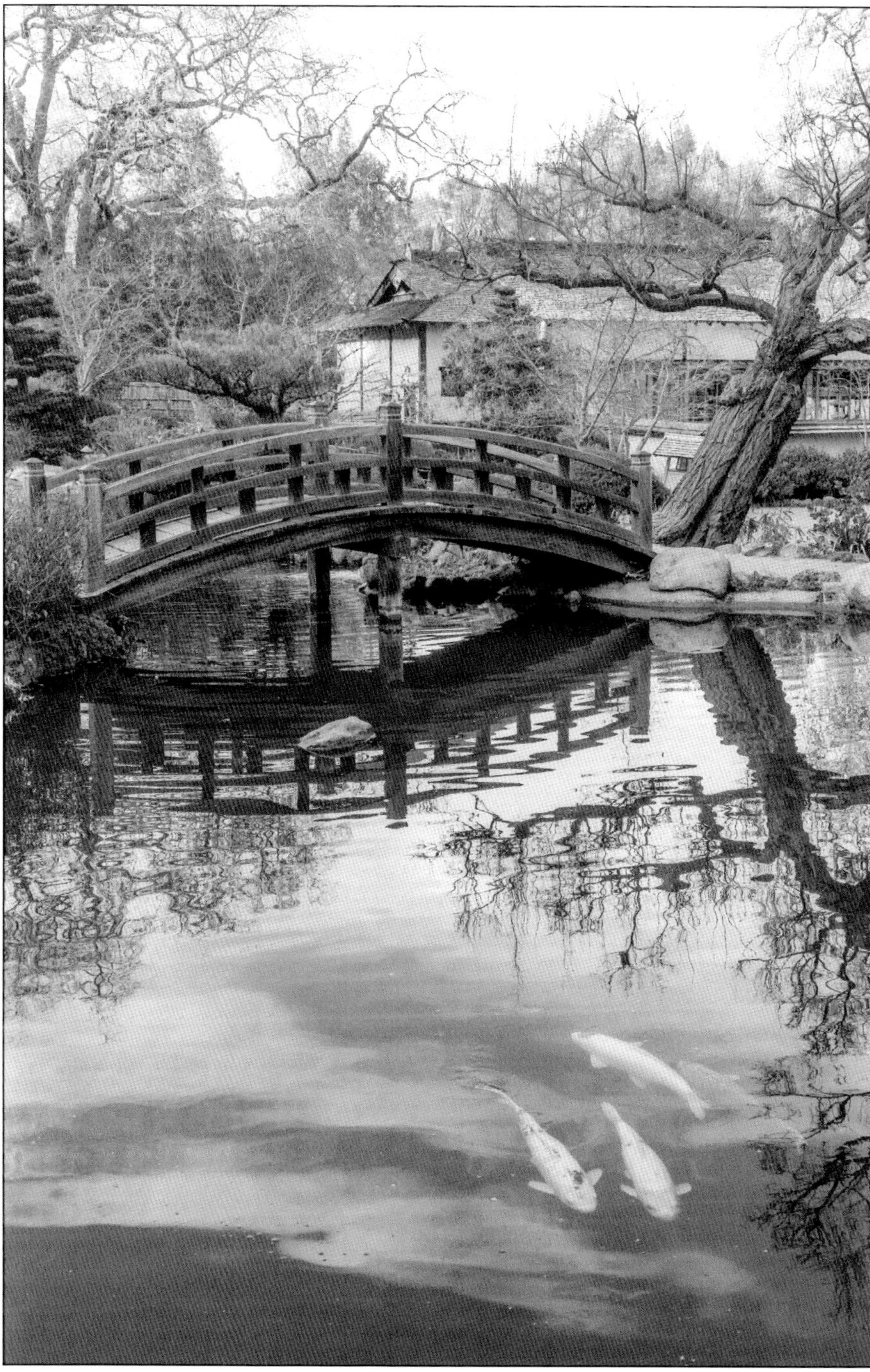

Every view of Hakone Estate and Gardens evokes beauty. In the foreground, the tranquil pond is graced with elegant koi and the venerable Moon Bridge. In the background is the Lower House with its walled Dry Garden. When standing inside the Lower House, visitors can view the exquisite Karensansui through large glass windows that slide open on warm days to give a timeless view and an aesthetic experience like no other. Isabel Stine's dream of a Japanese garden and estate becomes one's own. (Courtesy of Mike Story.)